CLEAN MOBILE ARCHITECTURE

Petros Efthymiou

ISBN: 978-618-86007-0-6

To Mom & Dad.

CONTENTS

Foreword

Anyone can be a software engineer. All it takes is a laptop, an internet connection and some time to go over some basic material, like Youtube tutorials. Then, off you go to build your first website or mobile app. Besides, there are tons of frameworks out there that make it really easy.

Let's consider our world for a moment. Software is just about everywhere. Without it, no plane can fly, no modern car can brake safely, there can be no online transactions whatsoever. There can be no taxing applications, email, social media, phones, smart TVs, ATMs. I could literally fill this foreword by keeping on listing things that are powered by software. I won't. I believe you already thought of some more on your own. The conclusion I am looking to draw is simple: software is really important to our lives. It's indispensable.

Not only is it ever-present in our lives, but it is a crucial part as well. Sure, software bugs can cause a web page not to render correctly, but they can do so much more than this. They can lead to plane crashes, as with the Boeing 737 Max in 2018 and 2019, resulting in 346 people dying. A severe bug in the ABS system of our car or a nuclear reactor could prove fatal. Defects in our web banking or taxing applications could lead us to an inconsistent and maybe irrecoverable financial state, wreaking havoc on our society. Sometimes, the ramifications of a software defect can be unforeseeable. Writing software is a serious job. A very serious job!

Having just considered this, one would expect a rigorous preparatory phase in a software engineering career, precisely like in any other job that carries a heavy responsibility load. No doctor performs an operation the day following their graduation. On the contrary, they have to spend years and years studying and working alongside experienced doctors before they can be allowed to perform an operation. No pilot flies a commercial jet on their first day at work. They need to spend a certain number of hours in a flight simulator and be co-pilots on several flights. No architect designs a building fresh out of college and no lawyer represents a client during their first month in the profession. However, there is no such process for software engineers.

This is an oxymoron, right? Such importance is attached to this profession, yet it is so easy to practice it. Are we missing something here? Not only does software play a vital role in our lives today, but I believe we agree that its importance constantly grows. We can only begin to imagine how dependent on software our lives will be in 10 years from now. Or even 20, or 30. This means that the need for software engineers will only increase and probably steeply. How are we going to make sure that these people meet the standards? How are we going to define the standards in the first place? Who is responsible for solving these tricky problems?

Perhaps our industry is too young to be able to give answers to these questions. Currently, one thing is certain: the responsibility of dealing with the problem lies with us, software engineers. And frankly, it is better this way. We are the ones who know what it means to write software. It is our responsibility to build a strong community, to exchange ideas and experiences relentlessly, and to make sure that this community grows wiser and more skilled every day. It is us who need to mentor each other, guide the younger engineers and make sure that today's mistakes will not be repeated in the future.

This is why I find it so inspiring that seasoned engineers, like Petros, take time and energy out of their personal lives to contribute to this great cause. They are sharing their experiences and their learned lessons. And I feel even more inspired that you are holding a copy of this book and are about to start the next step in your beautiful journey to mastery.

While reading it, I would like to urge you to keep the following in mind: writing working code is only part of our job. In fact, it is the bare minimum. It is a given. Our goal should be to write high-quality, well-crafted code.

Nikos Voulgaris, Software Craftsman
Athens, March 2022

Preface

If you don't build a building well, it will collapse.

It's a great metaphor for building software, a life, or a dream. If you don't build those things well, they collapse, too. Unlike buildings, though, life and software are malleable. A system's architecture is not set in stone. Each day we have the opportunity to reshape it and improve it.

I realized this early in my career. Apps that are architected poorly and don't improve each day eventually collapse. I have gone on a journey ever since to master software architecture. It's been a rollercoaster, and I still have a lot to learn. However, I had the chance to apply several architectural patterns in a number of production apps. I've seen what works and what doesn't. And I want to make this journey easier for you.

Platform Agnostic

The book is about software architecture and doesn't focus much on low-level coding details. It is targeted at Android, iOS & Flutter professionals. The coding repos and samples include both Android & iOS.

* * *

The Golden Circle

Simon Sinek's *Start with Why* inspired the way I structured this book. He emphasizes that to be successful in anything you do, you need to understand *why* you are doing it. You won't go far in any career unless you establish solid motivation. The same applies to software engineering. We need to understand why it's better to write quality software before we can achieve it.

After we understand *why,* we need to learn *how;* the motivation can get us going, but it's not enough to achieve results. We must learn about the Fundamental Software Objectives, separation of concerns, S.O.L.I.D principles, and other best practices that enable us to write quality software.

Finally, we need to learn *what* quality software means. We need to put the best practices together into actionable Architectural patterns that you can use to structure your next production application. Theory backed up by practice is called experience. That's what we are aiming for.

So as Simon Sinek suggests, I am navigating this book from the more abstract to the more concrete. I have split the book into three independent parts that describe:

I. *Why* write quality software.
II. *How* to write quality software.
III. *What* quality software means in the context of a

mobile app.

Each part is independent and can be read in isolation. If you are already convinced of *why* to write quality software, you can proceed to *how* and learn the fundamental principles. Or even go straight to *what* if you want to fast track to the Mobile Architectures. However, the book reads best when you follow the story from beginning to end.

Enjoy the ride!

About the Author

Petros Efthymiou is a software craftsman, instructor, and author. He has vast experience in building and architecting mobile apps of varying complexity. His experience includes lead engineering positions in startups and large multinational organizations. He has also worked as a partner software instructor in various institutions such as New York College, Hellenic American Union & Careerbuilder GR. Currently, he is working as a software instructor and consultant at software enterprises in the banking industry.

He is passionate about software architecture, XP practices, and pragmatism. Among others, he is the author of *Clean Mobile Architecture* and the best-seller Udemy course - Android TDD Masterclass.

Acknowledgments

Million thanks to the incredible people who helped me finish the marathon of writing a book:

Nikos Voulgaris, for the Foreword and the technical review.

Jovche Mitrejchevski, for the Android technical review.

Donny Wals, for the iOS technical review.

Christos Smpyrakos, for the Android technical review.

Nina Muzdeka, for academic and linguistic assistance.

PART I

Why - Cheap Code is Expensive

Introduction - A Spaghetti Story

I started my career as a consultant for a software vendor. Don't picture someone modernizing systems in Sandro Mancuso's Codurance. We were all labeled consultants as we were outsourced to customers and working at their premises in most cases. The consultant title added a sense of credibility.

I was a junior Android developer yet ambitious and eager to take on more responsibility. My employer welcomed this, as mobile engineers were scarce back then.

We kicked off the initial mobile team with two more mobile devs and a team leader. Our initial assignment was to develop the mobile application of a major Romanian telecom provider. Nine months and six production releases later, they switched to another vendor. They fell for promises that were not delivered if we fast-forward to the future.

Anyways, in the absence of a mobile project, my team got split into several backend projects. We weren't fond of the projects, neither of the teams. We were craving to get our mobile team back!

On a warm, Greek June's Wednesday, almost a year after the initial team's kickoff, my ex-team leader interrupted me and asked me to chat in private. I got goosebumps as I sensed what this was going to be about. He had just returned from a meeting with the senior management of a major telecom provider in Greece. We had good chances of hitting their mobile project!

The news was even better than I thought. Not only did we have a high chance of re-assembling our team, but we were after one of the largest apps in Greece. Millions of active users were using it, including friends and people I knew. And Greece is not Silicon Valley; you don't often get the chance to work on impactful products. On top of that, the client's premises were just 500 meters away from our offices. What more could I ask for?

Our only competitor was the vendor that took (stole if you asked me back then!) our previous mobile project. The vibes in the meetings were not the friendliest. Long story short, after several meetings and RFPs[1], we finally landed the deal!

Having the excitement of a 26-year-old junior developer, who is about to jump into an impactful project, I started project analysis!

The Project

The telecom provider was segregated into two parts: fixed and mobile telephony. They had decided that it was time to merge and consolidate their digital systems; our project was part of this effort. Our initial objective was to implement a single mobile application to serve both fixed and mobile telephony customers.

The mobile sub-company had designed the existing app. Thus, only

[1] A request for proposal (RFP) is a document that solicits proposals, often made through a bidding process.

customers of mobile telephony could use it. Our initial scope was to add support for landline customers. And yes, we hadn't yet adopted an agile mindset, neither us nor the customer. We were trying to inject agile elements in a waterfall-based approach. Adding landline support was the scope of our first iteration. Pretty huge to be considered an agile sprint.

Since the project's kickoff, we already knew that the company had decided to go big on their mobile app. Their strategy up to 2014 was centered around the web portal. But as the whole world was getting disrupted by the mobile revolution, they realized they had to switch to a mobile-first approach. An interesting statistic is the purchases of additional MB. The diagram below displays the shift in volume from the web portal to the mobile app:

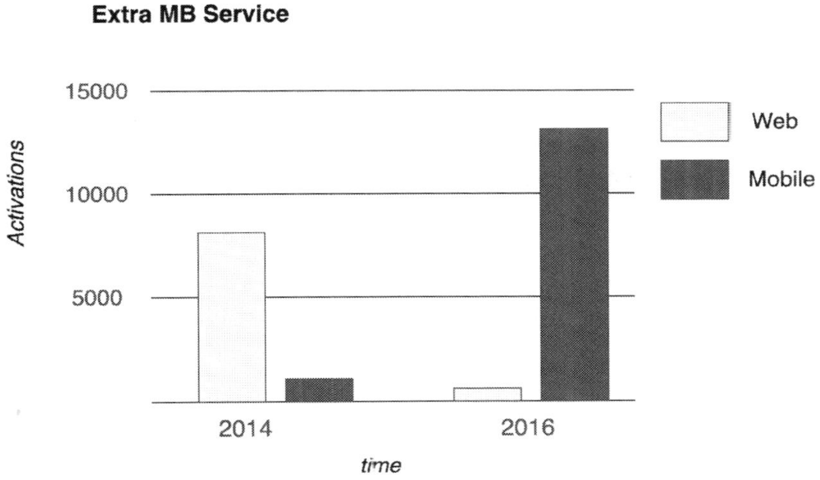

We knew that we were into something big!

The Execution

So, getting back to my youth excitement, we started reviewing the existing codebases soon after signing the contract. I started with Android and my team leader with iOS. Those projects were about three years old, none of the developers who participated were currently around. They were implemented by several software teams and cost quite a lot.

"Oh god!" That's exactly what came out of my mouth in the first 30 minutes of reviewing the code. The reaction of my team leader, even though he is one of the calmest persons I've ever met in my life, was even worse. Understanding how those software pieces worked together and building on top of them would be no walk in the park.

- The modules were tightly coupled to each other. There was no clear separation of concerns or any identifiable logical cohesion.
- The largest class was 5798 lines long! Five thousand seven hundred ninety-eight lines! It was responsible for the HTTP networking layer of the whole application. With, of course, several other unrelated responsibilities included.
- There wasn't a single automated test. Both the unit and instrumentation test folders were blank. Or, to be more specific, they included only the auto-generated tests.
- Undefined architectural pattern. To be fair, back in the day, we didn't have the same variety of mobile architectural patterns as today. Only MVC was somewhat popular. In our case, most of the project's code and business logic resided inside Activities and View Controllers. There is no excuse for that.
- I don't want to get into too many details, but you can probably imagine that the naming, functions' size and code formatting were pretty @# bad.

The situation was similar on the iOS side. We were both terrified by this monster and questioned if it was even possible to add any further functionality to this application. The answer was obvious. It would be a colossal waste of time, money, and effort.

We explained the situation to our client. But like most business people, they weren't fond of the idea of rewriting the whole project. The debate went on for a couple of weeks. It was typical management vs. tech series of arguments. Finally, despite the odds, we got them to agree to start a greenfield project! We falsely promised that we would reuse as much as possible from the previous app. We already knew, though, that this didn't make any sense. There wasn't a single well-made, cohesive component that was worth porting to our new polished codebase.

The Outcome

Fast-forwarding into the future, the project went on for about two years, two of the most productive and exciting years of my career. The mobile team grew from 2 to 16 engineers, and we adopted a three-week release cycle. We implemented:

- A clean, single-activity MVC architecture.
- Migrated from Eclipse to Android Studio. Yes, that was a thing back then.
- In iOS, we switched from Objective-C to Swift. That was also a thing back then.

It wasn't all rainbows and unicorns. The codebase wasn't a state-of-the-art masterpiece, but it was a decent app for the time. With our limitations in experience, environment, and industry immaturity, our application had its own flaws and downsides.

But overall, we managed to accomplish some truly amazing things. We have to consider that back in 2014; mobile development was the latest addition to the software family. The project, though, had the potential of getting refactored and improved. It could live a long and healthy life.

The Aftermath

The point to be taken from the story is that the cost of developing low-quality software is vast and often not visible early enough. Think of how much effort was wasted when the previous codebase was disposed of. All this effort could mean something if we could build upon it. If the initial app was built on practices that allowed us to:

a. Understand it.
b. Refactor it without the dreadful fear of breaking the existing functionality.

c. Quickly add extra features to it.

Instead, the project ended up in a discontinued internal repo, and we gave it a proper funeral. We did celebrate burying it but mourned for the effort of our fellow developers.

Writing cheap code ends up being expensive.

It's not easy to build a software product; it's even harder to build it well. In this book, you will learn the practices backed up by solid theory that will enable you to achieve it. Enjoy the journey!

> The only way to go fast is to go well. —Robert C. Martin

CHAPTER ONE

Loans are generally a bad idea

Every product, including software products, has a price. Taking a loan to buy it will only increase the overall cost.

> If you think good architecture is expensive, try bad architecture. —Brian Foote

Unless you are new to the software industry, you have probably been part of the following conversations:

Management - "Our priority now is to meet the deadline. We cannot spend time in code quality, refactoring, and tech debt."

Developers (under pressure) - "Let's get done with it fast; we will refactor it later."

Clients - "We were supposed to have the deliverables last week; why are you late? I cannot measure your code quality, but I can measure time to market."

The dangerous thing is that "quick and dirty" *works*! It works like a charm in the short term and while the team is small. It's basically like taking a loan with high-interest rates, you may enjoy the cash now, but you will end up paying more in the long run. Hence the term "Technical Debt." The interest is the additional effort to refactor a spaghetti app. If the loan is not repaid in time, it will eventually cause your "house foreclosure, "aka disposing of the project and rewriting it from scratch.

Every software product has a price that needs to be paid. Quick and dirty wins are not to be celebrated. Having said that, there are occasions where "borrowing" makes sense—for example, working for a startup with a capital runway of 12 months. Taking a technical loan to show progress and land funding makes sense. This should be a conscious and educated decision, though. With a complete understanding of the consequences, followed by a strategy to address them.

Contain cancer

Not every lousy practice or poor design decision has the same impact. In financial terms, they don't come with the same interest rate. In medical terms, there is cancer that spreads and threatens the application's life and cancer that is contained. Contained cancer refers to legacy code that is effectively isolated in specific layers. When we maintain a single point of contact with those layers, most of our codebase remains unaffected by the cancerous parts. This reserves the option to refactor/treat cancer at a later stage. This is not meant to excuse poor design decisions and cutting corners. But more of a pragmatic approach to the challenges that we face in a real-life project.

Usually, textbooks only refer to ideal scenarios and insist on perfect solutions from day one. We know that this is not always possible. Sometimes due to external limitations such as clients, managers, and deadlines. And sometimes due to internal limitations like our own experience. To understand this better, let's discuss a few examples of cancer that is contained:

1. Designing an application to be testable is crucial for its longevity. Omitting writing some tests is something that we can deal with later on.

2. Limiting the dependency on mobile frameworks (Android, iOS, Flutter, etc..) is essential. The same applies to third-party libraries. With this, I don't mean to limit the usage of third-party libraries,

particularly when they are helpful for our app. I mean that the majority of our codebase should be agnostic of them. Most architectural patterns, including Clean Architecture, banish those dependencies at the outermost layer of the system. The vast majority of the system should be platform agnostic and external libraries agnostic. The focus is on the business logic, the problem we are trying to solve. This is particularly useful when we need to change those libraries. Or when those libraries introduce breaking changes. Having a large part of the app depending on them will bring an extensive refactoring and re-testing effort. Recall when Google introduced AndroidX. Large-scale apps, heavily coupled to Android code, were a pain to migrate. On the other hand, when only a particular layer is aware it belongs in an Android app, then the "cancer" is contained. Such changes, like the introduction of AndroixX, don't affect us as much. I will display how to achieve this in Part III of the book.

3. Choosing the right high-level architecture is also essential. Not something that we cannot refactor later, and as a matter of fact, we often should. The app complexity keeps evolving over time. Alongside it, we must keep adjusting our architectural design. Getting the architecture right based on the facts can go a long way. A well-designed architecture is more effective in isolating cancerous and legacy parts. A way to mitigate the consequences of getting it wrong is to segregate the app into independent feature modules. This is something that we will touch on later in the book.

Again the point is not to make excuses for poor architectural decisions but to understand that not all of them are of the same importance. We need to make conscious and educated decisions on which corners we will cut and why. Cancer must be contained in specific layers, which can be reworked later. Letting cancer spread can prove to be fatal.

Products vs. Projects

Let's align on the terms software project vs. software product. Taken from Project Management Institute (PMI)[1]:

"A *project* is temporary in that it has a defined beginning and end in time and thus defined scope and resources. "

"A *product* is an object or system made available for consumer use; it is anything that can be offered to a market to satisfy a desire or need[2]."

Software development nowadays is mainly about building products. It involves many unknowns that make it hard for us to have the certainties projects require upfront. When we start working on a new app, we know the least about the software that we are building. Additionally, we are living in the digital transformation era. Businesses have realized that technology must be at their core. It's not a side hustle.

Software evolves constantly. Think of the apps you use in your daily life. We are continually receiving updates, whether for bug-fixing, adding new features, or improving the UX. Take as an example your favorite social media or telecom app; how much has it changed over the past two years? Does this fit into the definition of a project? Do these applications have "a defined beginning and end in time"? And how about scope and resources? Do they seem to have been fixed upfront?

Change and evolution are natural in products but not in projects. Projects don't welcome change. And software evolves constantly.

We can even go as far as saying that a software project can only exist as a subset of a software product. Any piece of software with a fixed scope and time will become obsolete. Regardless of how innovative the idea is, evolving competition will eventually increase, eating up the market.

In conclusion, we can't get away without paying our technical debt. This only happens in bankruptcy, aka project discontinuation.

Software is a compound word composed of soft and ware. Ware means product. Soft comes from the fact that it is easy to change and reshape. Or at least it should be!

> To fulfill its purpose, software must be soft. That is, it must be easy to change —Robert C Martin.

* * *

How to determine the technical price of a software product?

We usually refer to the complexity of a product solely based on the technical complexity and the number of features. Are those the only factors that define its overall complexity? Definitely not! There is a process, organization, and people involved in building a product. On a high level, three major factors define the technical price of a software product:

1. *The people.* This is probably the most significant factor in defining how elaborate or simple our architectural design should be. More specifically:

- The team's size. It's generally easier to understand the code that we wrote ourselves. Not always, but in most cases, something that made sense to us in the past will also make sense to us in the future. At least, it will make more sense to us than to someone else. As the team grows larger, we need stricter code practices to keep the codebase readable by *everyone*.
- The level of the engineers. Do we have the seniority to deal with elaborate designs and patterns, or do we need to stick to simple code? Is there a critical mass that can educate the more junior members? Essential factors to consider when you want to introduce fancy new design patterns to the codebase.
- The number of teams. It's a whole different situation when one or multiple teams are working on the product. Each team should have its own boundary of control over the app and be empowered to make their own choices based on the unique challenges they face.
- The retention of the team(s). Closely tied to the first point. People who quit take their knowledge with them. Newcomers should be able to get onboarded and understand the code fast.

2. *The amount & complexity of the features.* As expected, those are critical factors as well. What types of logic are required by our app (presentation, business, etc.)? How complex is the logic? How many features do we have to introduce, and how do they interact with each other? How many systems do we depend on, and what API do they

expose? Do the backend systems include the business logic, or do we have to add it in our app? Crucial factors that drive our architectural design.

3. *The longevity of the product.* Interest adds up in time. The longer the project goes, the harder it gets to deal with technical debt. Additionally, we tend to forget our own cut corners and dirty solutions. Given enough time, say a year, even we can't understand the spaghetti we wrote.

The above factors are essential to understand. From now on, when you see me mentioning product context, complexity, or technical price, I mean all the factors above combined. They are key in making architectural decisions.

I often discuss with developers who, based on their personal experience, advocate heavily against elaborate architectural designs. Their experience, though, is obtained by working primarily in startups or small teams. For sure, a small startup with a couple of developers requires a flexible and straightforward design. Lots of unnecessary interfaces and rigid system boundaries will cripple productivity. The case is fundamentally different in enterprise apps with several development teams involved. Without well-defined boundaries there, the teams can't be productive.

The architectural design is context-dependent. What works in a particular context does not work in another. Our own experience, when limited in variety, leads to biases that can harm the team's productivity.

It is also essential to understand that software architecture is not a boolean value. It is not something that we either have or haven't. It's instead a beautiful canvas of smaller and bigger design decisions that we continuously make. In time, each of those decisions proves to be right or wrong.

> Architecture is a hypothesis that needs to be proven by implementation and measurement. —Tom Gib

* * *

When you open your code written a few months ago...

In my life and career, I try to avoid being dogmatic and one-sided. I show empathy and understanding to solo-developers working to get a quick prototype out of the door. I've also been there with side projects. In this case, taking a technical loan makes perfect sense. Just make sure you repay it before you scale the company.

Where do successful startups fail?

Besides securing initial funding, what's the most dangerous phase that startups go through? Where do most *successful* startups fail? By successful, I mean the startups that have managed to secure series-A and sit on sufficient funds. You probably guessed right; they fail at scaling. Why?

This is a multi-dimensional answer—the way people organize and communicate needs to change. Also, the way that we communicate the code needs to change. Software architecture is primarily a communication medium. We communicate to other engineers the intention of our system. As more and more devs jump on board, we often double in size every year; the communication models we used in the past do not address the arising challenges.

At this point, the codebase often requires radical refactoring. What used to be tailored to the previous context is no longer able to facilitate the company's growth. What used to be over-engineering and an impediment to productivity is now necessary to enable multiple teams to work on a shared codebase. A new architectural design is required.

Software architecture is a communication medium. We communicate to other engineers the intention of the system.

Radical system refactoring is not an easy task, and it's often done poorly. It requires experience, effort, and iterations. It's often better to avoid rapid scaling in the first place. *More people does not mean more work is done.* Sometimes a small engineering team with the right people can be way more productive than a sizeable bureaucratic engineering department. First, try to avoid rapid growth in engineering numbers. When growth is necessary, pay the price to refactor the system accordingly. Accumulating technical debt will slow you down forever.

> *Writing cheap code ends up being expensive.*

Summary

Containing cancer by isolating legacy and third-party code is crucial for the longevity of a software product.

Unlike a product, a software project has a defined lifespan, scope, and resources. Modern software is mainly based on products; therefore, technical loans will eventually be paid.

To define how elaborate an app's architectural design should be, we must take into account its context, which includes:

- The people involved.
- The technical complexity.
- The intended lifespan.

CHAPTER TWO

Expensive code is also expensive

> "When your design or code makes things more complex instead of simplifying things, you're over-engineering." —Max Kanat-Alexander.[1]

I was once working for a USA-based healthcare startup. As with every startup, we didn't have much structure. Instead, we had an abundance of energy and enthusiasm about what we were doing. Whenever we received a new feature request, we engaged in stormy meetings to figure out the best way to implement it.

We had advocates of all styles, from "quick and dirty" to clean practitioners. It often got tense in the meeting room. An "inflexible" backend engineer was continuously pushing for the most complex solutions. Even for trivial cases. He wasn't exactly the type of person who would listen to different opinions. If he had read about a particular software practice in a book, that would be the global and only truth. He lacked the context-understanding and experience we talked about in the previous chapter.

Strict protocols, complex solutions, premature performance optimizations, and speculations about the future. Particularly the anxiety of supporting millions of concurrent users was crippling the team's performance. We had zero active users at that time.

The result was delayed releases and overly-complex systems that, in the end, did not even achieve the business goals. The backend system had to be re-written several times based on his framework preferences. Finally, it ended up being replaced by a Firebase system that could simply get the job done effectively. The effort and money waste were massive. Even worse, constantly arguing with that person took its toll on our mental health.

The definition

Over-engineering is building more than what is really necessary, based on speculation.

More often than not, writing code based on speculations proves to be unnecessary. Not just unnecessary but actively destructive for the team's performance. Specific practical examples of this are:

- Overusing Generics to support "future" cases. Generics in Object-Oriented Programming (OOP) are useful when we need extensible abstractions. However, they also add complexity. When we find ourselves passing null values, *, Unit, or Empty as a type, it must ring a bell that this generic is not serving a real purpose.
- Applying Design Patterns to support future requirements. Design patterns are also excellent tools that enable us to write better software. But as with every toolset, we need to know when to use it and when to avoid it. Let's understand this better with an example:

Consider the function below:

```
fun mapColorForOwedAmount(amount: Int): Int {
    if (amount in 0..49)
        return R.color.green
    else if (amount in 50..99)
        return R.color.yellow
    else if (amount in 100..199)
        return R.color.orange
    else
        return R.color.red
}
```

It receives as input the amount that a customer owes and returns the text-view color. Even though it is an "if/else" block, which is generally frowned upon, it is pretty clean and easy to understand. There's no need to apply a design pattern here. We could simply make use of some neat Kotlin features to refactor it and improve its conciseness:

```
fun mapColorForOwedAmount(amount: Int): Int {
    return when (amount) {
        in 0..49 -> R.color.green
        in 50..99 -> R.color.yellow
        in 100..199 -> R.color.orange
        else -> R.color.red
    }
}
```

But nothing more is required. Some developers may get tempted to refactor this code block with the Strategy Design Pattern. They argue that we will have to support more conditions in the future. This is an example of over-engineering. We don't know what the future holds and what business requirements we will need to support later. Even if we know what is coming down the road and anticipate it to happen four months later, it still doesn't make sense to pay the price now. We need to focus on our priorities and ship the current release as fast as possible. The business benefits more from working software in the hands of the customers right now. Besides that, there is a high chance that the priorities will change within four months. In the end, the product team may even decide that this feature is not required at all and remove it from the backlog.

Having said that, there are speculations with a high probability of materializing. For example, any decently sized mobile app will require data from multiple endpoints. Therefore, segregating the networking concern into single-entity Services from the very start is a safe call. While safe assumptions do exist, we should not overestimate our guessing capabilities and make a lot of assumptions early on. In most cases, when we try to predict the future, we fall short.

A principle originating from Extreme Programming describes the above situation; it's called YAGNI. "You ain't gonna need it." The principle states that a programmer should not be adding functionality to the software until deemed necessary. XP co-founder Ron Jeffries has said:

> Always implement things when you actually need them, never when you just foresee that you need them. —Ron Jeffries

Another term originates from U.S Navy back in 1960, called KISS - "Keep it simple, Stupid." Kelly Johnson reportedly coined the acronym. He was a lead engineer at the Lockheed Skunk Works, creators of the Lockheed U-2 and SR-71 Blackbird spy planes, among many others. The KISS principle states that most systems work best if kept simple rather than complicated. Therefore, simplicity should be a key goal in design. Unnecessary complexity should be avoided. [2]

Image: XKDC

The Mastery Path

Programmers generally pass through (at least) three stages of mastery —Junior, mid, and senior. At the junior level, we struggle to understand design patterns and apply them. Therefore, we just avoid them. At the mid-level, we are mainly able to understand and apply them. But in our excitement of acquiring this toolset, we tend to overuse it. Even in cases where they make the code more complex and harder to read. At the senior level, we have the experience and understanding to use them properly, in the right place and time. Complex code needs them; simple code does not benefit from them.

It's interesting how the developer mastery path coincides with the Dunning-Kruger effect[3].

* * *

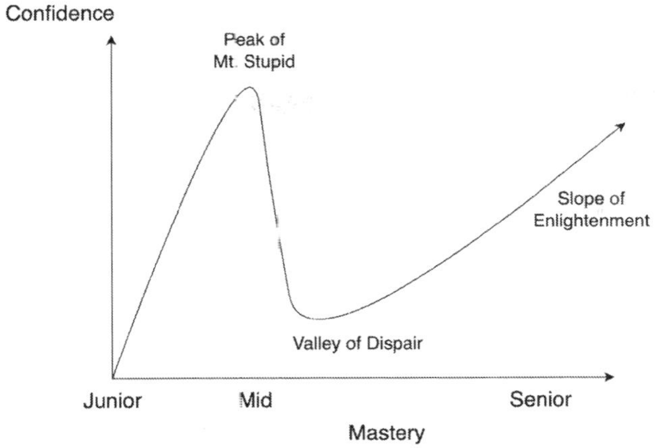

The Dunning-Kruger effect in software engineering.

The diagram above describes our confidence in our software skills vs. our actual skills and mastery. A junior engineer does not know much, and they are aware of it. A mid-level engineer has learned about "best practices" such as Clean, S.O.L.I.D, and design patterns. In their enthusiasm, they make use of them in every situation. This makes them feel like masters. Soon, they realize that by misusing those practices, the code has become hard to read, extend and maintain. This makes them fall into despair. They fall under the misconception that they have wasted their time learning them. They go back to believing that simple code is *always* better. Finally, enlightenment comes as we achieve mastery by experience and understanding of when each tool is helpful and when it isn't.

Design patterns are meant to simplify complex code, not complexify simple code.

Code that solves problems you don't have

Besides speculations about what is going to happen in the future; common cases of over-engineering are:

- Unnecessary performance optimizations. Sure, having a 50 ms response time in all user actions is great, but not something that should delay the release of critical features. You can spend the effort to optimize the time to load the Home Screen but don't spend the effort to optimize everything.

- Premature scalability optimizations. Don't put great effort into implementing a system that can support millions of concurrent users. First, create a product that people want to use.
- Configurability. Business people get overly excited about having the capability to configure the application at runtime. Without having to wait for a deployment. In most cases, they ask for a CMS that enables them to change the app's literals and images. Sometimes they desire the power of deeper configurations. Like runtime feature activation and deactivation. Technically, this includes fetching configuration files that drive runtime decisions on our application's behavior. In my experience, if we measure how many times those configurations were used in a year, we will conclude that they weren't worth the effort. I am not suggesting pushing back by default on such requests, but research should be done before implementing them.

How much should I pay?

> Time is money. —Benjamin Franklin

I purposefully used monetary terms to describe the terms under-engineering and over-engineering. First of all, as Benjamin Franklin stated, time is money. And engineering effort takes time. Secondly, as engineers, we often debate priorities with business people and product owners. Those people, before all, understand money. Therefore, it will help you make your case if you back it up with arguments closely tied to money. Speak their language. The next time you negotiate in favor of prioritizing a better dev-ops strategy, make sure to emphasize how much time and money the organization will save.

How much should I pay - in engineering terms - refers to how elaborate our architectural design should be. We seek to find the sweet spot, avoiding both under-engineering and over-engineering. We want to avoid costly loans while also avoiding paying for something that we don't currently need.

Now let's go back and build on top of our previous example, the function that calculated the color of the owed amount text-field. We will fast-forward ten months into the future. The product team eventually decided to add further business requirements to how this text field should be colored. The current state of our function looks like this:

```
fun mapColorForOwedAmount(amount: Int, customer: Customer): Int {
    if (amount in 0..49) {
        if (customer.type == CustomerType.PREMIUM ||
            customer.type == CustomerType.VIP)
            return R.color.green
        else
            return R.color.yellow
    } else if (amount in 50..99)
        if (customer.type != CustomerType.VIP) {
            if (customer.balance > 200)
                return R.color.yellow
            else
                if (customer.type == CustomerType.GUEST)
                    return R.color.red
                else
                    return R.color.orange
        } else
            return R.color.yellow
    else if (amount in 100..199)
        if (customer.balance < 100) {
            if (customer.type == CustomerType.PREMIUM ||
                customer.type == CustomerType.VIP)
                return R.color.orange
            else
                return R.color.red
        } else
            return R.color.orange
    else {
        if (customer.type == CustomerType.VIP &&
            customer.balance > 100)
            return R.color.orange
        return R.color.red
    }
}
```

Now the logic is significantly more complex. We have added two more factors to the equation, the customer type, and the customer balance. This piece of code is definitely not OK. You may call it spaghetti, abomination, technical debt, or any other fancy name. Regardless of what you call it, this code is hard to read, understand, test, and extend. Imagine the Product Owner asking a junior developer to add another business rule. The horror!

Above all, it violates the Open-Closed Principle. Adding new behavior requires modifying the existing function. This introduces the risk of breaking the current behavior. The best way to deal with this code is to refactor it using the Strategy Design Pattern[4]. The Strategy DP is an effective tool to clear up code cluttered with many conditionals. We will perform this refactoring in Part II, the Open-Closed chapter. For now, let's stick to the *why*.

Going back to our previous point, over-engineering is writing code based on speculations. When do you think is the right time to refactor this function? Is it when the code was in the initial state while speculating that the business will request for more rules in the future? We don't know that!

Or the right time is the final spaghetti state? Nope, that code is heavily under-engineered and very hard to understand. We will definitely pay the interest now to deal with this mess. Additionally, we face a high risk of breaking past functionality.

There is no - one size fits all. The rule of thumb is that: we refactor the code when it becomes hard to read. Usually, we notice it in the following moments of the development life-cycle:

1. While reviewing our own implementation, right before we commit it.
2. When a colleague complains that the code is hard to understand. This usually happens during code review or pair-programming.
3. When we receive a new requirement that affects the code significantly. It's more efficient if we perform the refactoring before adding the extra functionality.

From the above, I prefer point 3. In our example, I would refactor the function when the requirements included extra deciding factors. At the moment, the customer type and balance were added to the equation. At this moment, it's also easier to convince the business people. Avoid adding a task "Refactor function X." Instead, add the refactoring effort inside the task: "Adjust text coloring based on customer type and balance." A product owner can decide that something is not a priority. They can't pressure you to deliver something they asked for in a very short time, though.

This way, the refactoring efforts are kept at a minimum, and mostly we won't have to convince anyone. So small that hardly anyone (other than the devs involved) will have to know about them. Martin Fowler describes this with the term "Preparatory Refactoring" [5].

Summary

Over-engineering is writing code based on speculations or writing code that solves problems you don't currently have. It's as bad as under-engineering.

The Dunning-Kruger effect coincides with the software mastery path.

The ideal moment for refactoring is right before introducing a new feature that our codebase is not ready to support. This way, it's easier to convince other people as well as to motivate ourselves to do it.

CHAPTER THREE

Minimum Viable Architecture

I have come up with the notion of Minimum Viable Architecture, which is the technical equivalent of the Minimum Viable Product.

Minimum Viable Product

The Minimum Viable Product (MVP) is the simplest product (mobile app in our case) that makes sense to be released in order to validate an idea.

Let's assume that we are building an innovative new healthcare application. Our Product Owner has to carefully select the minimum set of features that constitute a releasable application. You want to get it out to the public as fast as possible to start receiving feedback from the actual users. This feedback is invaluable to determining whether the app is worth pursuing at all. If it's something that the market needs and is willing to pay for.

Additionally, the user feedback should be driving our prioritization. We want to identify the features that matter most to our users. The goal is to minimize the speculations, both on the technical and the product side.

> A minimum viable product (MVP) is a version of a product with just enough features to be usable by early customers. Those can then provide feedback for future product

development:— Eric Ries[1].

The idea of MVP is a concept derived from Lean Startup[2]. It stresses the impact of learning in the development of a new product. It is widely accepted by the Agile community and incorporated into the agile way of working. Before that, in the "waterfall" way of working, we used to release only when the product was "fully built." Sometimes the line between what constitutes an MVP or a "full product" is unclear. An experienced product professional, though, should be able to identify the minimum viable set of features. Everything else will have to wait. The risk of spending too much effort on developing something that the market does not need is high. We must either validate our idea or pivot[3] as fast as possible.

Minimum Viable Architecture

The Minimum Viable Architecture (MVA) is the simplest architecture that can support the clean implementation of the product.

The MVA is the manifestation of two equally important ingredients:

Minimum. First of all, it should be as simple as possible. We must avoid speculations about future requirements. Those usually lead to over-engineering. Additionally, a product backed by a small team of developers does not benefit from many rigid boundaries. For example, we should avoid segregating the codebase into feature modules from the start unless there is a need. So minimum stands for simplest. We need to support the planned scope; anything else is subject to change.

Viable. Besides minimum, our architectural design has to be viable. This means that our architecture should support the development of

---

[2] The Lean Startup is probably the best business book I have read. Written by Eric Ries in 2011 it provides a clear methodology and steps on how to maximize a startup's efficiency by quickly identifying what are the market needs.

[3] Pivoting in business means to make a shift or turn in a new direction. A product pivot, indicates a dramatic shift in direction of at least one aspect of the product.

the current scope while respecting the S.O.L.I.D principles, Clean Architecture, and other best practices that we will touch on later.

Those two powers have conflicting interests and are pushing to opposite directions. One leads to under-engineering while the other to over-engineering. Our duty as engineers and architects is to balance the dance between those two forces. It is often challenging, but as we explained in the previous chapter, it's literally what separates junior, mid, and senior developers. The pathway to mastery includes the ability to balance *minimum* and *viable*.

This balance changes over time; thus, the MVA has to evolve alongside the system's complexity. As the complexity increases, what used to be viable is not anymore. We must always stay alert and re-adjust the scale. The right time to do this is at each iteration's design or analysis phase. We first need to understand the new requirements deeply. Then, we have to determine if they can fit well within our current architectural design. If they can, meaning we can implement them without breaking the principles, then we go ahead and implement the features. If they cannot fit, we need to start the iteration by refactoring our system. The goal is to bring it to a state, ready to accept the new requirements.

So refactoring is our only tool to balance those two powers—usually, the system's complexity increases. Therefore we must refactor it to a more elaborate architecture. It's not *always* the case, though. Sometimes we realize that we have to downscale it and simplify our design.

MVA Example

Let's take a look at how an MVA can evolve alongside the app's requirements.

Generally, for a simple CRUD application, I consider the following as the starting point of an MVA:

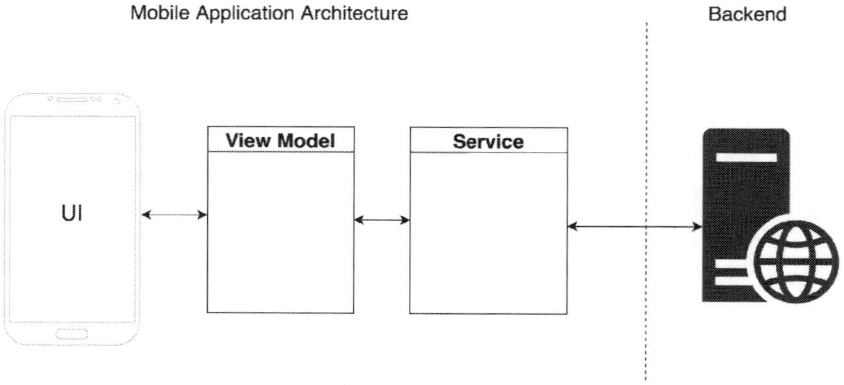

Simplest MVA.

UI is always necessary. Normally includes Fragments for android, View Controllers for iOS, and Widgets for Flutter. We also need a View Model (VM) or a BLoC to host the application's logic. The View Model is also obscuring the data topology from the UI. Finally, the Service is responsible for performing the CRUD operations. This is the minimum architecture that I would consider for simple CRUD applications.

Let's assume now that this MVA supported us in getting the MVP out of the door. We start receiving valuable feedback from our users. The initial feedback, though, is not favorable. Our users often need to use our app while offline, which is currently not supported. Additionally, they are experiencing massive delays due to backend performance issues. We could address it with HTTP caching if it were just the performance issues. Combining it with the off-line demand, we realize that we need to include a local database in our app. The new design looks like this:

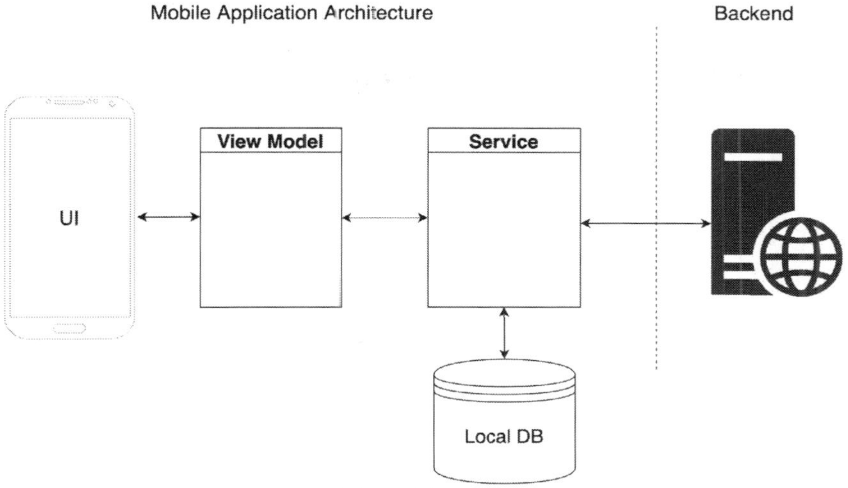

Bloated Service.

So now we have introduced the local database. Our architecture remains minimal, but it's not viable anymore. The Service has too many concerns. It is responsible for performing the HTTP operations and querying the database for information. Furthermore, it contains the decision-making logic on whether the data should come fresh from the backend or cached from our local DB. This layer has become bloated with too much code.

To make our architecture viable again, we introduce a new layer that handles the database communication. This layer will be "speaking" with our View Model in order to let the Service do what it can do best, communicate with the Backend.

* * *

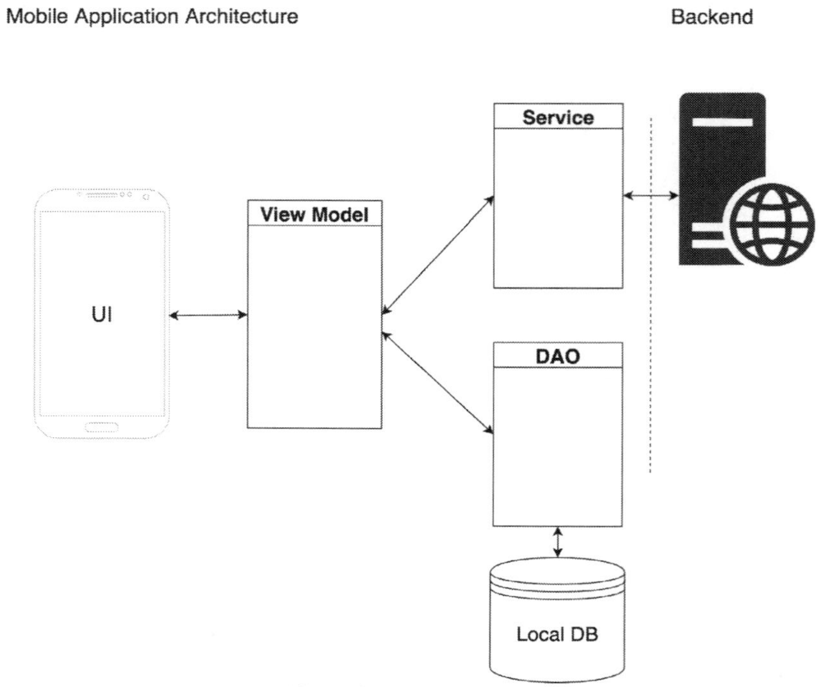

Bloated View Model.

The Data Access Object (DAO) layer is now responsible for retrieving and writing data from and to our DB. It is the only layer that is aware of the existence of a local database. Even though this version is an improvement and a good step to bring our architecture back to viability, it still doesn't feel right. The View Model has now taken on too much burden. First, it applies the application logic. It also bridges the UI with the data. Finally, it decides whether the data will come from the Service or the DAO. We need to introduce one more layer that will take that last concern away.

* * *

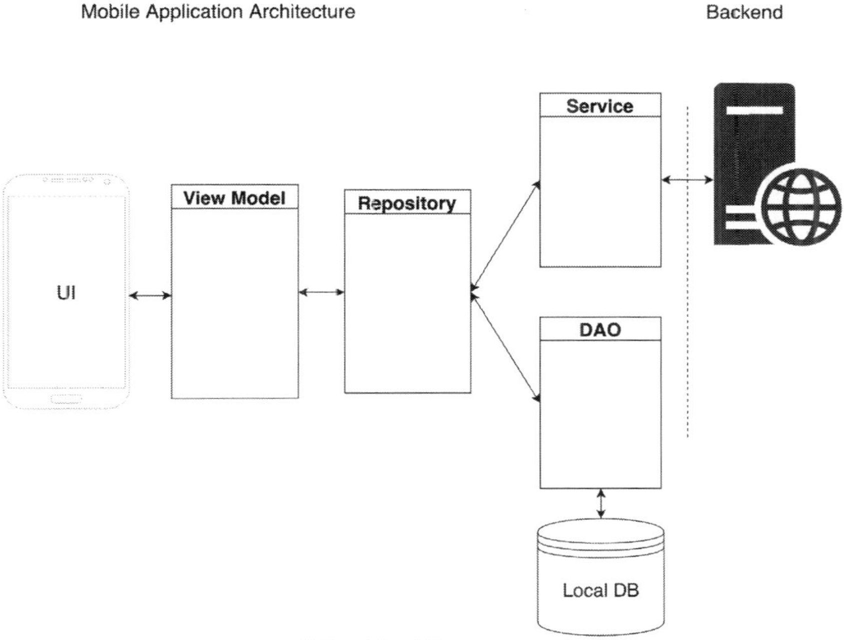

MVA with offline support.

Now, our MVA is viable again. The Repository has only one concern—decide whether the data will come from the DAO and/or the Service. It has all the caching and offline rules. It contains code like:

```
if (cachedTime > 10 mins)
  fetchFromService()
else
  getFromDao()
```

This MVA now can perfectly support caching and offline mode. Our users have noticed the improved response times and can use it offline. We are starting to receive several positive reviews and improving the store rating. Yay!

This architecture facilitates the app's development effectively for a couple of months. Then, our Product Owner brings another set of requirements that increase the overall complexity. The new requirements include making UI decisions based on the data. For example, changing the screen element's color based on the owed amount. We could keep adding this logic inside the View Model, but this would soon lead to a bloated and thick layer. To address this, we are going to introduce transformation mappers:

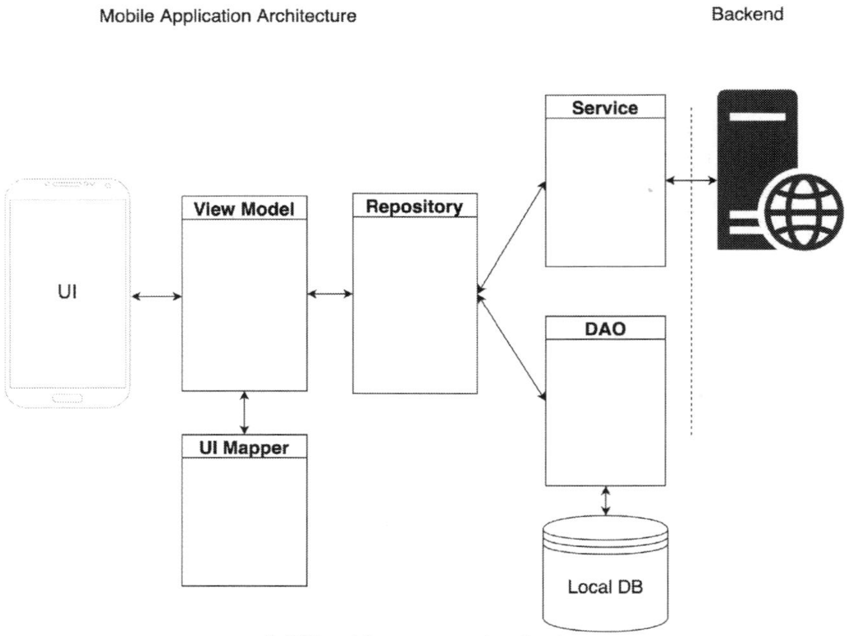

MVA with presentation logic.

The Mapper is now responsible for applying the presentation logic. It does so by inputting a specific model, say Customer, and mapping it to a CustomerPresentation model. The new model contains the required customer info, as well as a few additional fields that represent the color and size of our texts:

```
struct Customer {
    var id: String
    var fullName: String
    var phoneNumber: String
    var address: String
    var balance: Int
    var customerType: CustomerType
    var owedAmount: Int
}
```

```
struct CustomerPresentation {
    var id: String
    var fullName: String
    var balance: Int
    var balanceColor: String
    var balanceFontSize: Int
    var customerType: CustomerType
    var owedAmount: Int
    var owedAmountColor: String
    var owedAmountFontSize: Int
}
```

Notice how the CustomerPresentation struct contains information about the color and font size. Additionally, we have removed the fields *phoneNumber* and *address* since we don't need to display them on the screen. By not including unnecessary information, we conform to the Interface Segregation Principle. We will deep dive into this later. So our CustomerMapper class contains logic like:

```
if (customer.owedAmount > 400)
  customerOwedAmountColor = Colors.RED
```

By isolating all the presentation logic into a single mapper, we make it easy to find, test, debug and maintain. Here we assume that we combine Object-Oriented and Functional programming. But more on that later.[4]

The diagrams that I have been presenting in this chapter include layers. This means that every *Entity* must have its own Service, DAO and Repository. For the Article entity, for example, we have to implement the: ArticleService, ArticleDAO, and ArticleRepository. And so goes for the rest of our entities.

On the other hand, each *Screen* has its own UI (Fragment, ViewController) and View Model. E.g., HomeScreen, HomeViewModel.

---

[4] In a pure OO design, we should add the data operations—presentation logic, inside the presentation model, CustomerPresentation. And not on an external "service" or mapper—CustomerMapper . We will dive more on this concept later, for now let's assume that we have chosen to combine OOP and Functional Programming in our architectural design.

* * *

There is an asymmetry here. The data layer is built around the data topology, while the presentation layer is built around the UI/UX we want to provide to our users. The above architecture is clean only because every screen must display data from only one entity. In those cases, the UI has a 1-1 relationship with the data. If a screen requires combined information from both the Article and the User entities, someone must aggregate that data. And data aggregation is a concern not to be underestimated.

When we receive a feature that data aggregation is required, we can refactor our MVA in the following way:

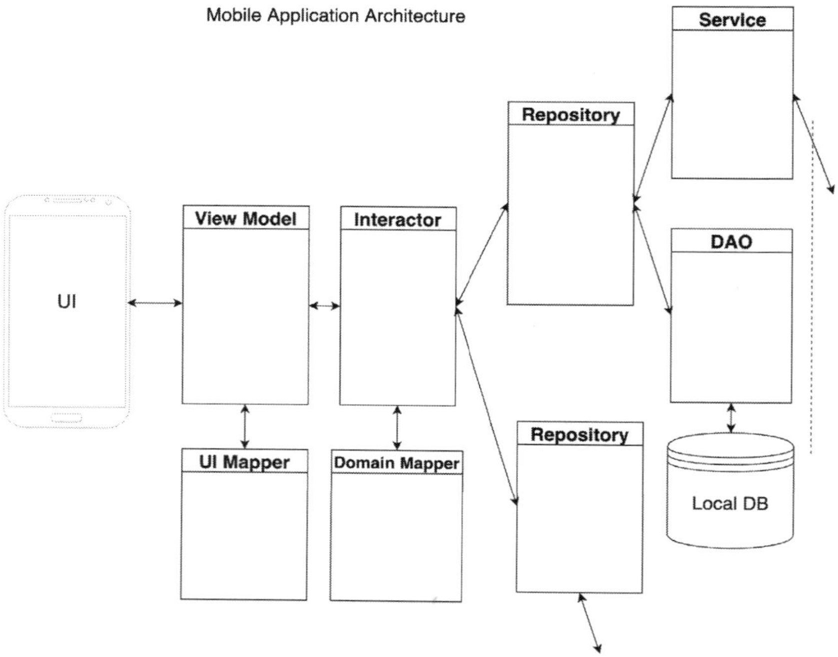

MVA with data aggregation.

So we have now evolved our MVA to include the Aggregator. This component combines unrelated models from multiple Repositories. It may also apply business logic via its mapper and then forward the data to our View Model.

* * *

Furthermore, we now include two mappers, one used by our View Model and one by our Aggregator. What kind of logic should each mapper contain? How do we differentiate them in order to maintain a single concern in each?

We should include what we call presentation logic in the View Model's mapper. We saw an example of presentation logic earlier. UI-related decisions like color, size, etc.. belong in the presentation layer. In the Aggregator mapper, we can add the application or business logic. Those include the business rules and the rules that a user is allowed to interact with the data.

So going back to our startup scenario, we receive a new feature request. We are tasked to display the customer's running balance. The running balance is calculated by subtracting the owed amount from the total balance:

```
runningBalance = balance - owedAmount
```

This is an example of business logic, not presentation logic. We don't decide how something will appear on the screen but rather what the actual data is. Now you might argue that this is something that the backend system should handle. While this is true, from time to time, we face situations where specific business logic algorithms are not included in the backend, and we have to apply them.

There are different examples of business logic as well. Let's assume that we restrict purchases to customers with a running balance below 50. Again, receiving an *allowPurchases* boolean field in the JSON response is preferable. It won't always be the case, though. The Aggregator mapper is responsible for combining the aggregated info and performing any kind of business logic. The result looks like this:

* * *

```
struct ArticleCustomerDomain {
    var customerId: String
    var customerBalance: Int
    var customerOwedAmount: Int
    var customerRunningBalance: Int
    var customerType: CustomerType
    var allowPurchases: Bool
    var articleId: String
    var articleTitle: String
    var articleDesc: String
    var articleContent: String
    var articleImageUrl: String
}
```

The Aggregator mapper contains code like:

```
if (customer.balance - customer.owedAmount > 50) {
  allowPurchases = true
} else {
  allowPurchases = false
}
```

Again this model does not need to include all the fields of the Customer and Article entities. Only the ones that we need in this specific use case.

This architectural design is by no means "final"; it will continue getting more fine-grained, and we will see more of it in the following parts of the book. But it is a decent MVA that can support complex applications. The architecture should evolve alongside the requirements. There is no point starting with an enterprise architecture for a small MVP. We don't know whether we will need offline support, data aggregation, or business logic in our application. A well-designed backend system should perform data aggregation and apply business logic. In that scenario, the front-facing applications would only contain the presentation logic, and our MVA would be significantly thinner. So let's start simple and keep refactoring and evolving it. It requires skills and experience to identify at each point in time what is the right MVA. You already have a head start by reading this book!

* * *

Not all products start from startups.

The above scenario is a cherry-picked example in which we are working for a startup. We start with a simple MVA while gradually upscaling it to enterprise architecture. This process is essential for the viability of the company itself. It is the perfect example of evolutionary architecture as we don't want enterprise architectures on minimal apps. They will slow us down with their complexity in the initial releases, leading to the startup running dry.

But not all applications start from startups. For example, we may get hired by a bank to implement their mobile banking application. They know their business, and there are several competing apps live. They might not yet know the best way to engage with their customers, but they have a good sense of which features are required. A banking app must display the accounts, transactions, card management, payments, etc. Again while building it and releasing it gradually, we will learn a lot from our users and how they engage with the app. This information will help us reprioritize and adjust the UX of the app. But still, this case differs significantly from a brand new innovative product intended to disrupt an industry. The industry now exists; we are just working to improve the efficiency of the value streams and customer engagement.

So how do we approach the app's development in the enterprise scenario? The answer is the same as before but from a different starting point. We will not start a banking app with the same minimal CRUD MVA. We should engage with the whole team and define our starting point based on the current information. We need to enable the parallel development of several independent teams and the implementation of complex features. Therefore, our starting point is a more sophisticated architecture from day one. The initial MVA is more complicated than the initial MVA of a startup's MVP.

But the same principles apply. We have a starting point, an initial MVA, which keeps evolving alongside the teams and the product. We may decide later that we need a more sophisticated architecture. We may also figure out that our starting point was over-engineered.

Don't get me wrong; I do understand that refactoring does not come for free. It's often presented like refactoring is a "get away from jail card." Sometimes refactoring can cost a lot, particularly when it touches fundamental parts of a large-scale app. On the other hand, sitting forever on inadequate architecture costs more. Is "getting it right from the start" important? Yes, it is; it will save time. Will we always "get it right from the start"? No, we won't. So what we should do is:

1. Try to "Get it right" based on facts.
2. Refactor and reshape our system when we identify the need.

In the "What" section, we will study practical examples of the above. So don't worry if you're still unsure how to apply them practically. Many of the questions you currently have will be answered there.

Summary

The MVA is the Minimum Viable Architecture that can effectively support the planned scope / requirements.

The MVA should be both minimum and viable. The simplest possible architecture that respects S.O.L.I.D, Clean, and other best practices.

The MVA keeps evolving alongside the requirements. Refactoring is our balancing tool between minimum and viable.

CHAPTER FOUR

So, Why?

I have a dream… —Martin Luther King Jr.

The people who have clarity on *why* they do what they do are called leaders. They are the ones who drive positive change in the world.

We explained how cheap code is expensive. We also talked about how expensive code is expensive. We analyzed the terms technical loan & technical debt. So if someone asks you: "Which are your motives behind becoming better at software engineering?" what would be your response?

* * *

I am not referring to the *why* we write software. This is a personal thing, and each individual has their own why:

One may want to leverage technology to revolutionize the healthcare industry. Or help people with a specific condition, say diabetes, as they have suffered from it. Personally, or through a close family member.

Someone else may want to elevate their career and land a higher-end job. We live in the golden era of software. Previously, we passed through the golden age of layers, bank employees, and others. Nowadays, the demand for quality software engineers is booming, and the offer cannot keep up. Particularly in countries with lower living standards, learning to code can be the ticket to a better life.

Another one may want to build a product on their own. In software products, business success depends highly on technical success. Regardless of how innovative the idea is, after it goes to production, it won't be long until competition arrives. A software product must be built on a solid technical foundation in order to stay competitive.

My personal motivation for becoming a software engineer is to leverage technology to advance humanity. In other words, solve problems that are not easily solved without technology. With this book, I hope that I am multiplying this effect. I intend to help many engineers produce software better and produce better software.

The *why* I am trying to tackle in this chapter, though, is why to become better at software engineering specifically. Not the *why* we build software. Let's establish a clear *why* that will be the motivation behind going through the book. Of course, you can answer this question with: "To serve better the purpose that I build software." Let's try to identify what *better* means.

In several blogs around the web, you read articles that advocate doing X to apply separation of concerns or doing Y to improve the system's cohesion or lower the system's coupling. But why should you care about reducing the system's coupling or separating the concerns?

* * *

Outcome Objectives

It's essential to always keep in mind that software engineering is engineering. It's not a science.

Science is the body of knowledge that explores the physical and natural world[1].

Engineering is the application of knowledge to design, build and maintain a product or a process that solves a problem and fulfills a need (i.e., a technology).

> Science is about knowing; engineering is about doing. —Henry Petroski

We write code to solve real-world problems. The way we work should maximize our effectiveness and efficiency in solving those problems. "The way we work" includes several aspects like:

- The way we identify what needs to get built and break it down to specific requirements.
- The processes and tools we follow as a team and as a company to communicate and collaborate.
- The way we write and test code.

Each of the bullets above is its own beast. This book is focused on the third: the way we write and test code. So on the *highest level*, we intend to maximize:

1. *Efficiency*. It is defined as the ability to accomplish something with the least amount of wasted time, money, and effort. It's competency in performance.
2. *Effectiveness*. Effectiveness is the degree to which something successfully produces the desired result. As far as software engineering is concerned, it's how close the actual system's output is to the intended system's output, given any input. Unintended behavior, otherwise called defects or bugs, reduces our system's effectiveness.

So effectiveness and efficiency are the main motivations behind our architectural decisions. I would also include in the objectives:

3. Improving programming experience. It's vital that we also enjoy our day-to-day work.

But much of our work experience depends on maximizing our effectiveness and efficiency anyways. As engineers, we are wired to do it :).

Measure Effectiveness & Efficiency

Knowing what we want to achieve is essential. It's also necessary to measure our success in achieving it. By measuring, we can identify which practices, under what context, help us build better software.

Let's first try to tackle the puzzle of measuring efficiency. Efficiency in software development can be translated as: How fast do we develop features. In software, we are trying to measure our efficiency with a metric called velocity. As of yet, we haven't found an effective way of measuring velocity.

Agile methodologies and Scrum have introduced the story points technique[2]. This technique tries to measure the team's velocity in relevance to the same team's velocity in the past. The steps of the method include:

1. Based on both analysis and speculations, the team agrees on the number of story points that a story is worth. Usually, the consensus is reached with a technique called planning poker[5]. Stories represent system requirements. Story points encapsulate the story's effort, risk, and complexity. A story worth ten story points should be roughly ten times more

[5] Planning poker, also called Scrum poker, is a consensus-based, gamified technique for estimating, mostly used for timeboxing in Agile principles.

In planning poker, members of the group make estimates by playing numbered cards face-down to the table, instead of speaking them aloud. The cards are revealed, and the estimates are then discussed. By hiding the figures in this way, the group can avoid the cognitive bias of anchoring, where the first number spoken aloud sets a precedent for subsequent estimates.

"complex" than a story worth one.

2. We track the number of story points we score in each sprint. We do this simply by summing the story points of all the *completed* stories.
3. We keep calculating the average number of story points that we score in our sprints. In time, as the law of large numbers[6] suggests, this average will become an accurate indication of the team's velocity.

This technique measures the team's delta. It doesn't make sense to know that a team's velocity is 40 story points; we don't get any information out of that. A story point does not hold any significance for the real world. We cannot tell whether a team scoring 40 points is an efficient team or not. It makes sense to know that after a specific change, the team's velocity went up from 40 to 45. It indicates improvement.

There are several pitfalls in the story points technique as well:

1. Estimation risk. The estimations are based both on assumptions and speculations. There are often unknowns and edge cases that cannot be calculated upfront.
2. It takes time until it shows results. Often the velocity that we calculate in each sprint varies significantly. Therefore, the

[6] In probability theory, the law of large numbers (LLN) is a theorem that describes the result of performing the same experiment a large number of times. According to the law, the average of the results obtained from a large number of trials should be close to the expected value and tends to become closer to the expected value as more trials are performed.
The LLN is important because it guarantees stable long-term results for the averages of some random events.

probability that we have calculated it wrong is high. We need to add a lot of sprints to the equation before we end up with an average that is highly likely to be accurate.

3. The team is changing in time. As the team members change, the criteria that we calculate story points, or otherwise complexity, change as well. We may notice an increase in velocity simply because the new team members calculate complexity more generously. This is called estimation inflation[7].

Regardless of its downsides, the story points technique does a somehow decent job at calculating team deltas. However, it cannot be used for a global velocity metric. In other words, it cannot calculate the relative velocity between two teams. Which team is faster and which is slower. A team that scores 40 points can be much more efficient than a team that scores 100 story points per sprint. Simply because the first team calculates complexity more conservatively.

So I would argue that the story points technique isn't a velocity metric at all. What it can measure is acceleration within the context of a specific team. Acceleration, in our case, translates as improvement or deterioration of the team's velocity. We need a stable point of reference to measure velocity, which we don't have. Our velocity is actually primarily "measured" by our intuition and past experience.

Remember that above, we discuss the good scenario where the organization correctly applies Scrum. More often than not, organizations adopt SCUM while maintaining a top-down mentality. They impose KPIs such as 30+ scored story points per print. This is actively destructive as it only adds pressure to the team. The team, in return, becomes defensive and protects itself by overestimating. In those cases, it's better if metrics can be avoided altogether.

Recently there has been a noticeable rise in the "#NoEstimatesMovements." It advocated against doing any

[7] Estimate inflation is when the estimate assigned to a product backlog item (usually a user story) increases over time. For example, today the team estimates something will take five points but previously they would have called it three points. Velocity increases, but the work done remains the same.

estimations at all. The reasoning behind this can be summed up in three bullet points:

- Accurate estimation is impossible.
- Estimates can put unnecessary and unproductive pressure on your team.
- Estimation is a waste, so better to spend as little time on it as possible.

Let's now try to tackle the puzzle of measuring effectiveness. Again, we lack a solid global metric. We primarily measure it with our intuition and experience. However, several indicators can help us like:

- The throughput of bugs that slip to production. Otherwise, the rate that production bugs are reported. The number of bugs divided by time.
- The impact of the bugs that slip to production:
  - How many users do they affect. A bug that appears in a particular type of user, in a specific scenario, and under a particular input is called an edge case. Edge cases commonly affect a small number of people.
  - How much do they affect the users. A bug that prevents a user from switching to dark mode causes insignificant inconvenience compared to a bug preventing a user from paying their due bill. The impact on our business is different as well.

The cost of a bug goes up based on how far down in the Software Development Life Cycle the bug is found. A bug identified in the development phase costs just a couple of hours from an engineer's time. A bug that reaches production can cost millions of dollars depending on the abovementioned factors. There are many examples of software bugs that ended up costing several hundred million dollars[3] [4]. The agile movement is trying to tackle this with a practice called left shifting[8].

The fact that we lack global, solid techniques to measure our efficiency

[8] Shift Left is a practice intended to find and prevent defects early in the software delivery process. The idea is to improve quality by moving tasks to the left as early in the lifecycle as possible. Shift Left testing means testing earlier in the software development process.

and effectiveness is what makes this profession so complicated. We know we have to maximize them, but we can't determine whether we have achieved it. Also, we can't be sure whether we achieved it in the short term at the expense of long-term success. Technical debt, I'm looking at you. Certain developers are advocates of lightweight, quick and dirty approaches. Others are in favor of full-fledged enterprise architectures. And we can't, mathematically at least, prove anyone wrong. Most of the decisions are very context-dependent. And the "context" is complex.

Our best shot is to:

1. Learn from the collective industry knowledge and the field's pioneers. That's why reading quality blogs and books can help us elevate our careers.
2. Apply those learnings and draw our own conclusions about what works and what doesn't.
3. Make use of the available techniques and metrics. Even though they are not perfect, they are helpful.

So from now on, we have established clarity on *why* to learn and apply the best engineering practices. We are after maximizing *effectiveness* and *efficiency* in whatever software we are inspired to build. In the following parts, I will lay down the collective industry knowledge on *how* to achieve this. I will try to make it as digestible as possible. First, I'll explain the theoretical background, as well as offer practical coding examples. Finally, I will also criticize and express my personal experience using those practices in production apps.

Summary

- The whole purpose of learning engineering practices is to maximize our effectiveness and efficiency in building software.
- We lack solid techniques for measuring effectiveness and efficiency. Most of the measuring is done by intuition and experience.

PART II

How - S.S.O.L.I.D Principles

Welcome to the second part of the book! By now, we know why picking an *adequate* architectural design is crucial. Emphasis on adequate, both over-engineering and under-engineering are equally harmful. This part of the book focuses on *how* we can achieve that—talking about *how* we are entering the technical realm. Inspired by the bestseller "Start with why" written by Simon Sinek, I am navigating this book from the more abstract to the more specific.

We will first talk about the Fundamental Software Objectives and how they enable us to write more effective code more efficiently. Then we will deep dive into S.O.L.I.D principles. S.O.L.I.D was first introduced in 2000 in Robert C Martin's paper - Design Principles and Design Patterns[1]. They are high-level principles that drive architectural decisions. They apply to any piece of software. We can apply them in any programming language, framework, and domain. We use them as a *"how"* to create software architectures and generally structure software. They are well established and widely accepted in the industry. Even their critics don't deny their overall importance.

* * *

Motivation

Learning the fundamental software principles and S.O.L.I.D will significantly help you write better software and elevate your career.

First of all, it will expand your horizons and make you a better engineer. Simply understanding the principle's rationale will improve your approach to writing software. Of course, you don't get much value by memorizing the names of the principles but by deeply understanding:

- How they work.
- What problems do they solve.
- How to use them.
- When to use them.

..you simply become a more powerful software engineer with more weapons in your arsenal.

Secondly, they are evaluated in almost any technical interview. I've seen countless companies that may not even include S.O.L.I.D, Clean, TDD, etc.. in their apps but still assess those skills in hiring interviews. Nowadays, you must prove your knowledge on these topics to get hired for a high-end engineering position, even if you will not use them day in and day out.

As we saw earlier, the word "Soft" in "Software" means that software should be able to change easily. Product requirements change rapidly; thus, software should be able to adapt to them quickly. There is a contrast here between SOFTware and S.O.L.I.D principles. Or is it? S.O.L.I.D principles are precisely here to make our software soft. S.O.L.I.D principles are here to stay. They aren't supposed to change often. They contain collective industry wisdom on the ingredients that make our software soft.

The approach

Initially, I will lay down the whole spectrum of fundamental objectives that define software quality. The Fundamental Software Objectives (FSO) drive the formation of every principle and modern architecture.

* * *

Then, we will deep dive into each of the S.O.L.I.D principles in a dedicated chapter. Each chapter will include the principle's theoretical background as well as practical examples. The coding samples will be mixed between Android and iOS. Those principles are framework-agnostic. Our focus is on the high-level engineering perspective and not on language features. Besides, Swift and Kotlin are very much alike.

We will understand how to apply those practices as well as include examples of violating them. It's often easier to understand the principle by understanding how to break it. I will also add criticism and my experience using the principles in production applications. The "best practices" are only best in a particular context. In a different context, they can be harmful. Breaking a rule is valid, so long as you know which rule you're breaking and the reason for doing so.

By the end of this part, you will have a clear understanding of what the S.O.L.I.D principles are, as well as how and when to apply them in your application.

CHAPTER FIVE

Fundamental Software Objectives

How to best architect software is a puzzle that has been troubling engineers for a long time. Alan Turing formalized the concept of computer science in the 40s. Since then, engineers have been trying to figure out the most effective way to structure software. The field of computer science that is trying to tackle this problem is software engineering. As we discussed in Part I, there is no such thing as one size fits all. Every software product is facing its own complexity and challenges. However, the spectrum of issues in software is common. Also, the foundation upon which we craft our clean solutions is the same, regardless of the programming language, the framework, or the business domain. We should avoid reinventing the wheel every time we build a new app. We must learn from the wisdom of the people who faced similar issues in the past in order to solve the problems we are facing now.

Luckily for us, due to the past work of some fantastic artisans, we do have a solid foundation to build upon.

Alan Turing; considered by many the father of computer science.

We have already established *why* we need to write Clean Code. That's to maximize our effectiveness and efficiency in whatever software we are inspired and/or paid to build. We now need to learn *how* to do it, and that's not a walk in the park.

You have probably heard about terms such as testability, cohesion, and coupling. "You must apply practice X to lower the system's coupling."

Then we just accept that lowering the coupling of the system is essential. Often, without fully understanding how it helps us improve our efficiency and effectiveness. We also don't fully understand when lowering the coupling is beneficial and under which conditions. Are there cases where reducing the coupling actually harms the codebase? Often people just try to sell their thing. Whether that's a practice, framework, or library and use buzzwords for marketing it.

Additionally, is lowering the system's coupling or improving the testability something that you can argue about with a nontechnical person?
"We need to focus on improving the system's testability."
"*Why?* I believe we need to implement more features that our customers need."

This is a common argument between tech and business. How can we effectively communicate with business people to make our case? In the end, we are all on the same team; we both want to make our product successful.

Finally, are those terms of equal importance? And do they all belong to the same level of abstraction?

In this chapter, we will put things in order. We will explain how those fundamental technical objectives can improve the quality of our code; how they make us more effective and efficient. And how to identify if the end goal is really achieved or if we optimized prematurely.

Fundamental Software Objectives (FSO)

So the collective industry knowledge indicates that to maximize our effectiveness and efficiency, we need to write code that is:

- *Readable*. We are constantly reading old code as part of the effort to write new code. Robert C Martin argues that the ratio of reading code vs. writing code is well over 10:1. Regardless of the exact number, we agree that we spend more time reading than writing code. And the ratio only increases as the system becomes more complex and the number of engineers grows.
- Testable. It should be easy to write automated tests that assert the system's behavior. The profound reason is that we don't want to spend too much time manually verifying that the system is effective. In other words, it has the intended behavior. As we discussed earlier, the cost of a bug goes up based on how far down in the Software Development Life Cycle the bug is found.
- Extensible. It should be easy to add additional functionality to the system. As we explained before, a big part of this comes from readability. Readability is a necessary but not a sufficient element to enable extensibility. We will learn several practices in the following chapters that maximize extensibility.
- *Robust*. Adding additional functionality should not introduce much risk of breaking existing functionality.
- *Maintainable*. When a defect is reported, it should be easy to

track it down and fix it.

- *Resilient and Durable*. Finally, we should be able to maintain the above qualities in time. As we discussed in Part I, our long-term efficiency drops dramatically when we are forced to rewrite the whole application.

> "Indeed, the ratio of time spent reading versus writing is well over 10 to 1. We are constantly reading old code as part of the effort to write new code. ...[Therefore,] making it easy to read makes it easier to write." —Uncle Bob[1]

The Fundamental Software Objectives are still high-level objectives. They don't require specialized technical knowledge in order to be understood. They are not as obvious to business people as efficiency, effectiveness, time, and money. But they are still able to appreciate their importance when appropriately explained.

Now that we found common ground on what we want to achieve, let's see how we can achieve it. We will move to *technical* objectives that will be difficult to explain to business people. In a debate with a business person, we should always point to their association with FSO and business objectives. Otherwise, they won't be able to understand their importance.

We can abbreviate the technical objectives as SCC. Separation of concerns, (High) Cohesion, (Low) Coupling.

The SCC signals the transition from the human to the technical realm.

Separation of Concerns

One of the most important concepts in software is the separation of concerns. Let's first try to understand what a concern is. We can explain concerns in different levels of abstraction; fine-grained concerns are aligned with coding tasks. On a high level, though, we can identify the concern categories below:

- *The business logic*. Aka, the real-world problem that our software is trying to solve. Let's take as an example a banking application. The business rules include making a payment, freezing a card, and more. It's why we are building the app in the first place.

- *The data.* Most apps require some sort of in-memory or persistent storage. It can range from storing minor configuration preferences locally up to building a relational database.
- *The user interface.* UI is actually a broad term representing the interface that a client uses to interact with the application. It can refer to the screens of a mobile or web app, but it can also refer to the REST API of a backend application. Since the clients of a back-end app are mobile and web apps, the back-end UI is the JSON requests/responses that it exposes. Console input is also UI.

The three bullets above are the most fundamental concerns an application can have. Most production apps often have to include two more high-level concerns:

- *Security.* Application security is also crucial nowadays.
- *Presentation logic.* The presentation logic includes the rules that define how something will appear on the screen.

As we explained earlier, we can go deeper than high-level and segregate each of those concerns into several micro-concerns. The principle applies to any level of abstraction. The separation of concerns indicates that all the concerns should be clearly separated in our codebase.

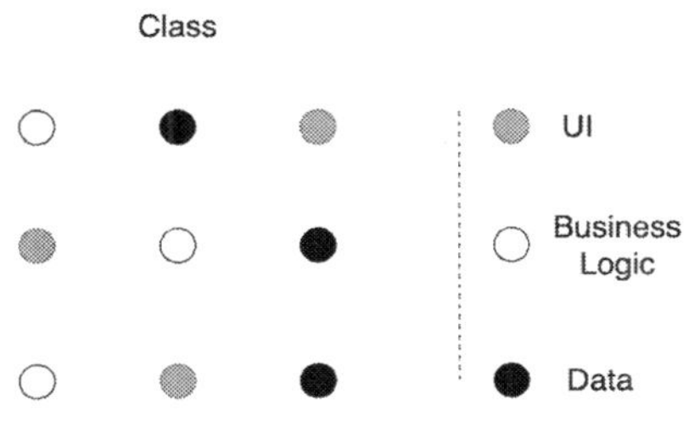

Mixed Concerns.

In the example above, we are mixing up the concerns. A single class is responsible for displaying UI elements, applying business logic, and performing data operations. The first symptom of this bad practice is that the class size will increase steeply. Secondly, its complexity will also increase exponentially. A human can hold at most nine objects in their working memory[9]. A class where the concerns are mixed can overwhelm quickly a developer trying to read it. The combinations of which the elements interact with each other increase exponentially. Increased size and complexity make a class hard to read, test, and maintain.

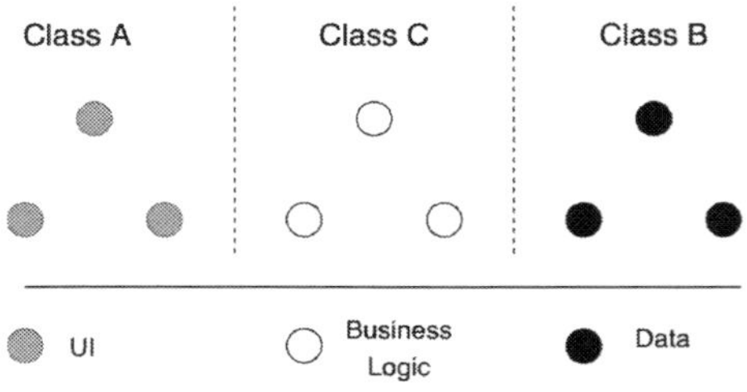

Separation of Concerns.

In this example, we have logically segregated the concerns into different classes. The code now is much easier to read, test, and maintain.

The *Single Concern* Principle (SCP) maximizes the separation of concerns. It tells us that only a single, fine-grained concern is allowed per file/class. We will discuss the SCP in detail in the next chapter.

> Separation of Concerns is not just a matter of good-looking code. SoC is vital to development speed. Moreover, it's vital to the success of your project. —Vladimir Khorikov

So as we can see, we separate concerns by drawing boundaries

[9] The Magical Number Seven, Plus or Minus Two: Some Limits on Our Capacity for Processing Information, is one of psychology's most highly cited papers. It was written by the cognitive psychologist George A. Miller of Harvard University's Department of Psychology and published in 1956 in Psychological Review. It is often interpreted to argue that the number of objects an average human can hold in short-term memory is 7 ± 2. This has occasionally been referred to as Miller's law.

between them. Before we move on to Cohesion and Coupling, let's first align on what a boundary is.

Boundaries, soft and hard

It's essential to understand what types of boundaries exist and how we cross them. At runtime, a boundary crossing is nothing more than a function on one side of the boundary calling a function on the other side and passing some data. The trick to creating an appropriate boundary crossing is to manage the source code dependencies and align the abstraction levels.

Technically, segregating code into two functions is drawing a boundary between them. Boundaries can be soft and hard, depending on how easy it is to cross them. Two functions within the same class are the softest type of boundary; even private functions can call each other. This boundary is so weak that it is often not regarded as a boundary at all.

The second softest type of boundary is two concrete classes under the same package or module, with one depending on the other. Private functions cannot be called, but the classes can depend on each other directly without an import statement. We can muscle up this boundary by separating those classes into different packages. Now crossing the boundary involves importing the dependency. Still, if the implementations change, the dependent class compilation can break.

To further increase the strength of our boundaries, we can draw interfaces between the concretions. This way, a concretion cannot change at will and cannot accidentally break other concretions. This is a pretty decent boundary that will lower the code's coupling (we discuss coupling next). Still, if the classes reside under the same software module, this boundary can be bypassed. We cannot prevent "illegal" boundary crossings. An implementation can, against the rules, import and use the other concretions.

* * *

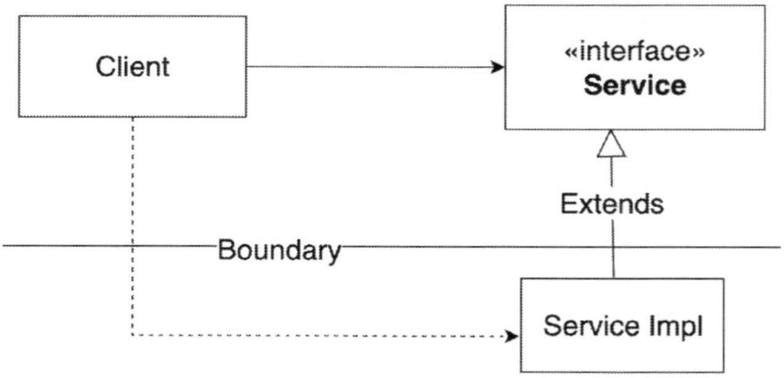

The dotted line represents a boundary crossing against the rules.

The most rigid boundary type is when we draw interfaces and segregate the code in different modules. Those modules can be developed, built, and deployed independently. They have their own build.gradle, or cocoa pods / Package.swift file. Those build files contain all the allowed cross-module dependencies. Those are hard boundaries.

It's also essential to understand that hard boundaries come at a cost. We increase the overall file count and lines of code, as well as the system's complexity. We don't always need them, nor are they always useful. Later in the book, we will learn to identify when we need to draw hard boundaries and when we can get away with soft ones or even no boundaries at all.

High Cohesion

Cohesion is a measure of how strongly related and focused the various responsibilities of a software unit are. Cohesive software units are easy to comprehend and are more reusable. A module that does only one thing (and does it well) is more likely to provide value in different contexts than a module that aggregates many unrelated behaviors. A software unit can refer to a software module, class, or function. As we explained, those principles apply at all levels of abstraction.

In essence, high cohesion means keeping parts of a codebase related to each other in a single place. In theory, the guideline looks pretty simple. In practice, however, you need to dive into the domain model of your software deep enough to understand which parts of your codebase are actually related. Perhaps, the lack of objectivity in this guideline is the reason why it's often so hard to follow.

Let's understand it better with an example:

```
class EmployeeInteractor(
    private val employeeRepository: EmployeeRepository
) {

    fun addEmployee(employee: Employee) =
        employeeRepository.addEmployee(employee)

    fun deleteEmployee(employeeId: String) =
        employeeRepository.deleteEmployee(employeeId)

    fun editEmployee(employee: Employee) =
        employeeRepository.editEmployee(employee)

    fun giveRaise(employeeId: String, amount: Double) {
        if (amount >= 0)
            employeeRepository.increaseSalary(employeeId, amount)
    }
}
```

This is an example of a cohesive class. We have an Interactor responsible for exposing specific business actions that belong to the Employee class. It's cohesive since its only responsibility is to contain all the business logic regarding a single entity.

* * *

```
class EmployeeInteractor(
    private val employeeRepository: EmployeeRepository
    ) {

    fun addEmployee(employee: Employee) =
        employeeRepository.addEmployee(employee)

    fun deleteEmployee(employeeId: String) =
        employeeRepository.deleteEmployee(employeeId)

    fun editEmployee(employee: Employee) =
        employeeRepository.editEmployee(employee)

    fun giveRaise(employeeId: String, amount: Double) {
        if (amount >= 0)
            employeeRepository.increaseSalary(employeeId, amount)
    }

    fun mapColorForAnnualSalary(amount: Int): Int {
        return when (amount) {
            in 0..60000 -> R.color.green
            in 6000..100000 -> R.color.yellow
            in 100000..150000 -> R.color.orange
            else -> R.color.red
        }
    }
}
```

The above represents a noncohesive version of the same class. We have added a function that calculates the color of a text field based on an employee's salary. It breaks the cohesion of the class because the rest of the functions apply business logic to the employee entity, while the *mapColorForAnnualSalary* function applies presentation logic. Responsibilities are mixed, and this class is not cohesive anymore. If we add all the responsibilities of the employee entity in a single class, soon, this class will become bloated with too much unrelated code.

The above is a cohesion violation, but not the worse type of it. A more severe violation would be adding a function to perform HTTP calls. The class then would combine business with low-level data logic.

High cohesion helps a lot with readability and reusability.

* * *

Low coupling

Coupling represents the degree to which a single software unit is dependent on others. In other words, it is the number of connections between two or more units and how strong those connections are—the fewer and softer the connections, the lower the coupling. Hard boundaries mean soft connections; soft boundaries are hard connections. High coupling is problematic. When everything is connected:

- A change in one portion of the system can break the behavior in another, distant part of the system. Imagine several classes depending on a single function that has to change its signature. All its clients now need to change in order to compile. This is the so-called ripple effect[10]. As Uncle Bob says: "This system exhibits the symptom of fragility."
- High coupling minimizes opportunities for reuse. Importing a module that depends on several other modules and third-party libraries makes you depend on all those as well. Those are called transitive dependencies[11]. We have all felt the pain of being unable to make use of two third-party libraries simply because they depend on a different version of another library. Version-classing is a high coupling symptom.
- Tightly-coupled units are hard to test. Testing a class with many collaborators often requires considerable setup and/or side effects. If we use mocks, having many collaborators heavily increases the effort to mock them. In case we avoid mocks, high coupling increases the number of side effects. That's because a class can be reported as defective, while in reality, the defect resides in one of its dependencies. This case will consume more effort since we will need to put more time into investigating and correcting the defect.

* * *

---

[10] Ripple effect: a spreading, pervasive, and usually unintentional effect or influence.

[11] Transitive dependencies are dependencies that we do not directly depend on. Instead we depend on a module that depends on them.

Let's take a look at an example to understand the above better:

```
class EmployeeInteractor(
    private val employeeRepository: EmployeeRepository
) {

    fun addEmployee(employee: Employee) =
        employeeRepository.addEmployee(employee)

    fun deleteEmployee(employeeId: String) =
        employeeRepository.deleteEmployee(employeeId)

    fun editEmployee(employee: Employee) =
        employeeRepository.editEmployee(employee)

    fun giveRaise(employeeId: String, amount: Double) {
        if (amount >= 0)
            employeeRepository.increaseSalary(employeeId, amount)
    }
}
```

We are re-using the previous EmployeeInteractor class; it also serves as an example of low coupling. The Employee Interactor has only one dependency, the Repository. It makes use of it in order to get data access. This dependency is necessary to comply with the high cohesion principle. Aka, not performing unrelated actions. Let's now take a look at an example of high coupling:

* * *

```
class EmployeeInteractor(
    private val employeeRepository: EmployeeRepository,
    private val employeeFile: File,
    private val employeeSharedPreferences: SharedPrefs,
    private val usersRepository: UsersRepository,
) {

    fun addEmployee(employee: Employee) {
        employeeRepository.addEmployee(employee)
        employeeFile.registerRecord(employee)
        usersRepository.addUser(employee.toUser())
    }

    fun deleteEmployee(employeeId: String) {
        employeeRepository.deleteEmployee(employeeId)
        employeeFile.removeRecord(employeeId)
        usersRepository.removeUser(employeeId)
    }

    fun editEmployee(employee: Employee) {
        employeeRepository.editEmployee(employee)
        usersRepository.editUser(employee.toUser())
    }

    fun giveRaise(employeeId: String, amount: Double) {
        if (amount >= 0)
            employeeRepository.increaseSalary(employeeId, amount)
        employeeSharedPreferences.registerRaise()
    }
}
```

It now has four dependencies the employee repository, file, shared preferences, and the UsersRepository. Those are unnecessary; the file and shared preferences dependencies should be moved to the Repository.

This example breaks the low coupling principle, the separation of concerns, and the high cohesion principle. The employee Interactor class now has more than one concern and knows about more than one business entity. Therefore, we can conclude that those objectives complement each other and often go side-by-side. A highly coupled software unit will most likely not be cohesive, and it will mix unrelated concerns.

Getting back to the connection between coupling & testability. If we used mocks, we would have to mock the behavior of all: Employee repository, Employee file, Employee shared prefs, and Users repository. Just to be able to test a single class. This is a lot of work, and it's increasing exponentially. Besides the happy path, we have also to test the error cases.

We also have the option to avoid using mocks, in accordance with the Chicago School of TDD[12]. Then, the Employee Interactor class tests could be reported defective for a bug in any of its dependencies.

Besides the number of dependencies, high coupling also depends on how tightly the dependencies are coupled. In other words, how soft or hard our boundaries are. Coupling with abstractions, interfaces, and protocols, is not tight. Coupling with concretions, classes, and implementations, is tight coupling. Depending on concrete classes reduces the reusability of the unit as we cannot use it in different contexts. A class that depends on interfaces/protocols rather than concretions is more flexible. It may have the same number of dependencies, but it's not tied to concretions; therefore, the coupling is lower.

Low coupling is also related to the Law of Demeter or the principle of the least knowledge. The Law of Demeter (LoD)[2] is an Object-Oriented design guideline for developing software. The LoD is a specific case of loose coupling in its general form.

Ian Holland proposed the guideline at Northeastern University

---

[12] These two main schools of TDD. They are commonly referred to as the Chicago School of TDD (or Classicist, state-based testing, Inside-out, black-box testing) and the London School of TDD (or Mockist, Interaction testing, Outside-in testing, white-box testing).

The Chicago school of TDD starts with an inside-out approach to testing. Testing begins at the unit level, and the design is supposed to "emerge" from the tests.
A key feature of the Chicago school is the avoidance of mocks.

towards the end of 1987. It is briefly summarized as:

- Each unit should have limited knowledge about other units: only units "closely" related to the current unit.
- Each unit should only talk to its friends; don't talk to strangers.
- Only talk to your immediate friends.

The fundamental notion is that a given object should assume as little as possible about the structure or properties of anything else (including its subcomponents). This comes from the principle of "information hiding" [3]. It may be viewed as a corollary to the principle of least privilege[4], which dictates that a module possesses only the information and resources necessary for its legitimate purpose.

Levels of Coupling & Cohesion

We have used the term *software unit* to define cohesion and coupling. In our practical examples, the unit was a class. But as we explained, cohesion and coupling apply to any level of abstraction. They apply to units as small as functions or classes and as big as software modules or even whole software systems.

We identify a tightly coupled module when:

1. It depends on many other modules.
2. Many of its classes depend on classes in different modules. When there isn't a single point, preferably an interface, that handles the external communication.

A tightly coupled module cannot be developed independently, and it is hardly reusable.

Moving to cohesion, we identify a non-cohesive module when the tasks it executes are not logically related. Cohesion is more subjective than coupling, but the two are closely related. We intentionally couple things that want to live together into cohesive units (types/classes/modules etc.).

> Cohesion = intentionally coupled units. —Jovche Mitrejchevski.

Types of code based on Cohesion and Coupling

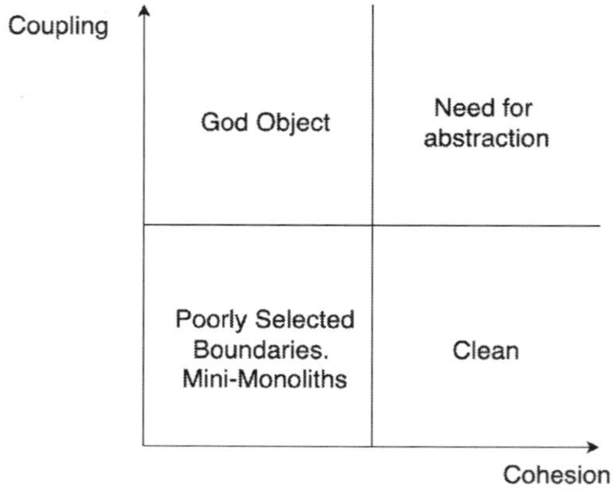

The diagram above categorizes the code based on cohesion and coupling.

- *High cohesion and low coupling* is the ideal, Clean situation.

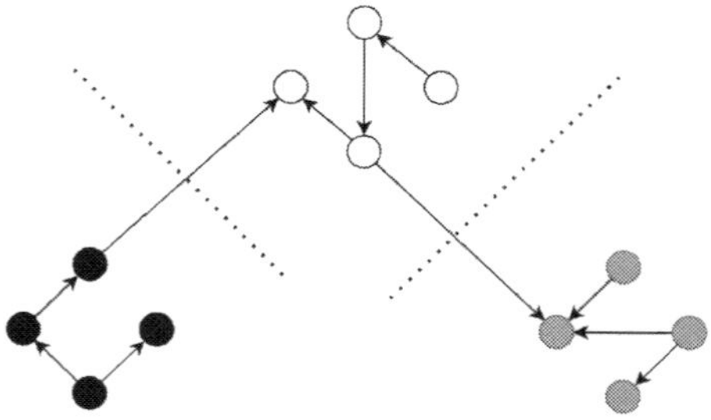

High Cohesion Low Coupling

- *Low cohesion and low coupling* indicate that we have separated our boundaries in a poor logical way. Thus we have introduced multiple monoliths within the system. The monoliths are not very dependent on each other; that's why we have low coupling. But the monoliths are also not focused;

that's why we have low cohesion. A monolith is doing much-unrelated stuff, making it harder to read, understand and maintain.

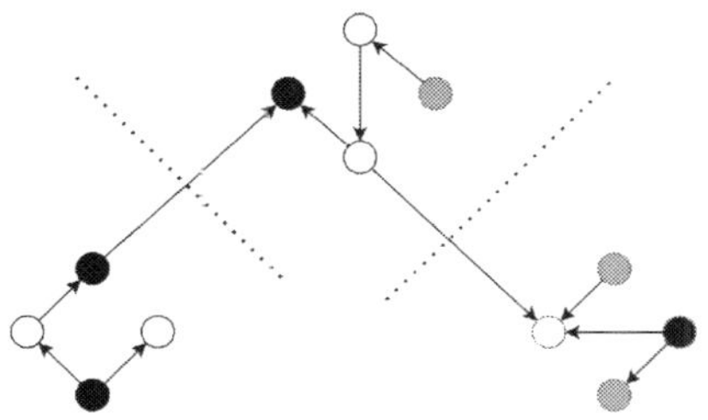

Low Cohesion Low Coupling

- *High cohesion and high coupling* indicate the need to introduce more abstractions and boundaries into our system. The units are small and cohesive but depend on concrete implementations rather than abstractions. In other words, there aren't enough boundaries, and the boundaries are soft. This makes them inflexible and more rigid to be reused in different contexts. We should also segregate and redesign those interfaces to minimize the number of dependencies.

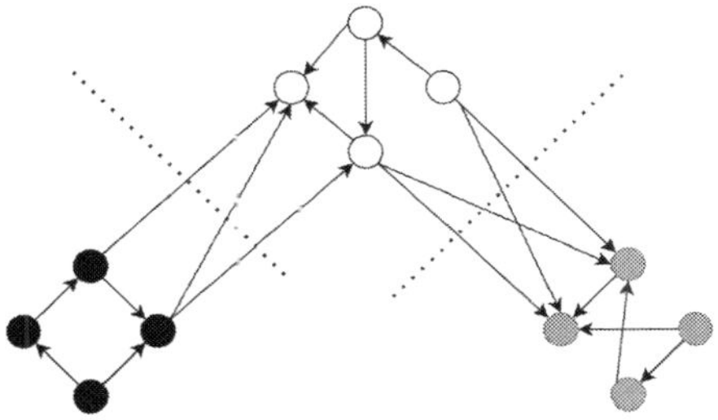

High Cohesion High Coupling

- *Low cohesion and high coupling* is the worst situation to be in. A code smell[13] that emerges from this situation is what we call

[13] A code smell is a surface indication that usually corresponds to a deeper problem in the system.
A smell is something usually easy to spot but it doesn't always indicate a

God object. A God object is an object that references a large number of distinct types and/or has too many unrelated or uncategorized methods. In other words, it's an object that does too much, knows too much, and is known by too many.

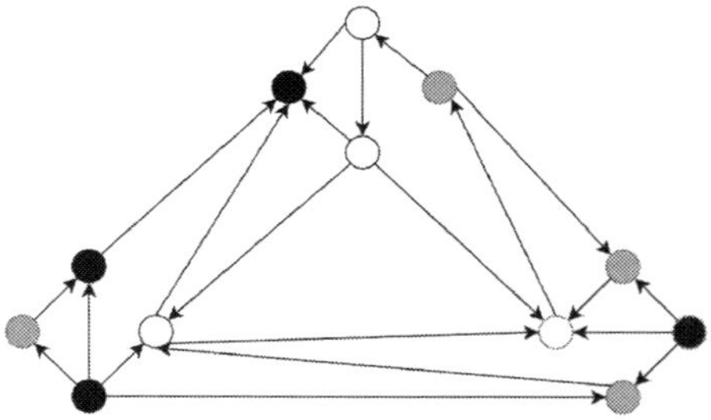

Low Cohesion High Coupling

Cohesion, coupling, and separation of concerns are interconnected. Usually, you achieve high cohesion and low coupling if you apply proper separation of concerns.

Most of the technical principles we will learn from now aim to achieve those high-level technical objectives.

Criticism

We discussed how high cohesion and low coupling are the fundamental technical objectives that drive our architectural design. But are there any downsides or points of consideration?

Regarding cohesion, I wouldn't say much. High cohesion means grouping related tasks together. The only concern is that it can be a subjective matter. Sometimes people may have different views on cohesion and how to design highly cohesive modules. But overall,

---

problem. Smells aren't inherently bad on their own - they are often an indicator of a problem rather than the problem themselves. The term was popularized by Kent Beck on WardsWiki in the late 1990s.

there aren't many objections on why to design a module to be cohesive.

Regarding low coupling, it can increase the complexity of our app when improperly achieved. Drawing boundaries in the code means implementing several interfaces and applying data transformations from one side to another. It doesn't come for free; it increases the file count and lines of code. Drawing a boundary needs to serve a purpose. Drawing interfaces between all implementations is futile. We must have a clear purpose and benefit for doing it, like:

i. Protecting stable, high-level code from volatile, low-level code. We will deep dive into this in the following chapters.
ii. Decoupling unrelated tasks and modules, high cohesion - single concern. The higher purpose is to increase the readability and testability of the system.
iii. Isolating legacy code or decisions that we don't want to affect a large part of our codebase. Contain cancer and deal with it later.
iv. Enabling independent teams to work in parallel. Drawing rigid boundaries can help teams to be less dependent on each other. It can reduce symptoms like inter-team merge conflicts. It can also enable the teams to decide on code style and third-party library usage. Similarly to leveraging microservices in a backend system. This can be helpful for the development of a large-scale enterprise app. However, It is not required when a small team of developers builds the app. Hard boundaries may slow the team down in this case.

Summary

We want to maximize our:

- Efficiency. The velocity[14] that we are delivering features.
- Effectiveness. To deliver code as close as possible to the intended behavior under any input.

* * *

[14] Velocity term isn't used here to describe the story points technique used in SRCUM. It refers to the actual speed that we deliver code outcomes.

How? By building systems that achieve the FSO. In other words, by writing code that is:

- Readable.
- Robust.
- Extensible.
- Testable.
- Maintainable.
- Resilient.

How? By building systems that achieve SCC. Otherwise, by structuring code that is:

- Highly cohesive.
- Loosely coupled.
- Applying proper separation of concerns.

How? By applying the S.O.L.I.D principle and other best practices that we will learn in the following chapters!

Finally, there is no need to decouple everything or apply S.O.L.I.D everywhere. It must serve one of the higher-level objectives. Whenever you find yourself adding a pattern, try to answer the question: "Which high-level objective does it serve and how?". If you can't answer this question, abandon it and write simpler code. MVA and evolutionary design can guide us.

CHAPTER SIX

Single Responsibility

> "...each individual can only do one thing well. He can't do lots of things. If he tries, he will be a jack of all trades, and master of none." —Socrates.

Socrates, in 400 BC, formed this argument for people. We may have to learn something from him in 20xx for machines.

The Background

The Single Responsibility Principle (SRP) states that every module, class, or function should have responsibility for a single part of that program's functionality and encapsulate that part. All of that module, classes, or function's services should be narrowly aligned with that responsibility[1].

Uncle Bob rephrased this principle as "A module should have only one reason to change"[2].

This definition is ambiguous. What exactly qualifies as "a reason to change." Some developers would argue that a bug fix is a reason to change the module, refactor the code, or add a new feature. It required a little bit more elaboration, so Uncle Bob rephrased the principle to:

"A module should be responsible for one, and only one user, or stakeholder."

This is also kind of ambiguous. Does the ownership of a module belong to a single physical person? Should we mention at the top of the file that it belongs to "John" and he is the SRP representative? This re-definition did not help much in clearing up the ambiguity, so the final version of the SRP Robert C Martin came up with is:

"A Module should be responsible to one, and only one, actor."

I can't say that the community has understood the SRP even after the last definition. Still, for many engineers, it's unclear what actor means. But if you read the book *Clean Architecture* or Uncle Bob's blog[3] he makes it a bit clearer.

An actor for Uncle Bob is a human role, position, or responsibility. For example:

- a CEO is an actor.
- a CFO is an actor.

- a CTO is an actor.
- a Product Owner is an actor.

Of course, at a given time in a company, a specific person fulfills each of those responsibilities. Thus we are still referring to actual people. However, people rotate in companies, and it isn't convenient to define a software module's actor with their name. So in the latest definition, we abstract the physical person. We define actors by a position/role or ownership of a particular domain, of certain business decisions. They are positions that decide how certain parts of the product must behave.

But a regulator can also be an actor. State regulations may also force certain parts of our product to change. So I think we can sum it up as follows:

An actor is a decision-maker who defines the desired behavior of a specified part of the software.

What does the SRP mean in code?

Let's focus on some code examples to understand this better. Let's assume that we are working on an e-shop app. We are selling products to both retail and business customers. We have a product class that looks like this:

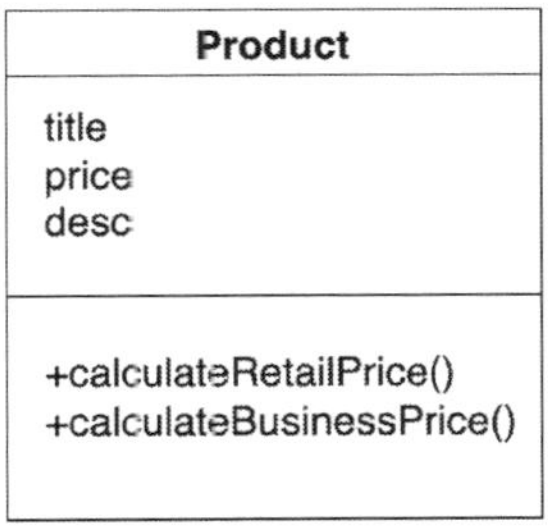

The product has the title, desc, and price attributes. It also has two price calculation functions, one for business and one for retail customers. The business customers have different rules and discounts than retail ones. This class violates the SRP because those two functions belong to different actors. Different actors decide the price calculations for the two groups. As we will see, different regulations govern them as well. In other words, those two functions change for different reasons.

Let's examine a symptom of the violation above. In every price calculation, we need to apply VAT. The VAT calculation is pretty simple; we just need to increase our final price by 24%. Therefore, to avoid duplication, we have implemented a shared function called *applyVat*:

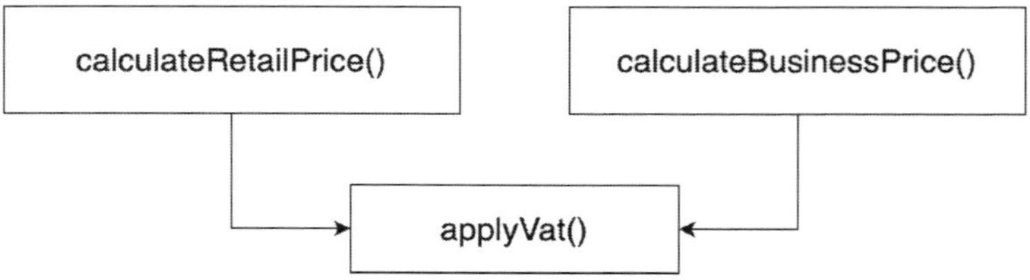

Now suppose that the regulations in our country or state change. The regulators decide that the VAT for business-to-business transactions will drop to 12%. So the development team working in the business department finds it convenient to change the *applyVat* function. It's as simple as changing a constant integer value from 24 to 12. It gets implemented fast and deployed to production to comply with the new regulations. What happens the next morning is that our retail customers are happily purchasing everything 12% cheaper than before. Our company is taking a hit on its earnings and is obligated to pay the price to avoid reputation damage.

Uncle Bob also refers to this case as accidental duplication. Accidental duplication happens when we use a shared function to avoid duplicating code when we actually should be creating two implementations, even if they are identical. This is valid for the case that two separate actors are responsible for the shared implementation. The functions are accidentally similar and will remain so for a "short" time. They change for different reasons, so they are meant to diverge eventually. Accidental duplication is the first symptom of violating the Single Responsibility Principle.

The second symptom is merge conflicts. When a class has multiple reasons to change, various developers will be writing code in the same file. When the code has to get merged and released, we will eventually have to deal with the dreaded merge conflicts. Particularly in a scaled project where multiple teams are involved, merge conflicts tend to introduce risk and increase our time to market. Therefore, we should be architecting in order to minimize them as much as possible.

How to comply with the SRP

There are multiple ways to refactor the code above to comply with the SRP and treat the symptoms mentioned. All the solutions involve segregating the business from the retail behavior. Each should be contained in a dedicated class. The most obvious solution is implementing two separate price calculators with access to the Product data.

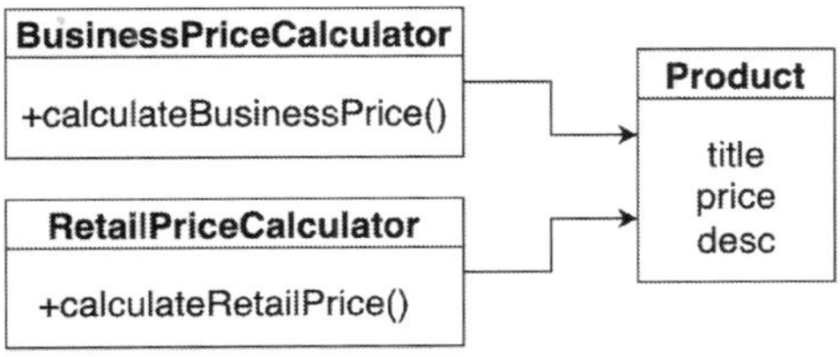

The issue with this approach is that the client of this code now needs to be aware of two extra classes. It's preferable when clients interact with a single interface, and we keep the dependencies at a minimum (low coupling). We can improve this by applying the Facade Design pattern[15]:

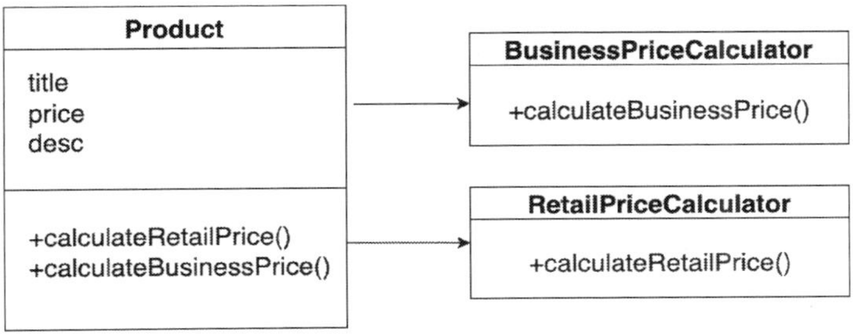

[15] Facade is a structural design pattern that provides a simplified interface to a library, a framework, or any other complex set of classes.

* * *

We keep the signature of the functions inside the Product class while moving the actual implementations to collaborative calculators. With this refactoring, changes in the business price calculation will not affect the calculation of the retail price. Furthermore, the files are different, so no merge conflicts or other side-effects can occur.

Our code is now compliant with the Single Responsibility Principle.

Criticism

In my experience, many engineers still find the SRP ambiguous and confusing. There are a lot of interpretations of what constitutes a "responsibility" and how to define if a module is pertaining to just one. It seems evident in carefully picked examples found in textbooks and blog posts. However, in day-to-day work on a production application, it feels hard and impractical to identify the actor of every module/class. It definitely is an important principle and deserves its place in S.O.L.I.D, but it is a bit abstracted, and it's not always clear whether we are violating it.

Its connection with "actors" who are real people makes it ambiguous. Usually, we receive requirements from a single Product Owner. Their job is to abstract the complexity of where the requirements are coming from. As far as the team is concerned, the requirements come from the single truth source—the PO or, anyways, a product professional. Sure, the team must discuss and refine them together with the PO, generally though the PO will do most of the work in the backlog. Therefore, it is not practical to think about every feature who may actually be the real stakeholder and possibly request changes.

The boundaries are often not so well-defined. In fact, it took me quite some thinking to come up with an example to describe the principle. Most blog posts use the same example as Uncle Bob first used in the original post[4]. In cherry-picked examples, it makes perfect sense, and it's crystal clear. In day-to-day work, you can give it a try and draw your own conclusions.

* * *

By no means am I saying that it is not a very valuable tool. Nor do I want to criticize the legendary Robert C Martin, whose experience surpasses mine by a few decades. Suppose we could measure experience in time, at least in the absence of another metric. I just want to state that I've seen a lot of confusion in the industry around this principle, and there is probably a reason for that. We often violate it and only realize it later while dealing with the symptoms.

Besides its ambiguity, I believe it still delivers value. It serves as the "business representative" in technical decisions. It reminds us, engineers, that not all technical decisions need to be driven by technical principles. The people/actors who drive the product decisions should also be taken under consideration while designing technical solutions.

Personally, what helps me more to define architectural designs in day-to-day work, is what I like to call the **Single Concern Principle (SCP)**. The drivers behind the SCP and what constitutes a reason to change are technical rather than business-oriented. They don't tie up to actual people. I will do my best to describe it below, and hopefully, you will also find it helpful when you design your application.

The Single Concern Principle

The SCP states that:

Each software unit should have one, and only one, technical, fine-grained concern.

To make sense, we should define what a technical concern is. A concern is either:

- The execution of a task or a group of related tasks.
- The delegation of a task or a group of related tasks.

When working with Functional(like) Programming[16], we can also

[16] Functional-like programming is what most of us are currently applying in mobile apps whether we know it or not. We will deep dive into this later and

include that a concern can be:

- Containing data that describes a business entity. This does not apply in pure OO designs as data and operations (task executions) sit together by the Data Encapsulation Principle[17].

With the term "task," I refer to any calculation the software needs to perform. Like:

- Applying business logic to solve a problem.
- Data accessing or modifying. Either locally or remotely.
- Drawing UI on a screen. Etc.

We can categorize our classes or files in the following categories using the above. A class can be either:

- An *executor* is a "class" that executes a task or applies logic.
- A delegator or *orchestrator*. It orchestrates the flow of control and delegates the tasks to the responsible executors.
- In pure functional programming, a data container. Those are our models, POJOs, or data classes.

If a class belongs in more than one category, it has more than one concern and violates the SCP. Another way to break the SCP is if it's a container, delegator, or executor of tasks that are *not related*.

Again we fall on the same ambiguity we fell before with the Single Responsibility Principle; what does "related" mean? We can use the same explanation; related tasks are tasks that change for the same reason. But here, we don't tie this to actual people, roles, regulations, or anything related to the real world and business requirements.

The SCP stays at the technical level, where things are more

---

explain why and how we are practically applying a mix of OO and functional programming to our apps. And this is not necessarily a bad thing. Kotlin as well as Swift and Dart are modern languages that have consciously decided to support both styles so we can enjoy the best from both worlds.

[17] Data encapsulation, also known as data hiding, is the mechanism whereby the implementation details of a class are kept hidden from the user. The user can only perform a restricted set of operations on the hidden members of the class by executing special functions commonly called methods.

straightforward. So how do we define that a group of tasks is related, they have a single concern, or otherwise change for similar reasons? The best way to understand this is by example. The example should be as generic as possible and not outline a specific scenario where the principle makes particular sense. In fact, we have already seen an example of it earlier in the MVA chapter. The evolution of the high-level architecture there was driven mainly by the Single Concern Principle.

Let's break it down and explain the evolution of our architectural design in terms of the SCP.

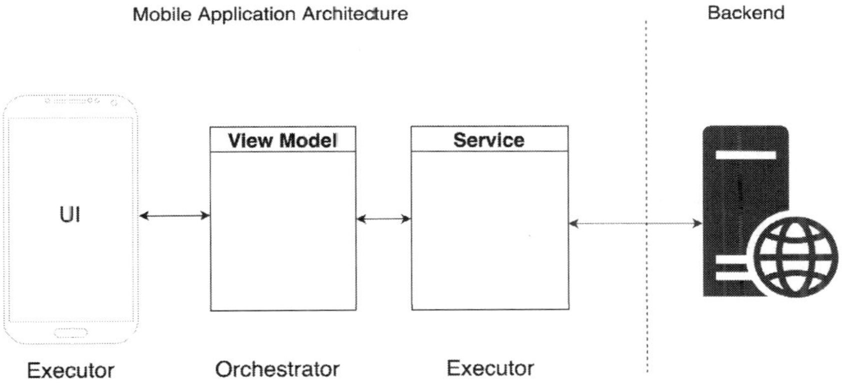

In the initial MVA, we can identify the UI layer as an executor. It carries out all the screen interactions, whether it's an iOS View Controller, an Android Fragment, or a Flutter Widget. Those tasks include drawing the UI as well as receiving user input. Those are related tasks; thus, they constitute a single concern.

The View Model is an orchestrator. It usually[18] facilitates the

[18] Generally, I've seen multiple types of View Models in apps; the important thing is to carry out only one responsibility. One responsibility is the aggregation of data from various services (Orchestrator). Another responsibility is the application of the presentation logic (Executor). It's important not to be both an Executor (applying logic) and an Orchestrator(delegating tasks). Then this layer becomes thick, and we break the SCP.

communication between the UI and the Service.

The second SCP condition suggests that a piece of software must execute or delegate *related* tasks. The View Model belongs to the presentation layer, whose purpose is to serve the view layer. Consequently, one View Model should be responsible for serving a single screen. A single screen can be apart from multiple Fragments or views, but it has to be a single screen. A View Model serving multiple screens falls under the accidental duplication that we discussed earlier. The two screens change for different reasons. Thus it will be causing the symptoms described earlier. The relationship between a screen and a View Model should be 1-1.

Finally, the Service is an executor. It is responsible for performing all the CRUD operations to our backend.

It's important to understand that the SCP is a low-level principle that applies to the class level. The service layer can be broken down into multiple components like the HTTP client, the JSON parser, and the higher-level API. In this breakdown, the high-level API layer would be an orchestrator. The HTTP client and the JSON parser would be executors as they perform a specific cohesive task. The diagram below depicts the full breakdown:

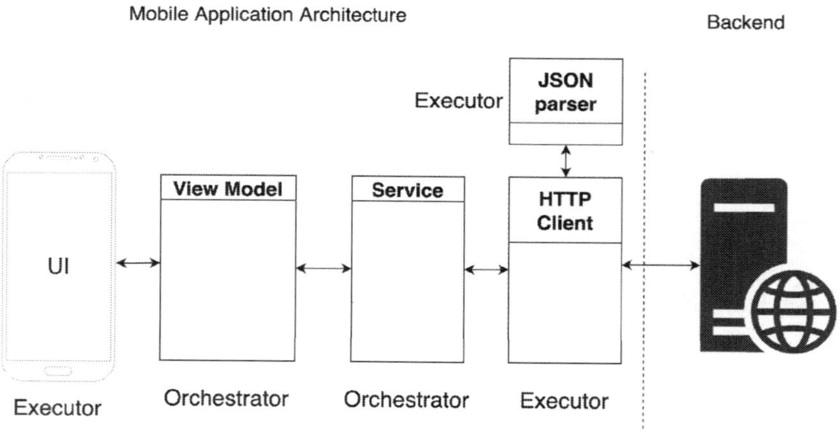

Later in our story, we received new requirements and identified the need for a database. Our first thought was something like this:

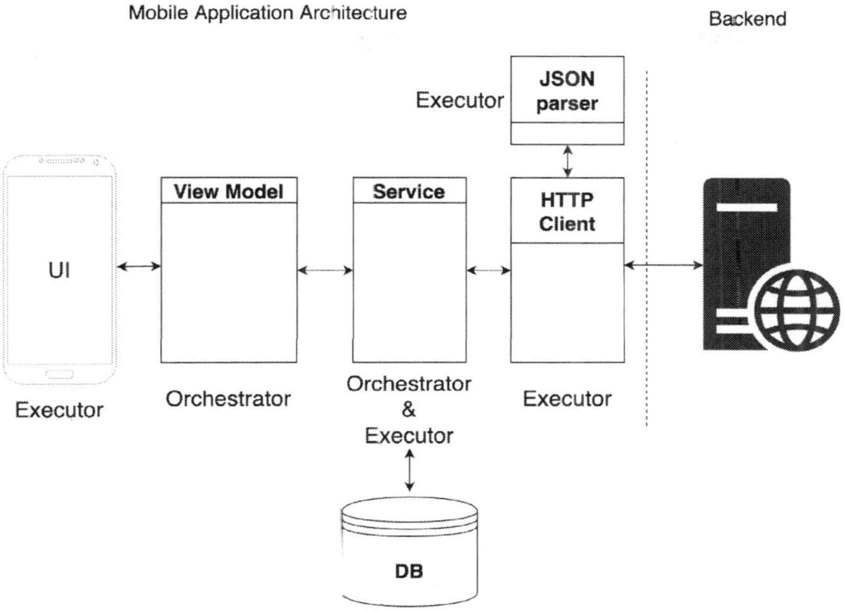

In this example, the service is responsible for two beefy concerns. One is to communicate with our backend, and the second is to execute queries and communicate with the database. This is a severe violation of the SCP, so we immediately refactored to:

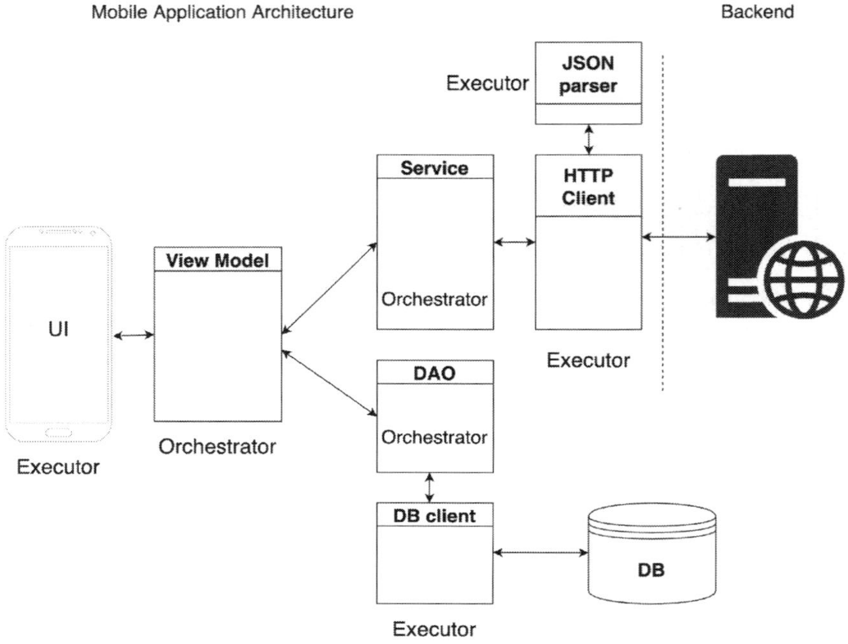

Communicating with the database has been moved to the DAO layer. This is an orchestrator; it provides an interface to interact with the DB. To comply with the SCP, we also include a separate lower-level DB client class. This is responsible for executing the actual queries. Thus, it's an executor. Some libraries like Android - Jetpack Room work with code generation; therefore, we don't ever get to see the actual DB client implementation.

In the example above, we can identify that all the classes have a single concern except the View Model. The View Model now also contains the offline logic, whether we have to fetch fresh information from the Service or reuse the local data from DAO. This concern is pretty beefy, and its implementation can become quite complex. Therefore, we must refactor our system to include another orchestrator that will take this concern away from the View Model. Furthermore, we need a dedicated component to take care of the presentation logic. This will be the Presentation Mapper. After the mentioned refactoring, the new MVA looks like this:

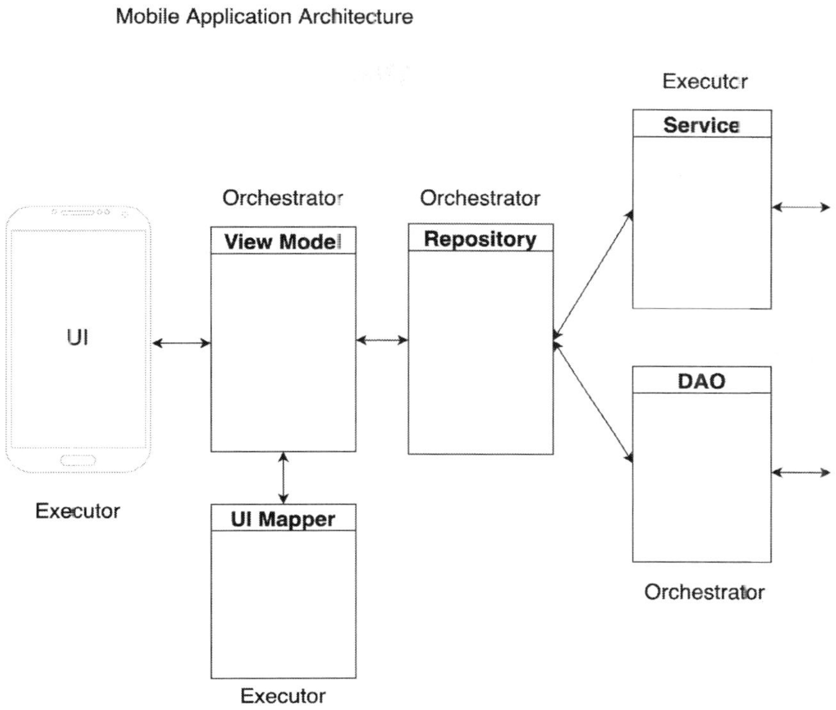

It's important to state that from the View Model and left, the layers serve the users of our app. While from the Repository and right, they serve the data. Therefore, we need to have a single View Model per screen and a single Repository per entity. For example, we have an ArticleRepository responsible for data operations related to articles. And an AccountRepository responsible for data operations related to the Account entity. A repository that mixes unrelated entities is breaking the second condition of the SCP; the tasks must be related.

We had to introduce data aggregation in the final version of the architectural design. A screen displayed unrelated information, so the 1-1 connection between ViewModel and Repository was broken. Furthermore, as the application became more complex, additional logic had to be included. We had to separate the presentation logic from the business logic to keep the implementations cohesive and simple:

Mobile Application Architecture

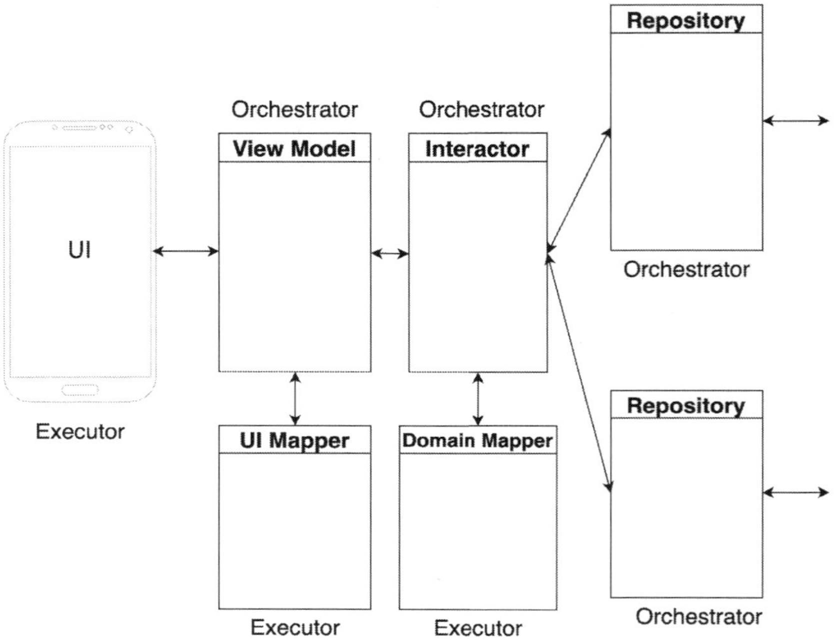

Here, we introduced another orchestrator, the Aggregator, sometimes also called Data Source. The Aggregator is responsible for aggregating the information from multiple Repositories. Remember that each repository handles one and only one entity. We have also introduced another executor, the Domain Mapper. Its unique concern is to apply the business logic.

It's also important to note that zero responsibilities means redundancy and should be avoided. If the View Model, for example, is not applying any logic, neither aggregating multiple data sources nor orchestrating other collaborators like data mappers, it is redundant. Having a View Model that simply interferes between the Service and the View without executing a concern is an example of over-engineering. This is described by a code smell called Middleman[19]. This is not a typical case for View Models, but I often see it in different layers. A layer should not just exist for the sake of architecture, but it should own one single concern.

One last thing to mention is that an app can function only by having executors. Executors perform the tasks. However, the meaningful introduction of orchestrators makes an app Clean. This is how we achieve separation of concerns, high cohesion, and low coupling; by having orchestrators orchestrating cohesive executors that perform a group of related tasks.

So we saw how the SCP can gradually guide us in designing a system where each file/class is pertaining to one and only one concern. By gaining experience in architecting software, it becomes easy to identify which tasks constitute a concern and when a class includes more than one.

Having said that, I also don't advise you to follow the principle blindly. Sometimes, we can consciously choose to let a layer have two concerns. Like a View Model orchestrating logic mappers and also performing data aggregation. Or allowing a single mapper to apply both the presentation and the business logic. In a simple application, we can live with that. However, it must be an educated and conscious decision. When our team or the app's complexity grows, we must take the time to refactor the app to comply with the SCP. Otherwise, the app will keep getting dirtier and the loan bigger.

A fun fact is that for several years I believed that the Single Concern Principle is the actual Single Responsibility Principle that Uncle Bob had defined. That's what I had understood from it, and many of my colleagues and friends were under the same misconception. Later I decided to study S.O.L.I.D in more depth, and I saw that it states something different than what I and many others had in mind. The SCP, as a misunderstood SRP, has been guiding me all this time to build clean systems. Therefore, I decided to describe it in detail here. I hope you will find it helpful in your day-to-day work.

---

[19] A Middleman is a class that is only delegating work to one specific collaborator.

* * *

Summary

Both the Single Responsibility and the Single Concern Principles aim for the same objective, high cohesion. The Single Responsibility Principle tries to tackle this issue from a business perspective. It introduces the business actors' notion and suggests identifying how many people can possibly ask for changes in a specific part of the code.

The Single Concern Principle looks at the same problem from a technical perspective. We assign a single concern to a "class" or "file." A concern is a related group of delegations or executions of tasks.

CHAPTER SEVEN

Open Closed

My personal favorites are the Open-Closed Principle (OCP) alongside the Dependency Inversion. In practical terms, I think the Open-Closed is the most pragmatic and delivers immediate results. While the Dependency Inversion is more abstract and drives high-level designs.

Bertrand Meyer is credited for the OCP. It first appeared in his book *Object-Oriented Software Construction*[1].

> "A software artifact should be open for extension but closed for modification."

As Robert C Martin states in his book, *Clean Architecture,* "Designing code to be extendable without modifying the artifact is the most fundamental reason we study software architecture." When we add new behavior to the system, we want the change to affect the existing codebase as little as possible. This reduces both the effort to understand the current codebase and the risk of breaking past behavior.

Closed for modification, in simple terms, means that when we add new functionality, we should not touch the existing files in the codebase. Of course, not touching them at all is impossible, but we should minimize the changes in the current codebase.

Open for extension means we should create classes that extend existing interfaces to add new features. The new concrete implementations include the desired behaviors. When we create a new implementation -> new file/class, we don't modify an existing class. Thus we avoid the risk of breaking past behavior.

Why?

Let's bring back the example that we saw in Part I. The poorly implemented function responsible for calculating the color of the owed amount text field.

* * *

```
fun mapColorForOwedAmount(amount: Int, customer: Customer): Int {
    if (amount in 0..49) {
        if (customer.type == CustomerType.PREMIUM ||
            customer.type == CustomerType.VIP)
            return R.color.green
        else
            return R.color.yellow
    } else if (amount in 50..99)
        if (customer.type != CustomerType.VIP) {
            if (customer.balance > 200)
                return R.color.yellow
            else
                if (customer.type == CustomerType.GUEST)
                    return R.color.red
                else
                    return R.color.orange
        } else
            return R.color.yellow
    else if (amount in 100..199)
        if (customer.balance < 100) {
            if (customer.type == CustomerType.PREMIUM ||
                customer.type == CustomerType.VIP)
                return R.color.orange
            else
                return R.color.red
        } else
            return R.color.orange
    else {
        if (customer.type == CustomerType.VIP &&
            customer.balance > 100)
            return R.color.orange
        return R.color.red
    }
}
```

We select the text view color based on the owed amount and the type of customer. Currently, the customer types are described by the enumeration below:

* * *

```
enum class CustomerType {
    GUEST,
    REGULAR,
    PREMIUM,
    VIP
}
```

The problem, well, one of the problems related to the Open-Closed Principle is the following: If the business decides to introduce one more customer type, say "Platinum," it will introduce new "ifs" to our *mapColorForOwedAmount* function. Therefore, we will have to modify the existing code and violate the "closed for modification" condition of the principle.

Why Closed for Modification?

First of all, when we keep modifying our code to add more functionality, we increase its complexity. And thus, we reduce its readability and testability. The current state is already hard to deal with; additional "if" statements will only make it worse.

Secondly, it hurts resilience and leads to error-prone systems. Modifying code always introduces risk. Whenever we add code to a function, we risk breaking the existing functionality. Imagine that we mess up the intended behavior for the "VIP" customers in our effort to add additional logic. This is likely to happen, especially with how complicated this function has become. Code reviews will not help much either, as the reviewer will hardly understand the change. If we don't have automated regression tests to act as a safety net, modifying code like this often causes more harm than good.

Finally, modifications cause merge conflicts. Assume that in the same release, we are tasked to both:

a. Introduce a new "Gold" customer type.
b. Change the existing logic for VIP and Premium customers.

Even worse, two different developers in different teams are tasked to perform the addition and the modification. At the time of the merge, this massive pile of conditionals will transform into a gigantic pile of merge conflicts. Thanks, I'll pass!

Open for extension

Okay, now that we understand why we should design our code to be closed for modification, we naturally question: "How to add more functionality if we are not allowed to modify our classes?!". And that's a pretty valid question if you haven't reencountered the topic. We can achieve this in several ways. I was craving to find a place to introduce Object-Oriented Design Patterns in this book, and I feel that they can help us here.

Design Patterns

Design Patterns are a vast topic; they deserve a book on their own. I am not going to deep dive into them here. I will get you in context and then solve the issue above with my personal-favorite design pattern—the Strategy DP.

"Software design patterns are general, reusable solutions to commonly occurring problems within a given context in software design"[2].

They sit close to the code level and offer specific low-level design techniques. They are practical and straightforward to apply. One of the best books I have read about design patterns is *Refactoring to Patterns* by Joshua Kerievsky[3]. He demonstrates how to refactor legacy code with design patterns and improve our codebase.

Strategy Design Pattern

The Strategy Pattern is a behavioral software design pattern that enables selecting an algorithm at runtime. Instead of implementing a single algorithm directly, code receives runtime instructions as to which in a family of algorithms to use[4].

* * *

The most common usage of the Strategy Pattern is to replace an "if/ else" block of code that has become hard to read. We must never forget that "expensive code is also expensive." We should avoid over-engineering as much as we avoid under-engineering. The key decision factor is that: the "if/else" block has become *hard to read and maintain.*

Let's now go ahead and see how we can refactor our previous function with the Strategy DP to conform to the OCP. The intention is to add extra functionality and support more user types without modifying our existing codebase.

The first step is to create the strategy interface or protocol in Swift. Remember that design patterns work on any object-oriented (supporting) language. I will use Kotlin for the sake of this example, but it works identically in Swift or Dart.

```
interface OwedAmountStrategy {
    fun execute(amount: Int, customerBalance: Int): Int
}
```

The strategy interface usually has only one function, typically named *execute.* Each user type is going to have its own concrete implementation. The execution of the strategy depends on two parameters, the owed amount and the customer balance. Let's now go ahead and implement this interface in concrete classes. We will create one implementation per user type:

```
class VipOwedAmountStrategy : OwedAmountStrategy {

    override fun execute(amount: Int, customerBalance: Int): Int {
        return when (amount) {
            in 0..49 -> R.color.green
            in 50..99 -> R.color.yellow
            in 100..199 -> R.color.orange
            else ->
                if (customerBalance > 100)
                    R.color.orange
                else R.color.red
        }
    }
}
```

* * *

We are starting with the strategy for our VIP customers. You can see how cleaner our code looks now. We have removed one level of complexity which is the customer type. This function is only concerned with the owed amount and the customer balance to calculate the color.

```
class PremiumOwedAmountStrategy : OwedAmountStrategy {

    override fun execute(amount: Int, customerBalance: Int): Int {
        return when (amount) {
            in 0..49 -> R.color.green
            in 50..99 ->
                if (customerBalance > 200)
                    R.color.yellow
                else R.color.orange
            in 100..199 -> R.color.orange
            else -> R.color.red
        }
    }
}
```

This is the implementation for our premium users.

```
class RegularOwedAmountStrategy : OwedAmountStrategy {

    override fun execute(amount: Int, customerBalance: Int): Int {
        return when (amount) {
            in 0..49 -> R.color.yellow
            in 50..99 -> R.color.yellow
            in 100..199 -> R.color.orange
            else -> R.color.red
        }
    }
}
```

The regular customers' logic isn't currently affected by the amount and balance. The implementation is minimal.

And finally, the implementation for the guest customers:

* * *

```
class GuestOwedAmountStrategy : OwedAmountStrategy {

    override fun execute(amount: Int, customerBalance: Int): Int {
        return when (amount) {
            in 0..49 -> R.color.yellow
            in 50..99 ->
                if (customerBalance > 200)
                    R.color.yellow
                else R.color.red
            in 100..199 ->
                if (customerBalance > 200)
                    R.color.orange
                else R.color.red
            else -> R.color.red
        }
    }
}
```

Now that we have all the concrete strategies in place, we need to create a "factory" that, based on the customer type, returns the appropriate strategy:

```
class OwedAmountStrategyFactory {

    fun makeFor(type: CustomerType): OwedAmountStrategy {
        return when (type) {
            CustomerType.GUEST -> GuestOwedAmountStrategy()
            CustomerType.REGULAR -> RegularOwedAmountStrategy()
            CustomerType.PREMIUM -> PremiumOwedAmountStrategy()
            CustomerType.VIP -> VipOwedAmountStrategy()
        }
    }
}
```

We have successfully applied the Strategy Design Pattern! Now to define the color of our text view, we only need to call the factory and execute the strategy:

```
private val strategy = factory.makeFor(customer.type)

private val color = strategy.execute(customer.owedAmount, customer.balance)
```

Let's take a look at the dependency graph:

* * *

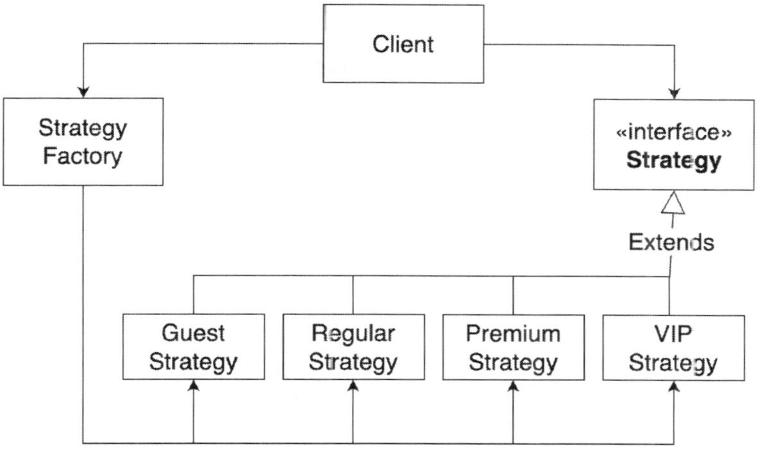

The dependency graph after refactoring with the Strategy DP.

Time to prove that after the refactoring above, the code is now closed for modification but open for extension. Let's assume that the business decides to add an additional customer type, the gold customer. The gold customer will sit in privileges in-between the premium and the VIP. We will first add it in the "switch" statement of our Factory:

```
class OwedAmountStrategyFactory {

    fun makeFor(type: CustomerType): OwedAmountStrategy {
        return when (type) {
            CustomerType.GUEST -> GuestOwedAmountStrategy()
            CustomerType.REGULAR -> RegularOwedAmountStrategy()
            CustomerType.PREMIUM -> PremiumOwedAmountStrategy()
            CustomerType.GOLD -> GoldOwedAmountStrategy()
            CustomerType.VIP -> VipOwedAmountStrategy()
        }
    }
}
```

This is a modification as we write code in an existing class. It is the bare minimum modification possible. Furthermore, this class is simple and conforms to the Single Concern Principle. Regardless of how many customer types we introduce, it will always be a trivial, one-line addition. It introduces minimum to no risk of breaking past functionality.

Now, we only have to *extend* the strategy interface and add another concrete implementation tailored to the gold customers:

```
class GoldOwedAmountStrategy : OwedAmountStrategy {

    override fun execute(amount: Int, customerBalance: Int): Int {
        return when (amount) {
            in 0..49 -> R.color.green
            in 50..99 ->
                if (customerBalance > 100)
                    R.color.yellow
                else R.color.orange
            in 100..199 -> R.color.orange
            else ->
                if (customerBalance > 300)
                    R.color.orange
                else R.color.red
        }
    }
}
```

As you can see, we did not *modify* the files of the other strategies. Therefore, we do not introduce any risk of breaking past functionality. Additionally, if we were tasked to modify the VIP customers' logic, it would not cause a merge conflict with the Gold addition.

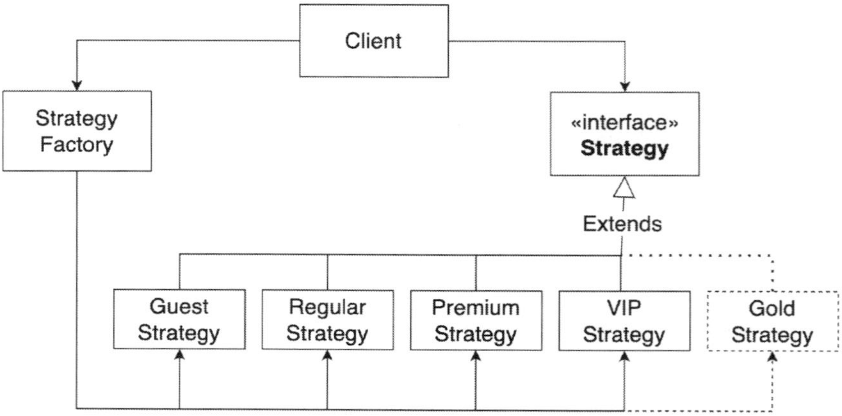

The dependency graph after we add support for Gold customers.

* * *

We have achieved our goal. We effectively isolated each customer's logic and made our app open for extension and closed for modification. By adhering to the OCP, we avoid modifying existing files to add new behavior. Therefore we also significantly reduce the amount of those pesky merge conflicts.

The OCP also goes along well with the Single Concern Principle. By implementing classes with a single concern, we avoid modifying existing ones. For example, we create a new Repository for the Customer entity rather than reusing/modifying the repository of the Product entity. After all, both principles achieve the same foundational objectives, high cohesion, and low coupling.

Criticism

The Open-Closed Principle is one of my favorites, to be honest. We just need to be careful not to get carried away with it and over-engineer our system. As Uncle Bob himself admits, we can only make our code open-closed if we know what types of changes will be coming, which is not often the case. It's easy enough to predict that another user type might be coming, but not all changes are that foreseeable. So, we can't be 100% compliant with the OCP, as this would imply huge over-engineering, defeating the purpose.

When a change request comes, and the code is not OCP-compliant, in other words, not ready to accept the change, then we should first refactor it. Exactly as Joshua Kerievsky advocates, which is by Kent Beck's "make the change easy, then make the easy change."

Using the example above, when the logic included just three conditions with few lines of code in each, it was readable and easy to extend. We don't need to introduce the Strategy DP in every type-based conditional. But at the moment that it becomes hard to read, which generally means that:

1. The number of types grows.
2. The logic for each type becomes more complex, including more lines of code.

3. Additional factors like the account balance and other variables are introduced.

..then we need to refactor the block before we add new functionality. Identifying the need promptly is critical.

Summary

The OCP states, "The code should be open for extension but closed for modification." Modification refers to writing code in existing files. Extension refers to adding new behavior via extending interfaces.
Modifying existing code should be avoided because:

- It introduces risk to break existing functionality.
- Introduces merge conflicts. Which, in return, increases the overall effort and adds additional risk.
- It increases the code's complexity and reduces its readability.

There are multiple ways to design a system to comply with the OCP. Design patterns like the Strategy DP are practical tools to achieve it.

CHAPTER EIGHT

Liskov Substitution

Definition

The Liskov Substitution Principle (LSP) enhances the Open-Closed Principle. It introduces rules on **how** to extend the behavior of the system in order to maximize resilience and robustness. As we will see, its definition is pretty scientific. Engineers usually tend not to understand and apply it correctly. By the time you finish this chapter, you will be able to put the principle into action in your own app.

The LSP was introduced by Barbara Liskov in her conference keynote "Data abstraction and hierarchy" in 1987. A few years later, she published a paper with Jeanette Wing in which they defined the principle as:

> "Let $\phi(x)$ be a property provable about objects x of type T. Then $\phi(y)$ should be true for objects y of type S where S is a subtype of T[1]."

If it's been a couple of years since you finished college, the above mathematical definition is probably not the easiest to read. It translates in plain English as:

If S is a subtype of T, then objects of type T may be replaced with objects of type S without breaking any of the desirable behaviors of the program.

* * *

To simplify it even further:

You should be able to replace any object in your app with any object of its subtypes without breaking your app's behavior.

Why apply the LSP?

The "why" to apply this principle is pretty straightforward: if not, you break the program's behavior. In other words, you introduce logical defects.

The trick here is to realize the difference between breaking type hierarchy at the logical or coding level. It's impossible to break code-level type hierarchy. The compiler will not allow you to compile and build the app in any strongly typed programming language like Kotlin, Swift, and Dart. But still, as we will see later in the examples, we are permitted to logically break the hierarchy and introduce defects that the compiler cannot detect.

How to apply the LSP?

There are multiple techniques and ways to design our code to comply with the Liskov Substitution Principle. Thorben Janssen spots an exciting correlation in his blog-post[2] between the LSP and Bertrand Meyer's Design by Contract[20].

Design by Contract

[20] Design by Contract (DbC), also known as contract programming, programming by contract and design-by-contract programming, is an approach for designing software. It prescribes that software designers should define formal, precise and verifiable interface specifications for software components, which extend the ordinary definition of abstract data types with preconditions, postconditions and invariants. These specifications are referred to as "contracts", in accordance with a conceptual metaphor with the conditions and obligations of business contracts.

* * *

A subclass's overridden function must accept all the inputs that the parent function accepts. This means that in the subclass, you are allowed to put in place less restrictive input validation rules. But you are not allowed to enforce stricter ones. If a subclass has stricter input validation rules and we put it in the place of a less restrictive implementation, the input will cause errors.

For example, let's assume that superclass Super accepts as inputs both paramA and paramB. Subclass Sub1 accepts both paramA and paramB like the parent, but subclass Sub2 accepts only paramA and throws an exception in paramB. If we replace inside our program an instance of S1 with an instance of S2, we have broken it.

Let's understand this better with a coding example. Assume that we have a price calculator class:

```
open class PriceCalculator {

    open fun calculatePrice(price: Int, discountPercentage: Int): Int {
        if (price < 0) {
            throw Exception("Price must be >= 0")
        }
        return price - (price * discountPercentage)
    }
}
```

This Price Calculator includes only one function that calculates a product's price based on a discount percentage. It has a single validation: the price must be a positive integer or zero.

Imagine that we are tasked to extend the logic and introduce different price calculations based on the customer type. To conform to the Open-Closed Principle, we decide to implement subclasses of this calculator. As we learned, our system should be open for extension but closed for modification. We want to introduce two more policies tailored for VIP and guest customers. In the guest's policy, we apply a half discount. In the VIP, we double the discount percentage but only if the price is above 10.000:

* * *

```
class GuestPriceCalculator : PriceCalculator() {

    override fun calculatePrice(price: Int, discountPercentage: Int): Int {
        return price - (price * discountPercentage / 2)
    }
}


class VipPriceCalculator : PriceCalculator() {

    override fun calculatePrice(price: Int, discountPercentage: Int): Int {
        if (price < 10000) {
            throw Exception("VIP calculator applies only for prices > 10.000")
        }
        return price - (price * 2 * discountPercentage)
    }
}
```

The code above violates both Meyer's Design by Contract and the LSP. If, for any reason, we substitute a GuestPriceCalculator with a VipPriceCalculator, and the price is below 10.000, the application will break. An overridden function must accept all the inputs that its super function accepts. In this case, to adhere to the principle, we should move the additional precondition to the caller of this function. And it them from the function itself.

Also, notice how we have removed the price validation entirely in the guest price calculator. This is perfectly fine based on what we've learned so far. We said that we are allowed to impose less restrictive input validations in subclasses. No validation is a less restrictive validation. But what happens if we receive a negative price input? We get a negative price output, which is a logical defect. Therefore, we do break the LSP. Here comes the second part of Design By Contract, which addresses this particular issue.

The *return* values of the overridden function must comply with the same rules as the superclass function. But for return values, you can decide to apply even stricter rules. The subclass may choose to return a small subset of what the parent returns.

In our case, the super function can only return positive integer values or zero. An overridden function is not allowed to return any value that is not a positive integer or zero. We can reduce the spectrum even more if we want, but not increase it. The output rule is precisely the opposite of the input rule. To fix this issue in our example, we can either add the same input validation to the guest calculator:

```
class GuestPriceCalculator : PriceCalculator() {

    override fun calculatePrice(price: Int, discountPercentage: Int): Int
        if (price < 0) {
            throw Exception("Price must be >=0")
        }
        return price - (price * discountPercentage / 2)
    }
}
```

Or depending on how we want our system to behave, we may add an output validation:

```
class GuestPriceCalculator : PriceCalculator() {

    override fun calculatePrice(price: Int, discountPercentage: Int): Int
        val finalPrice = price - (price * discountPercentage / 2)
        return if(finalPrice > 0)
            finalPrice
        else
            0
    }
}
```

Those modifications comply with both the Liskov Substitution Principle and Bertrand Meyer's DbC.

To sum it up: input validations cannot be more restrictive; they can only be more flexible. Output validations can only be more restrictive; they cannot be more flexible.

Risks of subclassing

The risks above exist only in subclassing. When a concretion extends from another concretion. Designing so that the parent is a pure interface (only containing signatures), the conditions above are always true. A signature of a function does not have any input or output validations. That's the reason why extending from interfaces is safer than extending from superclasses. James Gosling[3], the founder and lead designer behind Java, stated in an interview[4] that if he redesigned Java, he would consider removing concrete class inheritance.

We must be extra careful when altering the input or output validation rules in a superclass. This can effectively break the LSP without noticing it. Specifically, when in a parent class, we make input validations more restrictive or output more flexible. Then, we have to update or at least test whether we have introduced defects to its child classes.

We need to be particularly cautious when we extend from a class that we don't control, such as a class implemented in a third-party library. Updating the library to a version where the above validations have changed can introduce defects that we cannot anticipate. Unit tests that verify that our subclasses behave properly under any expected input can be gold in these situations.

> Rather than subclassing, just use pure interfaces. It's not so much that class inheritance is particularly bad. It just has problems. —James Gosling

Further LSP Applications

Initially, the Liskov Substitution Principle was only used to guide inheritance in OO designs. As demonstrated in the previous example. However, the LSP has morphed over the years into a broader principle of software designs that can be applied in any kind of interface. This includes a public interface of a software module, a third-party library, or even a REST API of a backend system. In other words, we should design software so that it doesn't break regardless of who is using it.

To understand this better, let's give an example of a backend API violating the LSP. Let's assume that we are building an open weather API. We have implemented a REST endpoint, "getWeather," that accepts the following JSON input:

```
{
  lat: Double
  long: Double
```

```
}
```

It returns the weather forecast for this region. Now let's assume that a big corporation called "Big Weather" has built a mobile app that aggregates and displays weather info from multiple providers. Their mobile app is performing the following HTTP request:

```
{
  lat: Long
  long: Long
}
```

As they are huge cooperation with millions of users, we agree to support their HTTP request and accept Long values. In order to avoid code duplication, we decide to stick to a single endpoint, and we modify it as below:

```
if (request.channelId == "Big Weather")
  parseRequestBodyAsLong(lat, long)
```

We have successfully broken the LSP! If other clients somehow end up in this code block, our application will crash. In other words, we can't substitute "Big Weather" with any other client, even though more clients depend on this endpoint. If Big Weather decides to:

- Rebrand.
- Gets acquired by another company.
- Or, for any reason, decides to change their channel id.

..the application will crash.

The example above also applies to software modules and third-party libraries. When implementing an independent module for internal or external use, we shouldn't include unique treatments according to which client is using it. If we absolutely must do this, we should provide a separate API dedicated only to this client. We should avoid adding conditionals in shared implementations. This also complies with the Single Responsibility Principle, different actors, different functions. It also complies with the Single Concern Principle. Clients with different requirements do not classify as a related group of tasks. Even if the functions are identical, it falls under the accidental duplication case that we discussed earlier.

Summary

The LSP complements the OCP and indicates how to design the extensions in order to be robust. Or, more specifically, how we shouldn't design them to avoid loose ends that can break our app in specific system inputs. Those bugs are pesky because they only happen in particular inputs. Therefore, they are hard to trace and fix.

The purpose of adding functionality with code extensions is to have isolated re-usable parts of business logic. But for this to make sense, those should be interchangeable. Tomorrow we may decide that certain "gold" users deserve "VIP" treatment on specific occasions. We need to be able to swap between them without breaking the app.

When subclassing, particularly from third-party code, it's beneficial to include unit tests that verify that the overridden functions behave appropriately in every input. Changes in the parent class input and output validations may break its subclasses.

CHAPTER NINE

Interface Segregation

"A client should not depend on stuff it doesn't need."

This principle is straightforward and almost profound. You shouldn't depend on anything you don't need. Right, do we need a principle for that? Well, while it initially seems obvious, it's sometimes not so obvious how to apply it. Or how to identify when you violate it at the time that you violate it. By the end of this chapter, you will clearly understand how to identify and correct the violations.

Similar to the LSP, this principle applies to multiple levels of abstraction. At the low level, the public interface of any implementation should be as minimal as possible. It should expose only the essential functions and information while hiding everything else under private implementations. Some IDEs can be helpful with this, as they prompt us to add the private keyword in functions and variables that are not accessed from outside. It is not sufficient, though. Multiple clients may depend on the same interface, with each client using just a subset of this interface. In this case, no functions appear externally unused. But we are violating the Interface Segregation Principle, as a client that only needs a subset of this interface ends up depending on all of it.

This principle is also applicable at the module level. Each module should only expose the minimal/necessary information to the other modules via its cross-boundary interface.

* * *

The principle also applies at the system level. A back-end API should only expose the necessary information to mobile clients. When the API exposes unnecessary information, it causes two kinds of symptoms. First, the response contains junk which reduces its readability. The primary factor that should drive the design of a public API is to be easy to read and understand. It should be as expressive as possible to enable other developers to use it without reading extra documentation.

The other symptom which is even worse is production issues. In the past, I worked for a healthcare startup responsible for implementing its Android application. In a specific HTTP endpoint, the backend was exposing unnecessary information. At some point, a backend developer comes into my office and asks me if he can remove the unused information. I replied to him, "Yea, sure, we are not using this field." He then proceeded with the implementation and deployed the change to production. The following day we realized that we had broken the iOS client. The information was unused, but those fields were included in the JSON parsing and validation. I consider the interface segregation principle more critical at the system level than at the low level. When different teams are involved, amateur mistakes like this happen easier than when we work on a single codebase.

How to segregate interfaces/protocols

Let's now discuss an example of interface segregation at the lower level. Let's assume that we are working for an airline company and are developing a system that tracks the status of its fleet. We have implemented the following protocol, which describes the function of an airplane:

```
protocol Airplane {

    func takeOff()

    func land()
}
```

It contains only two functions, one to take off the plane and another to land it. Our airline currently operates only two airplanes:

```
class AirbusA220 : Airplane {

    func takeOff() {
        code
    }

    func land() {
        code
    }
}
class Boeing777X : Airplane {

    func takeOff() {
        code
    }

    func land() {
        code
    }
}
```

The airline is making plans to expand its business and include a seaplane. Seaplanes are fixed-wing aircrafts capable of safely taking off and landing on the water. So what we decided to do is introduce two extra functions in the airplane protocol that describe the new types of taking off and landing.

```
protocol Airplane {

    func takeOff()

    func land()

    func takeOffFromWater()

    func landOnWater()
}
```

And then we proceed with the implementation of the seaplane that recently joined our fleet:

* * *

```
class AG600 : Airplane {

    func landOnWater() {
        code
    }

    func takeOff() {
        code
    }

    func land() {
        code
    }

    func takeOffFromWater() {
        code
    }
}
```

While we celebrate the introduction of the new seaplane in our system, we have broken the implementation of the rest of our fleet. They are now required to implement two functions that they cannot possibly execute. This introduces junk code. One option is to print an error log when we incorrectly call water-related functions to non-seaplanes. As the error is severe, though, we most likely want to throw an exception in those cases. We don't want to release code that allows a Boeing777X to land in the sea!

```
class Boeing777X : Airplane {

    func takeOff() {

    }

    func land() {

    }

    func takeOffFromWater() {
        throw NSError(domain: "This plane cannot take off from water", code: 0)
    }

    func landOnWater() {
        throw NSError(domain: "This plane cannot land on water", code: 0)  ⊗ Er
    }
}
```

* * *

But now the compiler complains. We need to change the signature of the *landOnWater* and *takeOffFromWater* functions and declare that they may throw errors. This will also affect the seaplanes that aren't supposed to throw errors. From now on, the clients of seaplanes will need to catch those errors and handle them with empty implementations. It's clear by now that we have introduced a lot of junk code and added unnecessary complexity to our system. It's time to segregate the protocols. We will create a new protocol tailored to the seaplanes. This protocol will also conform to the generic airplane protocol as the seaplanes are also capable of taking off and landing on land.

```
protocol Seaplane : Airplane {

    func takeOffFromWater()

    func landOnWater()
}
```

And finally, our only seaplane will conform to the seaplane protocol while the rest of our fleet to the airplane protocol. This way, the airplanes that cannot land on the water will avoid including this function at all. No exceptions will be thrown; our code will be cleaner and our passengers safer!

```
class AG600 : Seaplane {

    func landOnWater() {
        code
    }

    func takeOff() {
        code
    }

    func land() {
        code
    }

    func takeOffFromWater() {
        code
    }
}
```

* * *

Code smells of ISP Violations.

Specific code smells help us identify the need to segregate our interfaces.

> A code smell is a surface indication that usually corresponds to a deeper problem in the system. —Martin Fowler

1. *Bulky Interfaces.* Interfaces (literally) or public class interfaces that have too many functions. In other words, a file that is doing too many things. Violations of Single Responsibility/Single Concern Principles often lead to bulky interfaces and violations of LSP as well.

2. *Unused dependencies.* This smell has two variations. The most obvious is when a class depends on another class that is not used. Those are easy to identify as the IDEs typically indicate them. The other variation is passing "null" input in a function. This usually indicates that we should overload the signature of that function or add default values. Passing null input or even allowing null values as input makes our code harder to reason about. It also leads to unnecessary null-checks and error handling blocks.

3. *Functions throwing exceptions.* As we saw earlier, functions throwing exceptions often indicate that we should segregate our interface. Having a "throw implementation" is useless; it doesn't provide any value to the users of the app. Even more, it makes the client's code more complex than it should. It must now include a "try/catch" block even for the valuable cases that don't throw exceptions.

4. *Empty overridden functions.* When a class extends from an interface or an abstract parent, it has to override all its functions in order to compile. Inheriting unnecessary functions will end up adding empty implementations. This pollutes our codebase and makes it harder to reason about. Getting into this habit may also lead to forgetting to add an implementation when it's actually needed.

* * *

Summary

The Interface Segregation Principle, in theory, is straightforward and obvious. One should not depend on anything they don't need. But to:

a) Identify when we break it.

b) Refactor our code to comply with it.

..can be more challenging. It requires some experience and a deep understanding of the principle.

The principle applies to multiple levels of abstraction.

- Functions should not depend on input they don't need.
- Classes should not depend on other classes or functions that they don't need.
- Modules should not depend on interfaces they don't need.
- Systems should not depend on information and endpoints that they don't need.

Code smells can help us identify the need for segregation.

CHAPTER TEN

Dependency Inversion

The Dependency Inversion Principle (DIP) alongside the Open-Closed is, in my opinion, the two most important S.O.L.I.D principles. The DIP is more complex and harder to understand than the OCP. It is a bit more abstract and higher-level. It took me quite a while to understand it deeply and apply it correctly. By the end of this chapter, you will be able to use this technique in your own application and draw proper boundaries between its layers.

The principle

It was defined by Robert C Martin and has two parts[1]:

"High-level modules should not import anything from low-level modules. Both should depend on abstractions (e.g., interfaces)."

"Abstractions should not depend on details. Details (concrete implementations) should depend on abstractions."

In other words:

"The Dependency Inversion principle tells us that the most flexible systems are those in which source code dependencies refer only to abstractions, not to concretions."

The purpose of this book is to enable you to act on those principles, but before we get to the practical examples, we need to understand a little bit of theory…

Code Layers

The DIP implies that the code is segregated into layers, with each layer belonging to a different level. Some modules sit on a higher level than others for some reason. How do we define those layers and the level they belong to?

Let's go back 30 years ago for a moment when most banks did not have any online presence. As customers, we want to apply for a loan to fund our business. We have to schedule a meeting with a bank representative and visit a physical branch.

1. First, we need to authenticate ourselves by displaying a physical id.
2. The representative will ask us questions and request us to complete a few printed forms. In other words, we have to perform data input describing our petition.
3. The representative will then apply some logic based on our data. For example: if our annual income is higher than 100.000$, they will approve the loan. If not, we still have the option to put our house on mortgage. If our home is worth more than 500.000$, we can also receive the loan.
4. If we fulfill the terms above, the bank representative will approve our loan request. Both parties will sign the papers, and the signed contract will be stored in a physical place at the safe premises of the bank.

Coming back to the present, the bank has recognized the necessity for digital transformation. We are hired to build their mobile application. The banking application must perform all the business operations previously done manually. When we build a mobile application, we are actually automating and scaling the business while also (trying to) improve the UX of the customer.

But it's the same process following the same business rules:

1. We need to authenticate the customer and make sure that they

are authorized to perform the action, the loan request.

2. We ask for the same user input, not by filling a paper form but by filling a digital form presented on their screen.
3. We then automatically apply the same business logic as the bank representative would do manually. This is important; the business rules describe the business and not our application. The rules for approving or declining a loan request are the same regardless of the medium. Irrespective of whether we apply for it at a physical branch or from the comfort of our home and our mobile phones.
4. Finally, if the loan request gets approved by the business rules, we digitally sign it, and it is stored securely in a database.

Let's try to categorize the tasks above into layers. The first layer describes the business. We usually have dedicated classes that represent the business structure; we call those entities—for example, the Loan entity, Payment entity, Customer entity, etc. We also have the business rules, logic, and actions that we can apply to those entities. For example, the action *requestForLoan* and the rules that allow it or decline it:

```
annualIncome > 100.000$ || mortgageValue > 500.000$
```

This kind of code describes our business regardless of whether our bank is a bricks-and-mortar institution or a NEO bank. We usually call this layer domain. In pure OO designs, the entities and actions sit together to conform with the Data Encapsulation Principle. We may extract the actions in different classes when mixing OO and functional programming.

Then, we identified the need to interact with the users. We will call this UI or view layer. You may also find people calling it presentation layer, but I personally reserve this term for logic—more on that in the "What" part of the book.

Finally, we need to store the information. All the data storage, retrieval, and update concerns belong to the data layer.

This is probably the most straightforward layer cake. Domain, UI, and data. We could fine-tune it even further and break our code down into several thinner layers but for the sake of this example, let's keep it simple:

i. Domain layer: describes the business.
ii. View layer: contains the UI and user I/O.
iii. Data layer: responsible for storing the information.

Level of code

Now that we defined the layers, we need to identify which layer is a "high-level" layer. In order to answer this question, we first need to define the criteria that drive the categorization.

High-level code is code that we want to protect.

Protect from what? You may ask. We want to protect it from changes in the low-level code. We know that depending on others imposes risks when they are not reliable. This applies to people as well as systems. Focusing on systems, it applies to all layers of abstraction. It can be a class depending on another class in the same codebase or our app depending on another system to retrieve data. When class A depends on class B, changes in class B may break the behavior or even the compilation of class A. Let's take a look at an example to understand it better:

We have a Loan entity:

```
data class Loan(
    val id: String,
    val date: Date,
    val rate: Double,
    val amount: Int,
    val paidAmount: Int
)
```

And the business Use Case of paying a loan installment:

* * *

```
class PayInstallment(
    private val service: LoansService
) {

    operator fun invoke(loanId: String, installmentAmount: Int)
            : Int {

        val loan = service.fetchLoan(loanId)
        val updatedLoan = loan.copy(
            paidAmount = loan.paidAmount + installmentAmount
        )
        service.updateLoan(updatedLoan)
        return updatedLoan.paidAmount
    }
}
```

It is a function that:

1) Retrieves the loan from the Service.
2) Calculates the new "paid amount" by adding the previous and current payments.
3) Saves the changes at the Service.
4) Returns the updated total paid amount to the caller.

The PayInstallment Use Case depends on the Loans Service. It receives an instance of it and uses it to perform operations. Consequently, our domain or use case layer depends on the data layer.

Finally, we have the Service which is responsible for retrieving and updating the data from and to our server:

```
class LoansService {

    fun fetchLoan(id: String): Loan = fetchLoanFromServer(id)

    fun updateLoan(loan: Loan) = updateLoanAtServer(loan)
}
```

Changes in the public API of the LoansService will break our PayInstallment Use Case. If we decide to change the above function signatures, the Use Case will face compilation issues that we'll need to address. As we have described earlier, whenever we change a file, we introduce risk to the file itself and any file that depends on it. Additionally, the Use Case unit tests will probably face compilation issues and require refactoring to run again as we will have to change the way we mock the LoansService.

It goes even beyond that. We may decide to restructure our data layer and introduce offline support. In this case, we will have to introduce a new component that will retrieve data both from the Service and local storage. This component is typically called a Repository. So we have to modify the PayInstallment Use Case to remove the Service dependency and introduce the Repository dependency. The modifications include:

1. Adding the new Repository dependency.
2. Using the repository functions to apply data operations. Those functions can potentially differ significantly from the Service. They may have different types of input and output.
3. Refactor our unit tests.

```
class PayInstallment(
    private val repository: LoansRepository
) {

    operator fun invoke(loanId: String, installmentAmount: Int)
          : Int {

        val loan = repository.getLoan(loanId)
        val updatedLoan = loan.copy(
            paidAmount = loan.paidAmount + installmentAmount
        )
        repository.updateLoan(updatedLoan)
        return updatedLoan.paidAmount
    }
}
```

So when class A depends on class B, class A becomes more error-prone to change. It needs to change not only for reasons related to the logic it contains. But it may also need to change for reasons related to class B. The same applies to layers. When layer A depends on layer B, it may need to change because of it. Dependencies introduce volatility and risk.

* * *

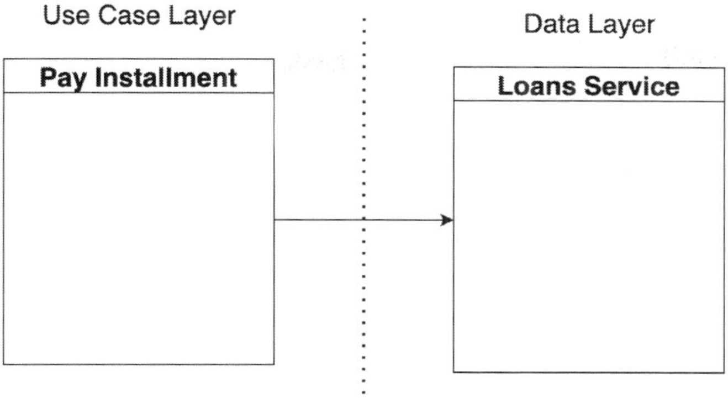

The dependency graph.

As we defined earlier, high-level code is code that we want to protect from change. If layer A is higher level than layer B, then A should not depend on B. Only B is allowed to depend on A if it needs to.

So from the layers that we have discussed so far, domain, UI, and data which one do you think is less volatile and should be protected the most? You probably guessed right; it's the domain layer. The one that describes our business alongside the allowed actions and operations. This layer is at the heart of our system. The business rules change only when the business itself changes. They don't care about our mobile or web apps. They don't care if a customer is paying the installment digitally or at a physical branch. Those rules should be protected from changes in the volatile UI or database.

Statistics show that mobile apps get majorly redesigned on average every two years. A redesign of the app does not, in any case, affect the way the business runs. Therefore, it should also not affect the code that represents the business. Ideally, we should not touch any domain layer classes while performing a complete app redesign. Besides the frequency, the UI is also changing for less critical reasons. Changing the color of a text field is much less critical than calculating the owed amount correctly. Customers can bear with a minimal design; they won't accept paying more. Furthermore, our business may face legal issues when the business rules are defective. *Changes in the UI layer should not, in any case, affect the domain layer.*

* * *

The same goes for the data layer. The fact that we decided to include offline support in our mobile app does not - in any way - affect the way the business runs. Therefore, it must not affect the code that represents the business. Our domain layer doesn't care if it initially received data from a local file, and we later decided to include a complete relational database. The classes belonging to the domain layer and their testing suites should be agnostic of those kinds of changes. They should not run any risk when they occur. Same as the UI, the data layer changes for less significant reasons. It is not crucial to our customers if the application is storing the data using SQLite, Room, or core data. They care more about calculating the amounts correctly.

The code example above, though, which represents most of the apps I see in the industry, does not reflect that. The domain layer retrieves information from the data layer. Consequently, it depends on it. This is the most common mobile example where the DIP can improve our architectural design.

Dependency Inversion

The Dependency Inversion technique does precisely what its name implies; it inverts the dependencies. We will make our data layer depend on the domain layer and the domain utterly agnostic of the data. We will use a powerful Object-Oriented tool called polymorphism.

First, we introduce an interface:

```
interface PayInstallmentDataSource {

    fun getLoan(loanId: String) : Loan

    fun updateLoan(loan: Loan)
}
```

This Interface is designed to cover the data needs of the PayInstallment Use Case. It is not intended to contain all the data operations on the loans. It delivers the data in the most convenient format for the Use Case. In other words, it is built around the Use Case and not around the data. It will only change when the needs of the Use Case change and not when the database or the remote API change.

Next, we refactor our Use Case to depend on this interface while removing any dependency on concretions:

```
class PayInstallment(
    private val dataSource: PayInstallmentDataSource
) {

    operator fun invoke(loanId: String, installmentAmount: Int)
            : Int {

        val loan = dataSource.getLoan(loanId)
        val updatedLoan = loan.copy(
            paidAmount = loan.paidAmount + installmentAnount
        )
        dataSource.updateLoan(updatedLoan)
        return updatedLoan.paidAmount
    }
}
```

The Use Case now depends on an interface designed specifically for its needs. This also complies with the Interface Segregation Principle. A Service or Repository implementation, which is built around the data, contains a lot of functions that our Use Case does not need. They contain functions like *getAllLoans, deleteLoan,* etc.. which are not useful to our PayInstallment Use Case. With the solution above, the Use Case depends only on the subset of the operations it needs; thus, we comply with ISP. This is important. If we simply create an interface that exposes everything the Service does, it's not proper Dependency Inversion. This is a mistake many developers make. The interface and the data it exposes should be in the format *most convenient for the Use Case.*

Finally, we will make our Service implement the data source interface:

* * *

```
class LoansService : PayInstallmentDataSource {

    override fun getLoan(loanId: String): Loan =
        fetchLoanFromServer(loanId)

    override fun updateLoan(loan: Loan) =
        updateLoanAtServer(loan)
}
```

This is it; we have successfully inverted the dependency! As you can see, the data layer now depends on the use case layer. The dependency graph now looks like this:

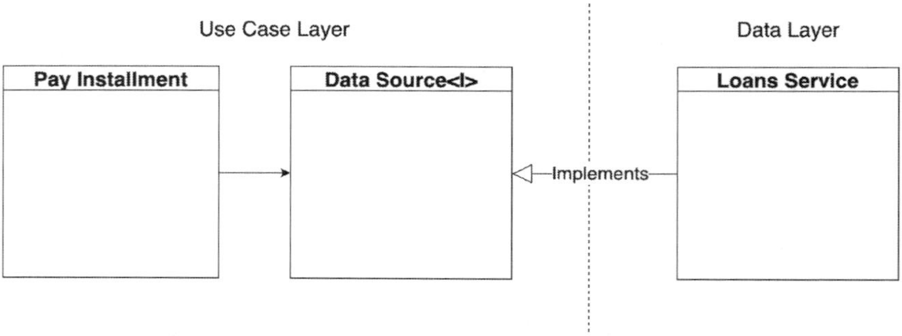

The dependency graph after Dependency Inversion.

The arrow doesn't point from the use case layer out to the data layer but rather from the data layer "upwards" to the use case layer. If the interface changes, which will happen only for business-related reasons, the Service will have to change. On the other hand, a change to the Service cannot impact our Use Case. The Service has to conform to the data source interface no matter what.

Note that the DIP tells us that low-level code should not depend on high-level code either; both should depend on abstractions. This is true in our example, as the DataSource is an interface/protocol and not a concrete implementation.

Criticism

* * *

I don't have any criticism for the technique itself. Whenever we identify the need to invert the dependencies in our architectural design, we can use this technique to achieve it. We just need to understand when it's needed and how to apply it correctly.

Building on top of the previous example, let's understand how the data layer will be affected if our application grows significantly. The Services eventually will either become too bloated with code or lose their ability to be reused.

Imagine that we need to implement ten Use Cases that require information regarding the loans. Each Use Case has different needs; one may only need to read information, another update, and another delete it. According to the Interface Segregation Principle, each Use Case should have its own data source interface tailored to its needs. Then, the Service would have to conform to all those data sources. That would clutter it with too much code:

```
class LoansService :
    PayInstallmentDataSource,
    ViewMyLoansDataSource,
    DeleteLoanDataSource,
    ViewDueLoansDataSource {

    override fun getLoan(loanId: String): Loan = fetchLoanFromServer(loanId)

    override fun updateLoan(loan: Loan) = updateLoanAtServer(loan)

    override fun getLoansFor(userId: String): List<Loan> {
        TODO( reason: "Not yet implemented")
    }

    override fun deleteLoan(id: String) {
        TODO( reason: "Not yet implemented")
    }

    override fun getDueLoans(): List<Loan> {
        TODO( reason: "Not yet implemented")
    }
}
```

In the example above, we have only implemented four data source interfaces. The implementations are minimal, and the code already looks very dirty. Imagine what it would look like for an actual production application. This situation is not viable; the Services should be designed around the data operations and not around the Use Cases. A Service should only know how to fetch, update, and delete information to our backend.

A solution to this issue is to introduce another layer that will contain only the implementations of our data source interfaces. Those implementations will be unique to each Use Case, and they will depend on the reusable Services to perform the actual operations. Furthermore, they could potentially apply data aggregation from multiple Services when the Use Case requires it. Remember that the Use Case is built around the needs of the business and the customer; it should be agnostic of the data topology:

```
class PayInstallment(
    private val dataSource: PayInstallmentDataSource
) {

    operator fun invoke(loanId: String, installmentAmount: Int)
            : Int {

        val loan = dataSource.getLoan(loanId)
        val updatedLoan = loan.copy(
            paidAmount = loan.paidAmount + installmentAmount
        )
        dataSource.updateLoan(updatedLoan)
        return updatedLoan.paidAmount
    }
}
```

The Use Case remains unchanged no matter what. We protect it by keeping it agnostic of any implementations. It only depends on an interface tailored to its needs. It's a high-level business policy. Now, we introduce a new class:

* * *

```
class PayInstallmentDataGateway(
    private val service: LoansService
) : PayInstallmentDataSource {

    override fun getLoan(loanId: String): Loan
        = service.fetchLoan(loanId)

    override fun updateLoan(loan: Loan)
        = service.updateLoan(loan)
}
```

The implementation of the data source can be called PayInstallmentDataSourceImpl or PayInstallmentDataGateway. We can also choose another name as long as it indicates its intended purpose. The purpose is to implement a unique data source interface designed for a specific Use Case and provide the data. It depends on the Service; therefore, it belongs to our data layer. It could, if needed, aggregate data from multiple Services and deliver them in the format most convenient to the Use Case. The Use Case is the boss.

Finally, the Service is unique and contains only the data operations. It's not concerned about who will use it or how:

```
class LoansService {

    fun fetchLoan(loanId: String): Loan = fetchLoanFromServer(loanId)

    fun fetchAllLoans(): Loan = fetchAllLoansFromServer()

    fun updateLoan(loan: Loan) = updateLoanAtServer(loan)

    fun deleteLoan(loadId: String) = deleteLoanAtServer(loadId)
}
```

This solution is clean but maybe not suitable for smaller projects as it increases the number of classes that we have to implement.

* * *

An alternative is to apply the Repository pattern[21]. Now again, if we don't apply Dependency Inversion, the Use Case will depend directly on the Repository class, which is not an abstraction but a concretion. This is not an example of Dependency Inversion. But being pragmatic, it's a viable solution, particularly for smaller projects. But how can this be possible? As we described earlier, having a high-level business module depending on low-level data details introduces risk.

The secret lies in the implementation of the Repository. If done correctly, it can still hide the details of the data layer and expose clean information.

```
class LoansRepository(
    private val service: LoansService,
    private val localDataSource: LoansLocalDataSource
) {

    fun getLoan(id: String): Loan {
        //return loan from server or from local data source
    }

    fun getAllLoans(): List<Loan> {
        //return loans from server or from local data source
    }

    fun updateLoan(loanId: String) {
        //delete loan from both server and local data source
    }

    fun deleteLoan(loanId: String) {
        //delete loan from both server and local data source
    }
}
```

The Repository is responsible for exposing a public interface that contains data operations. It orchestrates both remote services and local data sources to carry out those operations. If appropriately designed, it

[21] The Repository design pattern is a technique that hides the data layer's implementation details from any other layer that requires access.
In most cases, it is used to protect the application business logic from details like external APIs or local storage implementations.

can be agnostic of the details of the backend API and the particular local storage that we are using. This means that even though the Use Case depends directly on it, it is somehow protected from changes in those layers.

Again this is not an example of Dependency Inversion. This example is an alternative, lightweight approach to provide change protection to our business rules. Its advantage is simplicity. We avoid introducing and implementing several interfaces, effectively reducing the amount of code. Its disadvantage is that it doesn't offer the same level of protection as DI, and the code is not that clean. It's the dilemma of soft vs. hard boundaries that we discussed earlier. Furthermore, interface segregation is also not appropriately applied. The Repository contains all the data operations of a particular entity, while a Use Case does not require all of them.

As described in Part I, there is no one-size-fits-all solution. I want to provide you with the whole spectrum of viable solutions. You have to decide which one fits best to your app, depending on its complexity. Also, remember that as the project evolves, you can decide it's time to refactor the previous solution and apply another that fits best to the latest requirements.

Summary

The code can be categorized into layers based on its responsibilities/ concerns. The most straightforward layer cake we can bake is UI, data, and domain layers.

The layers are sitting on different levels. High-level layer indicates that we intend to protect it from changes in lower-level layers. So high-level code should not depend on low-level code. It's even better if low-level code does not depend on high-level code either (concrete classes). They both should depend on abstractions (interfaces, protocols).

To apply DIP, we need to create an interface that covers the needs of the high-level concretion. The high-level class depends on this interface, and the low-level class implements it. By applying this technique, the dependency is magically inverted, and the arrows now point upwards.

Keep in mind that the end goal is to protect the high-level code. DI is the cleanest way but also the one that introduces the highest amount of files and code. It fits better to complex applications. Alternatively, you may consider the Repository design pattern.

CHAPTER ELEVEN

Reactive Programming

Reactive Programming (RP) is a declarative programming paradigm concerned with data streams and the propagation of change[1].

RP is based on the Observer Design Pattern[2]. The Observer pattern is a software design pattern in which an object, named the subject, maintains a list of its dependents, called observers. The subject notifies the observers automatically of any state changes, usually by calling one of their methods. It is mainly used for implementing distributed event handling systems in "event-driven" software.

As much as we all love formal definitions, let's try to make things simple. Understanding is more important than sounding cool.

"Reactive programming is programming with asynchronous data streams."

You can think of a data stream as a pipe that delivers events; each event contains some information.

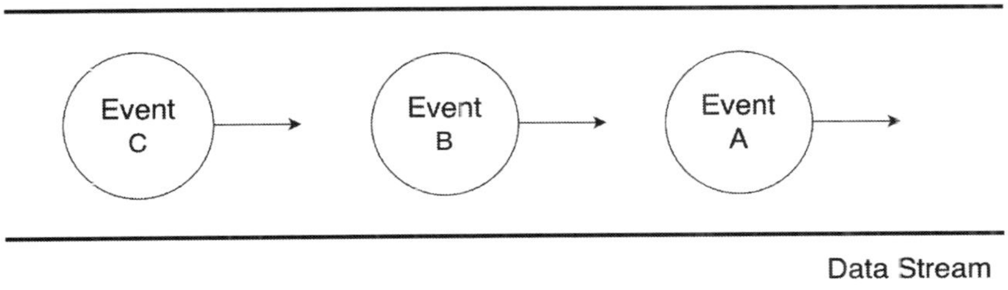

* * *

Several libraries can help us apply RP in mobile apps. The most popular is the ReactiveX family. ReactiveX[3] is a library for composing asynchronous and event-based programs using observable sequences. It extends the observer pattern and adds a lot of powerful operations for data manipulation and thread management. It's available in almost every language. As far as mobile is concerned: RxKotlin, RxSwift, RxDart, RxJava, and RxJs.

Besides Rx, we can use native frameworks like Kotlin Flow, Swift Combine, Live data, and more. Each comes with its own set of pros and cons.

RP includes many details that make it hard to master; understanding the basics, though, will go a long way. Before we deep dive into RP, let's first understand why we should use it and what problems it solves.

Why use Reactive Programming in a Mobile app

Mobile applications are, by nature, event-driven. Event-driven comes from the fact that a user is orchestrating their flow. Instead of having the main function sequentially calling other functions, a user clicks buttons. Those user actions are called events. The events orchestrate the execution of our code. Consequently, by definition, we need to follow some sort of Event-driven programming[22] [4] in a mobile app.

Mobile applications are also, by nature, asynchronous. As the user is firing events at will, those run in parallel. The only way to avoid parallel execution is to block the UI until the event completes. However, this would cause a horrible user experience and is avoided in modern applications. Additionally, those parallel events often take a

---

[22] Event-driven programming is a programming paradigm in which the flow of the program is determined by events such as user actions (mouse clicks, key presses) or messages passing from other programs or threads.

Event-driven programming is the dominant paradigm used in graphical user interfaces and other applications (e.g., web and mobile applications) centered on performing specific actions in response to user input.

long time to execute and require post-processing. They usually include an HTTP request, which can take several seconds to complete. After receiving the result, we perform further processing until the data comes in a meaningful shape. Alongside asynchronous and parallel programming come their evil children, race conditions[23]! UX-wise, a race condition often translates to an application crash, unexpected behavior, and a terrible user experience.

There we have our first *why*. Reactive Programming is an event-driven paradigm that helps us implement safe concurrency. In other words, it facilitates the execution of asynchronous events in a thread-safe manner. It does not apply safe concurrency by default, but it simplifies it by a lot. It is easier to achieve it with RP than with other asynchronous mechanisms. On top of that, it provides us with a fantastic toolbox of functions to combine, create, filter, and asynchronously process the data. RP adds both power and safety.

The second *why* is that RP helps us lower the system's coupling. We already know the benefits of reducing the system's coupling, we just need to understand how Reactive Programming can help us with it. Let's understand this better with an example…

Reactive Programming vs. traditional approaches

Let's assume that we have a class called Producer. The Producer is responsible for performing a heavy, asynchronous operation that must not block the UI/main thread. After the task is completed, it should notify another class, the Consumer, to post-process the data. In order to achieve this, the *produce* function does not have a return type. Instead, it receives an instance of a Consumer and notifies it via a callback function called *handleValues*:

* * *

[23] A race condition or race hazard is the condition of a software system where the system's substantive behavior is dependent on the sequence or timing of other uncontrollable events. It becomes a bug when one or more possible behaviours are undesirable.

```
class Producer {

    func produce(consumer: Consumer) {
        //asynchronous blocking task
        let values = [1,2,3]
        consumer.handleValues(values: values)
    }
}
```

The Consumer is requesting the data from the Producer and is responsible for handling the data after it is returned:

```
class Consumer {

    let producer = Producer()

    func requestForValues() {
        producer.produce(consumer: self)
    }

    func handleValues(values: [Int]) {
        for value in values {
            print(value)
        }
    }
}
```

As we can see, both classes are tightly coupled to each other. The Consumer depends on the Producer and vice versa. If the Producer decides to change the *requestForValues* function signature, the Consumer will break. Also, if the Consumer chooses to change the *handleValues* signature, the Producer will break. A Producer, though, should not be dependent on its consumers. We need to lower the system's coupling.

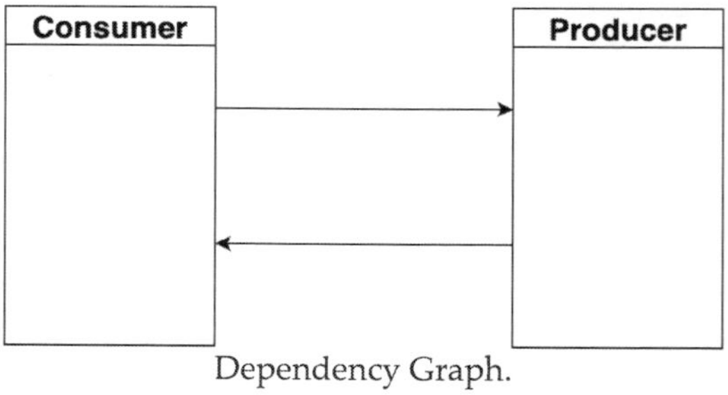

Dependency Graph.

* * *

Let's refactor our system with the help of Reactive Programming and Rxswift[5].

```
class Producer {

    let observable = Observable<[Int]>.just([1,2,3])
}
```

The Producer now does not hold a reference whatsoever to the Consumer. It exposes an observable stream that emits a single event, an array of three integers. An observable is a stream of data, a pipe that emits events. In our case, an event contains an array of integers, and our stream only emits once.

```
class Consumer {

    let disposeBag = DisposeBag()

    let producer = Producer()

    func consume() {
        producer.observable.subscribe { element in
            print(element)
        }.disposed(by: disposeBag)
    }
}
```

The Consumer subscribes to the Producer's observable. By calling subscribe, it can collect all the events that the observable will emit. In this case, it will catch the single event containing an array of three integers and print it on the screen. We can also see that we add the observable in a *disposeBag*. This is not mandatory, but we do it to avoid memory leaks. When the *disposeBag* is disposed of, it will cancel all its subscriptions.

Our dependency graph now looks like this:

* * *

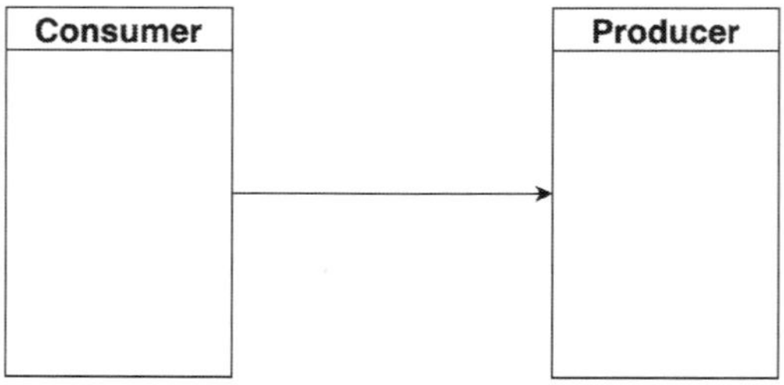

Dependency Graph with RP.

We have successfully reduced the coupling of our system and made the Producer reusable for potentially more consumers. Note that this is not the only way to achieve this result. There are other techniques like Async/await, Coroutines, and protocol-based callbacks. Each has its pros and cons. Reactive Programming has a steeper learning curve but is more potent than the other techniques.

Reactive Programming Components

As we saw in the previous example, RP includes the following main components:

1. *Datastream.* A data stream is a pipe that emits events. It can emit any amount of events, and it remains open until it's explicitly disposed of. Events are strongly typed; we define what data type it carries when declaring the Observable<TYPE> data stream.
2. *Producer.* A producer is a source of data. It exposes data streams to consumers. It is agnostic of the consumers and does not depend on or know anything about them. Anyone is free to subscribe to its streams.
3. *Consumer.* A consumer is a component that accepts and post-processes events from the data streams. Events can travel only from the producer to the consumer.

* * *

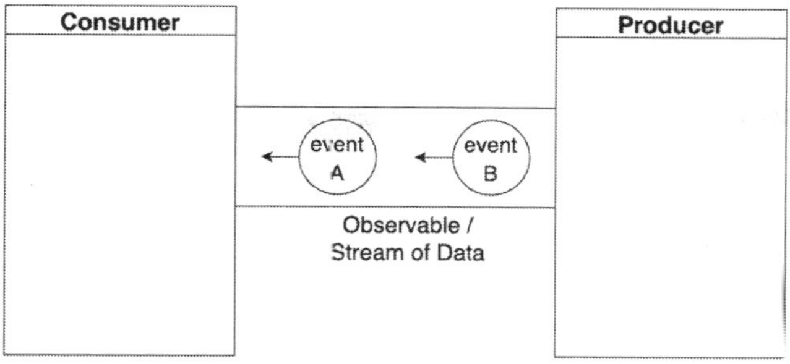

Hot and Cold Streams

On a high level, there are two types of data streams.

Cold streams are lazy. They don't do anything until someone starts observing them. They only begin emitting events when a consumer begins consuming them. Cold streams represent asynchronous actions that won't be executed until someone is interested in the result. An example would be a file download. It won't start pulling the bytes if no one consumes and process the data.

Hot streams are active before someone starts consuming them. The data is independent of an individual subscriber. When an observer subscribes to a hot observable, it will receive all values in the stream emitted *after* it subscribes. All the values emitted prior to the first subscription are practically lost. We should utilize hot streams when the events include write operations to a database or backend system. Regardless of whether a user observes the result, write operations must be carried through.

Immutability

Immutability is crucial in Reactive Programming and generally in any functional and asynchronous programming paradigm. Immutable objects are objects whose state cannot be changed after their declaration. On the other hand, mutable objects are variables whose state can be altered over the program's execution.

We usually recognize them as follows:

- In Kotlin, immutable objects are declared as values, val. Mutable objects are declared as variables, var.
- In Swift, we declare immutable values using let. To declare mutable variables, we also use the var keyword.
- In Dart, we use the final keyword to declare immutable objects and again var for mutable.

When performing asynchronous operations, immutability is key to avoiding issues related to concurrency. The first issue we face working with mutable objects is race conditions. When multiple threads try to change the value of the same variable simultaneously, the application crashes. This is particularly likely to happen when we apply operations to large arrays and lists, as they take time to complete.

The second issue we can face with mutable variables is unpredicted changes. Thread A can read the state of variable V and decide that will make a specific change. Meantime, thread B may change the state of V. Then, thread A may apply the change without knowing that thread B has altered its state. This may not lead to a crash but a logical defect.

Both issues are tough to identify and fix. As in every execution, the specific timing that the operations will take place is different. For example, we may aggregate data from multiple endpoints. The timing that those endpoints will respond is different in every execution; we are talking milliseconds here. Therefore, we may test the application several hundred times without noticing an issue. A user who will be unlucky enough to hit the wrong timing will experience a crash or a logical defect. As this bug is hard to reproduce, it's also tough to trace & fix.

In RP, I wouldn't say that it's even a choice whether to go with mutable or immutable objects. We must go with immutable. We use the map operator when we need to apply any operations to the data. This returns a new immutable object instance that includes the calculated immutable values.

Besides RP, it's preferable to use immutable values whenever possible. It simplifies the code and reduces the chance of state-dependent bugs slipping to production. The modern declarative UI frameworks like SwiftUI, Jetpack Compose, and Flutter also embrace immutability. We must always assume that all UI elements are immutable, and when we change something, everything is being recreated on the screen. In reality, they utilize clever caching and diffing mechanisms that don't redraw the unchanged elements, but this isn't something that affects the way we use those frameworks. As far as we are concerned, everything is being redrawn to the screen when a single element changes.

State management is a complex thing—possibly the most complex thing in mobile development. Immutability is key in simplifying it.

Common Reactive Programming Usages

The most common usage of RP in a mobile app is to retrieve and process data, either from a database or from a backend server. Most modern HTTP libraries and databases support RP out of the box. The queries or responses can expose data streams instead of traditional callbacks or Futures[24]. Those streams serve as single sources of truth. Multiple screens can subscribe to them and receive information regarding an entity, e.g., articles. As we explained before, a vast toolset can be applied to those streams. Both on composing them and on manipulating the data that they carry. We can use this toolset to achieve easy and safe data aggregation and transformation:

* * *

[24] Future or promise refers to constructs used for synchronizing program execution in some concurrent programming languages.
They describe an object that acts as a proxy for a previously unknown result, usually because the computation of its value is not yet complete.

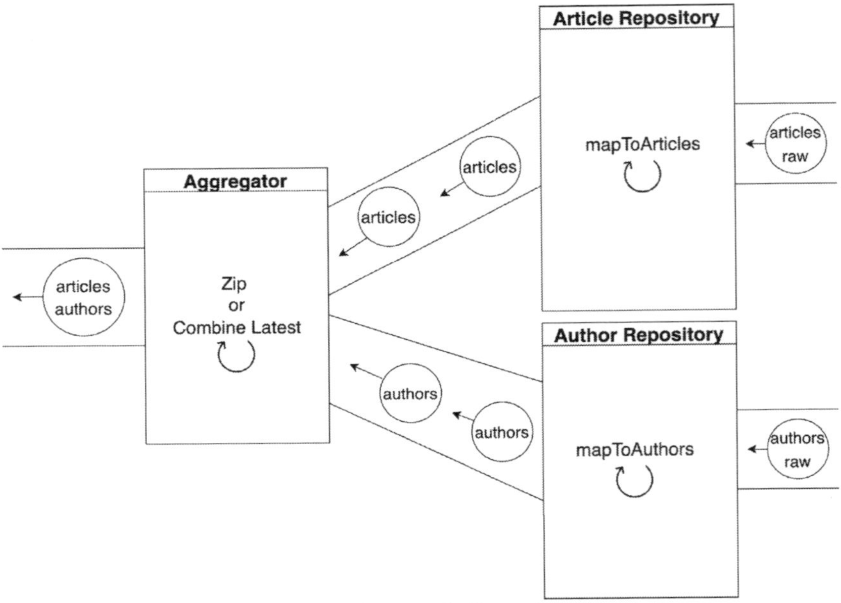

Aggregate & process data with Reactive Programming.

As we can see, the Repositories receive raw/unprocessed information as the Services are fetching it from the backend API. Using Functional programming, they process the data and map it to more convenient formats for our application. We could also use other operations like filter, sort, reduce, etc. Then, the Aggregator merges the information in a single stream that is exposed to the UI. Multiple operators combine data from various streams. The most common ones are:

- *Merge*. The merge operator can be used only in streams of the same type. If two streams emit events of, e.g., Article. Merging them means that the new stream will emit all the emissions from both.
- *Zip*. The zip operation can be applied to streams of different data types. We provide a function that inputs Article & Author and combines them in a new model. The new model can be called ArticleAuthor, and it contains attributes from both.
- *Combine Latest*. This operation is similar to Zip, with the difference in the timing that it emits events. The Zip operator will only emit when it receives an equal number of events from both streams. For example, if the authors stream emits six events and the articles stream two events, the Zipped stream

will only emit two events. The Combine latest stream instead combines a new emission from one stream with the latest (no matter how old it is) from the other. In the case of six and two events, it will emit seven times.

Another common usage is the case of "live data." I mean data that changes in real-time and triggers changes in the UI in return. For example, the value of a stock or crypto. We need to have some kind of asynchronous mechanism in place to fetch the new values. It can be:

- A polling mechanism that performs an HTTP request every X seconds to fetch the updated values.
- Long polling[25].
- A socket implementation where our backend pushes data directly to our client.

After the data is fetched, it must be processed, and the screens must be updated automatically. With RP, this becomes much easier than with other traditional approaches.

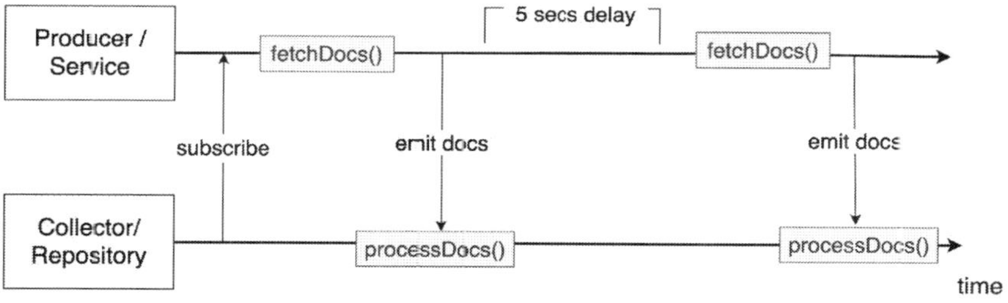

Polling example with Reactive Programming.

Assuming that the service stream was inactive before the repository subscribed to it, it is an example of a cold stream.

Finally, RP and data streams work well with declarative UI techniques

---

[25] Long polling is essentially a more efficient form of the original polling technique.

Rather than performing multiple HTTP requests every X seconds, the client performs one HTTP request with a huge timeout. The connection remains open until the backend responds or the request times out. Then the client performs another similar request in anticipation of new data.

like SwiftUI, Jetpack Compose, and Flutter.

Concerns

Let's discuss the downsides of Reactive Programming:

Steep learning curve. RP introduces a new way of thinking and many new concepts. It works in a functional fashion which is different from the OO approach that most of us are used to. It also follows an event-based programming paradigm instead of code controlling the flow with function calls and callbacks. It takes some time and effort to introduce it to an app and even more to master it.

Complexity. With great power comes great responsibility. Most RP implementations, especially Rx, provide many cool operator functions. It's easy to lean towards the "dark side." Chaining flatmap, retry, map, filter, debounce, zip, etc.. makes you feel like a ninja... BUT, never forget that good code needs to be readable by other developers.

```
service.getUserById(id)
    .flatMap { user ->
        service.getUserCart(user)
            .flatMap { cart ->
                val products: Observable<List<Product>> =
                    service.getProducts(cart)
                val pastProductPurchases:
Observable<List<Purchase>> =
                    service.pastProductPurchases(cart)
                products.zipWith(
                    pastProductPurchases
                ) { p, c -> CartPurchasesModel(cart, p,
c) }
            }
            .flatMap { model ->
                service.getDiscounts(model)
            }
    }
    .subscribe(
        { content -> displayContent(content) }
    ) { err ->
        Log.e("Unable to render campaign view", err)
    }
```

* * *

The example above is brutal to read, test and debug. It chains several asynchronous operations (flatmap), joining another set of operations (zip). Reactive Programming first requires a mind shift. You are notified of asynchronous events. Then, the API can be hard to grasp (just look at the list of operators). Don't abuse its power.

Summary

Reactive Programming can significantly assist in mobile development. It's event-driven and can enable us to perform asynchronous operations safely. Furthermore, it can also help us decouple our system and improve the code's conciseness.

Data streams act as single sources of truth; multiple screens can be updated simultaneously by a single stream that is exposed by a single Repository.

Initially, it has a steep learning curve. But when we get a good understanding, it can significantly increase our efficiency.

Avoid chaining multiple operators, one after another. The operations are powerful and concise, but they can hurt readability and debugging when overused.

CHAPTER TWELVE

Inversion of control

Definition

Inversion of Control (IoC) is a broad software principle that includes inverting the flow of control when we want to decouple two or more components.

Control generally means execution, the flow of control is the flow of execution. When class A calls a function of class B, we say that class A controls class B. In other words, the action, execution of code, passes from A to B. The same applies when class A calls the constructor of class B and creates an instance of it; then class A controls class B.

With inversion of control, we try to decouple those two classes so that one does not control the other. To solve issues related to function execution, we use *Dependency Inversion*. For issues related to class instantiation, we use another technique called *Dependency Injection*.

First, let's clarify the difference between the flow of control and the "flow" of dependency.

Flow of Control VS. "Flow" of Dependency

To understand how the DIP can help us here, we first need to understand the difference between the flow of control and dependency.

* * *

Let's assume that we have a simple, three layered application:

- UI, responsible for displaying the elements on the screen.
- Application, responsible for applying the business logic.
- Data, responsible for fetching the data from a remote server.

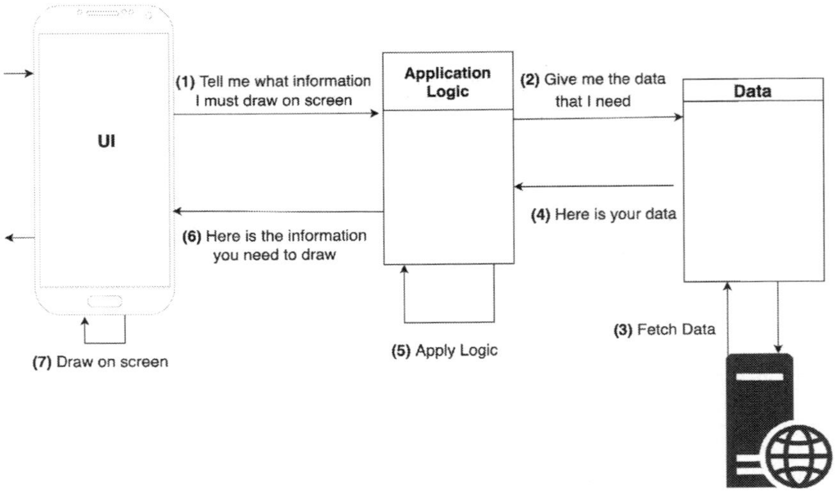

Flow of Control.

The flow of control typically kicks off from the user who opens up the application. Remember, we are dealing with event-driven programming. Then, the screen must display some information. It requests the data from the application layer; it can be a View Model, Interactor, or a Use Case. For the sake of this example, we will keep the layering simple. We will implement a Use Case that contains all the application logic. The Use Case, in return, will ask for the data from the data layer. The data layer, our Service, will fetch the information from a remote server. Then the data will return to the Use Case, which will apply the application & business logic. Finally, the data will end up on the screen and to the user. Note that there can be many more layers involved, but this is a simplification for the sake of this example.

This flow of control cannot change, ever. It will always start from the user, end up at the data layer, and then follow the same way back to the user.

* * *

"Flow" of Dependencies

Naturally, we assume that the dependency arrows follow the same flow. Which means:

- The UI depends on - knows about - the application in order to ask for information.
- The application depends on the data to ask for data.
- The data depends on the application to pass back the fetched data.
- The application depends on the UI to pass back the processed information.

In other words, the layers that share direct communication know about each other. In our case, though, as we will see, the dependency graph is more complex than the flow of control. It contains more arrows, and the layers are heavily coupled. Specifically, the UI depends on the Service even though those layers do not share any direct communication.

Let's demonstrate this in an iOS application:

Data Layer

```
class ArticlesService {

    func fetchArticles(useCase: GetArticlesUseCase) {
        Task {
            do {
                let articles: [Article] = try fetchArticlesFromServer()
                useCase.handleArticles(articles: articles)
            } catch {
                //handle error case
            }
        }
    }
}
```

The Service fetches data from a server. After the data is fetched, it is passed to the Use Case for post-processing. Both the GetArticlesUseCase and Article belong to the application layer;

consequently, the data layer depends on the application layer.

Application Layer

```
class GetArticlesUseCase {

    let service: ArticlesService
    let view: ArticlesViewController

    init (view: ArticlesViewController, service: ArticlesService) {
        self.view = view
        self.service = service
    }

    func getArticles() {
        service.fetchArticles(useCase: self)
    }

    func handleArticles(articles: [Article]) {
        //apply articles business logic
        view.displayArticles(articles: articles)
    }
}
```

The GetArticlesUseCase depends on the ArticlesService, the ArticlesViewController, and the Article. We don't mind much about the Article dependency since they both belong to the same layer. But the Use Case depending on both the Service and the View Controller means that the application layer is dependent on both the UI/view layer and the data layer. This is not an ideal situation.

UI / View / Framework Layer

* * *

```
class ArticlesViewController : UIViewController {

    lazy var useCase: GetArticlesUseCase = self.makeUseCase()

    func makeUseCase() -> GetArticlesUseCase {
        return GetArticlesUseCase(view: self, service: ArticlesService())
    }

    override func viewDidLoad() {
        super.viewDidLoad()
        useCase.getArticles()
    }

    func displayArticles(articles: [Article]) {
        //display articles on the screen
    }
}
```

Finally, our UI or View or Framework layer has two dependencies, the Use Case and the Service. This means that it depends on both the application and data layers. The Use Case is needed to receive data. On the other hand, the Service dependency exists so it can instantiate the Use Case dependency. This is unnecessary as the two don't share direct communication. If we change the Service constructor, our View Controller will break. This is a symptom of tight, unnecessary coupling.

If we take a look at the dependency graph, it looks like this:

* * *

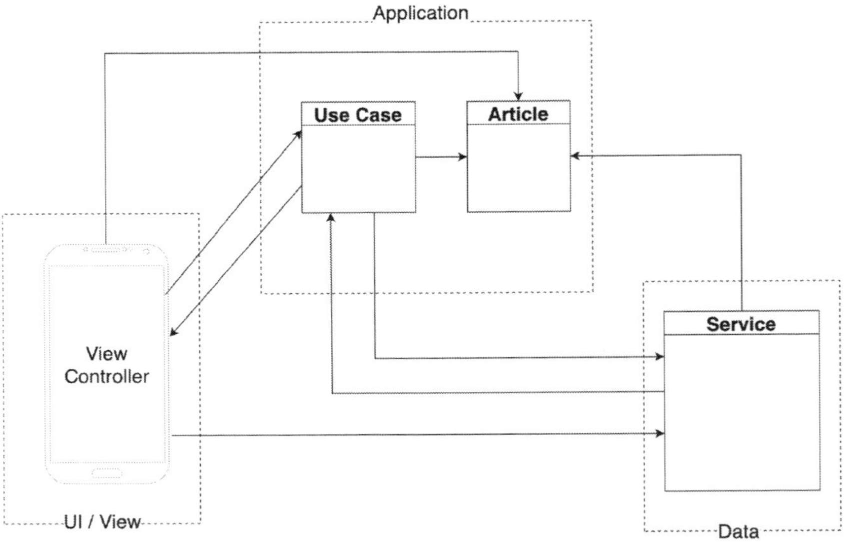

Dependency Graph.

It's a mess. Does it ring a bell? It's the case of high cohesion - high coupling. Our layers are cohesive, but they are also tightly coupled. We even have circular dependencies[26], the View Controller depends on the Use Case, and the Use Case depends on the View Controller. Circular dependency is one of the worst anti-patterns in software engineering.

I will try to simplify the graph to compare it with the flow of control. I will omit the classes & include only the layers. This will allow us to

---

[26] Circular dependencies can cause many unwanted effects in software programs. Most problematic from a software design point of view is the tight coupling of the mutually dependent modules, which reduces or makes impossible the separate re-use of a single module.

Circular dependencies can cause a domino effect when a small local change in one module spreads into other modules and has unwanted global effects (program errors, compile errors). Circular dependencies can also result in infinite recursions or other unexpected failures. Circular dependencies may also cause memory leaks by preventing certain primitive automatic garbage collectors (those that use reference counting) from deallocating unused objects.

https://en.wikipedia.org/wiki/Circular_dependency#cite_note-:0-1

make the comparison more easily:

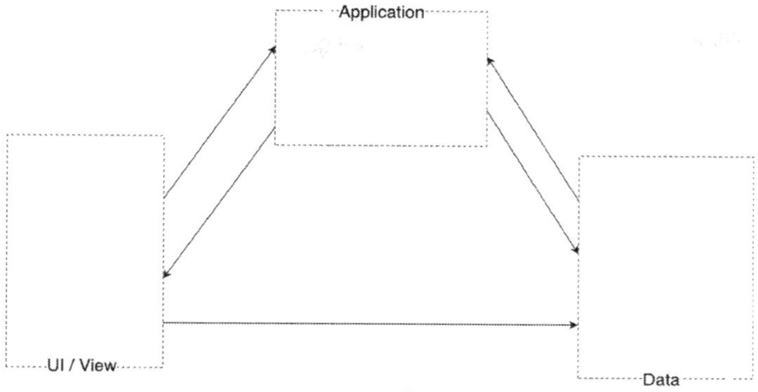

Dependency Graph, layers only.

The example above is the worst possible case. The flow of dependency is more complex than the flow of control. It contains one additional arrow pointing from the UI to the data.

There are multiple ways to improve the above situation and lower the system's coupling. I would prefer to first remove the dependency between the view and the data layers since those two layers do not share any direct communication. We need to apply the IoC technique called Dependency Injection to achieve this. Usually, this is a straightforward refactoring, but in our case, it is complicated due to the circular dependency between the View Controller and the Use Case. That's one of the reasons that we want to avoid circular dependencies. So let's focus on eliminating this one first.

We can decouple the circular dependency in several ways. Reactive Programming is an excellent pattern that can help us decouple our system and apply safe concurrency simultaneously. By applying RP:

- The View Controller (UI) depends on the Use Case (domain)
- The Use Case depends on the Service (data)
- The View depends on the Service (data)

* * *

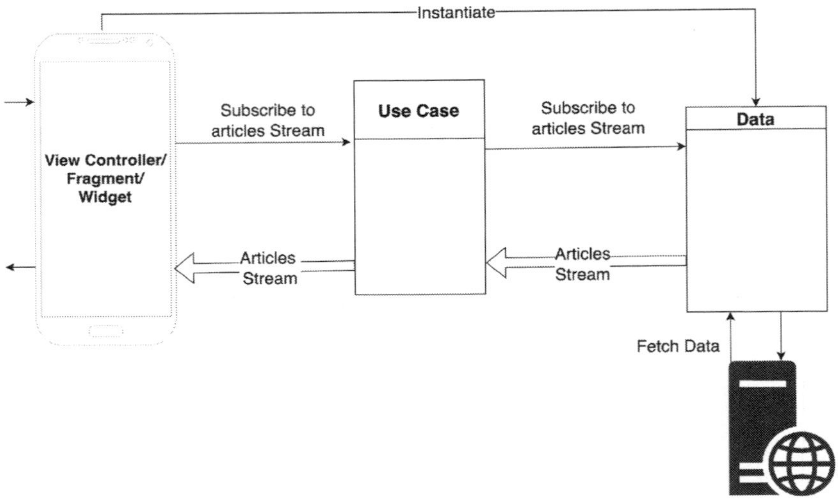

Reactive Programming.

As we have explained, the flow of control cannot change. The "flow" of dependencies can. In this diagram, the "thin" arrows represent the dependencies. We have reduced them from five to three. Most importantly, we have gotten rid of the circular dependency between the View Controller and the Use Case!

RP is generally a great way of implementing mobile applications. As we already covered RP in the previous chapter, now I will display another technique to decouple the components using *async/await*. *Async/await* is available on iOS and Flutter; for Android, we can achieve the same result with Kotlin Coroutines.

Let's refactor our implementation to make use of *async/await*.

Data Layer

```
class ArticlesService {

    func fetchArticles() async throws -> [Article] {
        let articles: [Article] = try await fetchArticlesFromServer()
        return articles
    }
}
```

* * *

Await suspends the function's execution until we fetch the articles from the server. After we fetch the articles, the execution resumes with the return statement. *Async/await* is an improvement on using completion closures. The Service now depends only on the Article. We have removed the Use Case dependency. It wasn't exactly a hard circular dependency as the Service was not holding a sticky reference to the Use Case. Nevertheless, changes in the Use Case will now not affect the Service.

Application Layer

```
class GetArticlesUseCase {

    let service: ArticlesService

    init (service: ArticlesService) {
        self.service = service
    }

    func getArticles() async throws -> [Article] {
        let articles = try await service.fetchArticles()
        //business logic
        return articles
    }
}
```

We have removed the View Controller dependency from our Use Case. This is an outstanding achievement since we released the circular dependency and decoupled the application layer from the view Layer.

UI / View / Framework Layer

* * *

```
class ArticlesViewController : UIViewController {

    lazy var useCase: GetArticlesUseCase = self.makeUseCase()

    func makeUseCase() -> GetArticlesUseCase {
        return GetArticlesUseCase(service: ArticlesService())
    }

    override func viewDidLoad() {
        super.viewDidLoad()
        Task {
            do {
                let articles = try await useCase.getArticles()
                displayArticles(articles: articles)
            } catch {
                //handle errors
            }
        }
    }

    func displayArticles(articles: [Article]) {
        //display articles on the screen
    }
}
```

Our view layer hasn't changed much. We mostly applied low-level code changes to handle the result of our async functions.

Let's take a look at the current state of the dependency graph:

* * *

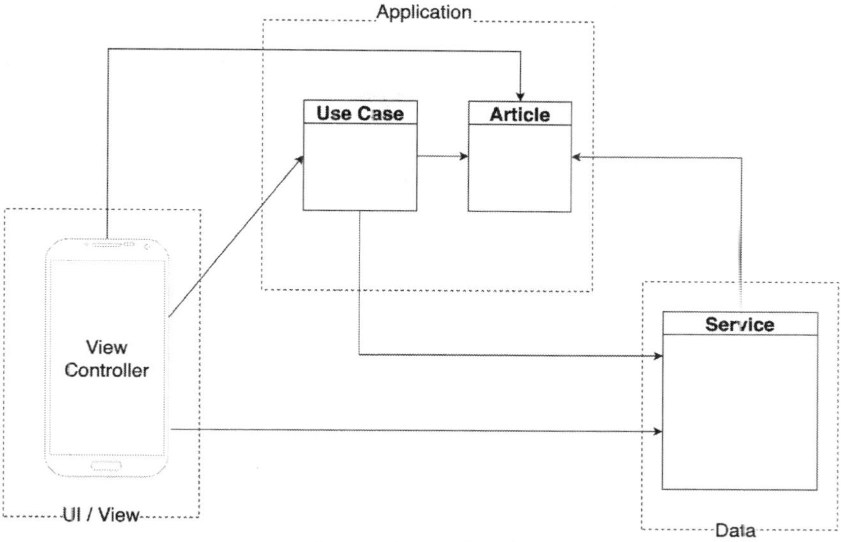

Dependency Graph.

As we can see, the situation has been improved. Our system is not so tightly coupled anymore. Let's also take a higher-level look, focusing just on the layers:

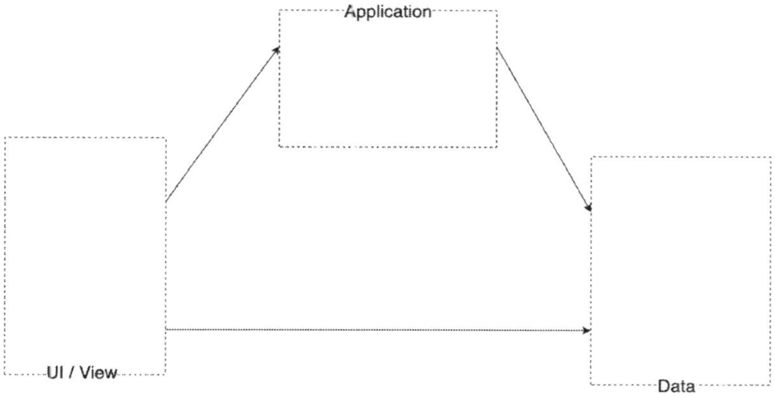

Dependency Graph, layers only.

We learned earlier that higher-level modules should not depend on lower-level modules. In our example, the Use Case - application layer depends on the Service - data layer. The application layer is the one that contains the business logic. That's the layer that we want to safeguard from change. Therefore, we need to apply Dependency Inversion to invert the tip of this arrow.

As we learned in the previous chapter, we need to implement a protocol tailored to the needs of our Use Case. It must deliver the data in the most convenient form & way to the Use Case. This is the difference from the Repository pattern that many developers apply. The Repository exposes an interface that contains all the related data operations; in proper DI, the interface is tailored to the business needs:

```
protocol GetArticlesDataSource {

    func fetchArticles() async throws -> [Article]
}
```

We will change the implementation of the Use Case to depend on this protocol:

```
class GetArticlesUseCase {

    let dataSource: GetArticlesDataSource

    init (dataSource: GetArticlesDataSource) {
        self.dataSource = dataSource
    }

    func getArticles() async throws -> [Article] {
        let articles = try await dataSource.fetchArticles()
        return articles
    }
}
```

And finally, the Service must conform to the protocol:

```
class ArticlesService : GetArticlesDataSource {

    func fetchArticles() async throws -> [Article] {
        let articles: [Article] = try await fetchArticlesFromServer()
        return articles
    }
}
```

We have successfully inverted the dependencies. Now the Use Case is agnostic of the Service, but the Service implements the Data Source. Our data layer now points upwards to the application Layer:

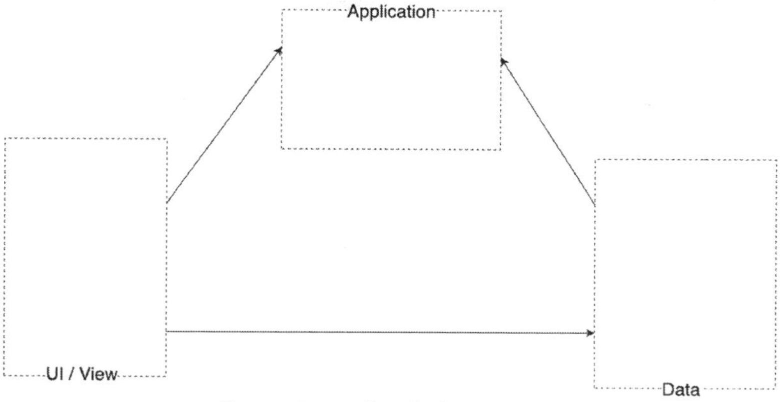

Dependency Graph, layers only.

This is the first part of Inversion of Control with the help of Dependency Inversion. A higher-level abstraction now controls the Service. The "flow" of dependencies goes against the flow of control.

Dependency Injection.

Dependency Injection is a technique where an object receives all of its dependencies instead of instantiating them itself. It involves three parts:

- The object that requires the dependencies, called client.
- The object that provides the dependencies, called injector.
- The dependencies.

* * *

In other words, when class A requires an instance of class B, instead of creating one, it should receive that instance from another class which is the injector. Furthermore, class A should be agnostic of the injector. It should not depend on it or be aware of its existence at all. It's the injector's job to know:

i. How to instantiate the dependencies.
ii. Which classes need those dependencies, and how to inject them.

The client is only aware that it requires an object of type <A>, and *someone* will inject it. There are two types of Dependency Injection:

1. Constructor injection: the dependencies are provided in the client's constructor.
2. Setter injection: the client exposes a setter function or variable that the injector is using to provide the dependency.

Examining all of the classes we implemented in our example, they are already receiving their dependencies in their constructors. Most of them are already in the ideal state. The injector, though, is our View Controller, and this is something that we have to fix.

* * *

```
class ArticlesViewController: UIViewController {

    lazy var useCase: GetArticlesUseCase = self.makeUseCase()

    func makeUseCase() -> GetArticlesUseCase {
        return GetArticlesUseCase(dataSource: ArticlesService())
    }

    override func viewDidLoad() {
        super.viewDidLoad()
        Task {
            do {
                let articles = try await useCase.getArticles()
                displayArticles(articles: articles)
            } catch {
                //handle errors
            }
        }
    }

    func displayArticles(articles: [Article]) {
        //display articles on the screen
    }
}
```

The View Controller requires an instance of a Use Case; it doesn't need to know how to instantiate it, nor does it need to know anything regarding its dependencies. In other words, the *makeUseCase* function must be removed.

We could implement a Dependency Injection mechanism on our own. It takes time, though, and it mainly includes writing boilerplate code. Several third-party libraries can carry out this responsibility perfectly.

- Hilt library for Android developers. Hilt is a library created by Google based on its predecessor Dagger 2.
- Resolver library for iOS developers.
- Provider or GetX for Flutter developers.

Every library has its own API, but they do the same thing behind the scenes. The Resolver library requires you to implement a function that registers all the dependencies:

* * *

```
import Resolver

extension Resolver: ResolverRegistering {
  public static func registerAllServices() {

    register { ArticlesService() }
    register { _, service in
        GetArticlesUseCase(dataSource: service())
    }
  }
}
```

And now, we need to go back to our View Controller and inform it that someone else will provide the Use Case dependency. It must be agnostic of who. We usually do this with the @Injected property wrapper:

```
class ArticlesViewController: UIViewController {

    @Injected private var useCase: GetArticlesUseCase

    override func viewDidLoad() {
        super.viewDidLoad()
        Task {
            do {
                let articles = try await useCase.getArticles()
                displayArticles(articles: articles)
            } catch {
                //handle errors
            }
        }
    }

    func displayArticles(articles: [Article]) {
        //display articles on the screen
    }
}
```

That's it! We successfully removed the View Controller's dependency on the Service and the concern of instantiating the Use Case. Our dependency graph now looks like this:

* * *

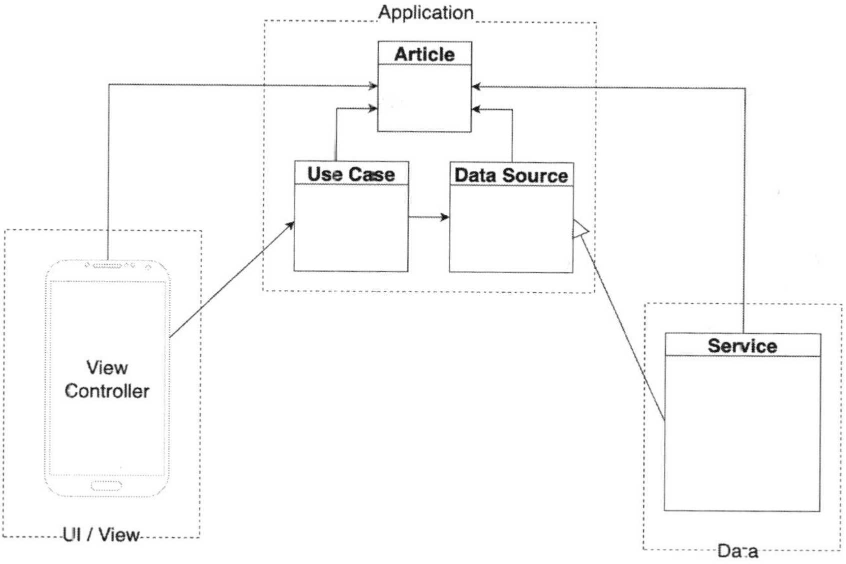

Dependency Graph.

And if we keep it on a high level:

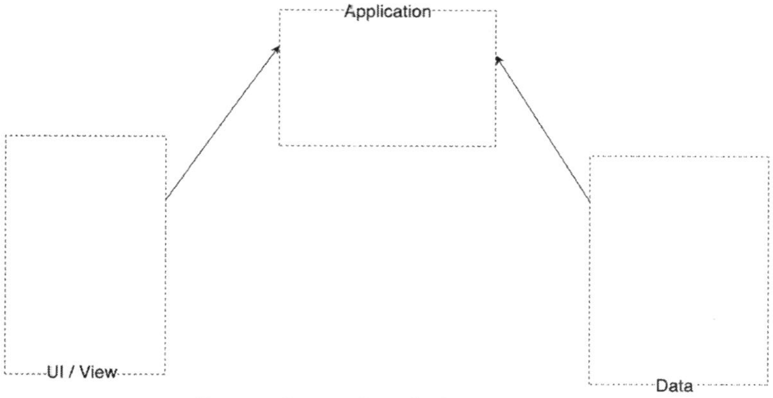

Dependency Graph, layers only.

That's much cleaner than what we started with. The coupling has been reduced significantly, and the high-level code is safeguarded from changes.

* * *

So if I asked you now: How is Dependency Injection related to Dependency Inversion? What would your answer be?

Dependency Inversion states that concretions should depend on abstractions. Without Dependency Injection, as we saw earlier, this is often impossible. When class A depends on protocol B, without Dependency Injection, it has to instantiate a concrete object itself. By knowing how to instantiate the object, it depends on the concrete implementation as well.

On the other hand, with Dependency Injection, class A can only depend on a protocol instance, and it will receive a concrete object from someone else. Class A remains utterly agnostic of any concretions. Consequently, Dependency Injection is the enabler of Dependency Inversion. It enables the concretions to depend on abstractions rather than other concretions.

Let's take a look at an example to understand this better:

```
protocol Abstraction {

}

class Concretion : Abstraction {

}
```

We have a protocol called Abstraction and a class called Concretion. The Concretion conforms to the Abstraction protocol. Then we have a client that depends on the Abstraction:

```
class Client {

    private var abstraction : Abstraction

    init() {
        self.abstraction = Concretion()
    }

}
```

Since it has to instantiate its dependencies, it also depends on the

Concretion. We can refactor this with Dependency Injection as follows:

```
class Client {

    @Injected private var abstraction : Abstraction
}
```

Now the client is agnostic of the Concretion. So Dependency Injection has enabled Dependency Inversion. Both of them combined achieve the Inversion of Control.

Benefits

Dependency Injection and Inversion of Control can help us:

1. Lower the system's coupling.
    - By reducing the number of dependencies between the classes and the layers.
    - By enabling the classes to depend on abstractions rather than concretions - soft boundaries.
2. Improve separation of concerns and cohesion. It removes the concern of dependency instantiation, making the client more cohesive.

As we explained in a previous chapter, we improve our app's readability, testability, maintainability, and resilience by reducing coupling, increasing cohesion, and separating concerns.

Inversion of Control is a powerful technique that should be used widely. Particularly the Dependency Injection part. As modern libraries have rendered its implementation trivial, there aren't any reasons to avoid it. On the other hand, Dependency Inversion should be used only when we identify the need to protect high-level modules. It comes with the cost of increasing the file count and overall lines of code.

Summary

* * *

Inversion of Control (IoC) is a broad principle that includes Dependency Inversion and Injection.

With Dependency Inversion, we turn the dependency flow against the flow of control. We do it when we want to protect a high-level module from changes in a lower-level module.

With Dependency Injection, we make the clients agnostic of how their dependencies are being instantiated. All they know is that an Injector will somehow provide them.

IoC is a powerful tool to reduce coupling, improve cohesion, and separate concerns. It can enable the Single Concern Principle.

CHAPTER THIRTEEN

Testing & TDD

Testing

It's time that we talk about testing. Testing refers to the implementation of automated tests that verify that the app's behavior matches the intended behavior. We explained how architecting an app to be testable is crucial for the app's longevity. Let's understand why this is important.

First of all, a testable app is also an app that is easy to read. Regardless of whether we have actually added the automated tests or not, simply by designing it to be testable, we improve its readability. We need to properly separate the concerns and keep our units small and focused in order to enable testability. By units, I am referring to classes and functions. A complex function that executes many unrelated tasks is hard to test. Additionally, to improve the app's testability, we need to apply techniques like Dependency Injection, which further increases cohesion and reduces coupling. A testable app is, by rule, a well-architected app.

Of course, we also have to add the automated tests in place and integrate them with our build system in order to get the maximum value. The benefits of an automated testing suite include:

- Acts as a safety net when we release new versions. A new release is always introducing the risk of breaking past behavior. Designing the code by the OCP can help a lot, but it cannot always guarantee that we haven't broken anything. A regression testing suite can catch all those pesky bugs before they reach production.

- Saves a lot of time in the long run. The most common counter-argument against implementing tests is that they take a lot of time. This is true. On the other hand, continuously testing and debugging the application manually takes more. We are constantly testing the app both while developing and prior to releasing it. An automated testing suite can take most of this burden away from us. I am carefully using the term time instead of effort here; I will explain this shortly.
- Enables us to deal effectively with legacy code. This argument is closely tied to the first one, but I want to emphasize that tests are more critical in legacy or unfamiliar systems. How many times have you encountered code that you fear touching? Or have you encountered code that appears to be unused, but no one dares to remove it? Having a test suite that verifies that the past behavior hasn't broken can give us the confidence to deal with cancerous code. In his book *Working Effectively With Legacy Code,* Michael Feathers goes as far as stating that: "Legacy code is code without tests"[1].
- Tests also serve as technical documentation. The trick to achieving this is to name the test functions to describe their intention. Something like "viewModelShouldEmitAllArticles." Then, by a quick scan of a class's test file, we can understand what this class is supposed to be doing. Most importantly, tests serve as living, executable documentation. They do not rot and get outdated, unlike any other written documentation. At the moment they get outdated, they ring the "test failed" alarm.

It's important to keep in mind that we are not allowed to modify the production code to write a test. Our application should be testable by design. Configurations inside production code that look like:

```
if(test) -> logic
```

..are forbidden. They clutter our application with code that is not delivering user value.

* * *

> The drastically shortened feedback loop fuelled by automated tests goes hand in hand with agile development practices, continuous delivery, and DevOps culture. Having an effective software testing approach allows teams to move fast and with confidence. —Martin Fowler

Tests & Effort

While listing the advantages of the automated test, I avoided using the term *effort* but rather stated that they save up a lot of *time*. A common argument against writing tests is that they require a lot of effort. Let's try to figure out the truth while being honest and unbiased.

First of all, it's widely accepted that manually re-testing every feature in every release takes more time than having an automated test suite in place. And to be professional, we should *know* that we haven't broken past behavior rather than assuming it. At least be as sure as we possibly can.

The thing is that manual testing does not add any severe cognitive effort. Running the app on a mobile device and asserting its behavior is often perceived as a pleasant task and a break from intense coding. On the other hand, implementing automated tests adds a similar cognitive effort to writing production code. It can make someone feel overwhelmed. This, together with the Principle of Least Effort[2], which we will discuss in-depth at the end of this chapter, makes a lot of developers avoid tests.

On the other hand, while manual testing can be pleasant, debugging is not. The value of tests does not only reside in flagging that something doesn't work as expected, but they usually also indicate what exactly goes wrong. This can effectively reduce both the time *and* effort to apply the fix.

Regardless of whether you belong in the group that loves automated tests or hates them, it's probably good to touch on time and (cognitive) effort separately when advocating in favor of your opinion.

* * *

Types of Tests

There are three types of tests that are intended to tackle different problems. Let's discuss them one by one.

1. Unit tests. Unit testing involves running tests on individual components or functions in isolation to verify that they are working as expected. They are the most lightweight form of tests. Unit tests should be focused and test tiny parts of behavior, like a single function output under a specific input. Unit tests are platform-agnostic. They shouldn't be aware that they test an Android or iOS codebase, nor should they require an emulator to run. For example, we could port the Android tests and run them in any JVM environment. This is one of the reasons that we are trying to keep as much of the codebase as possible platform agnostic. It enables unit testing, which is fast, reliable, and easy.

Unit tests can be of two categories:

i. White-box testing. White-box testing involves isolating a single class acting as the System Under Test (SUT). All the SUT dependencies are mocked, meaning they are not real objects but rather fake or test-doubles with defined behavior. White-box tests add more effort when we refactor the system, as we also have to refactor the mocks. The advantage of this method is that they indicate the precise bug's location when a test fails. Everything except the SUT is mocked; we can instantly identify and fix the issue. Furthermore, using mocks makes it easier to test the error cases and how all the components behave.

ii. Black-box testing. Black-box tests do not include any mocks except for the system boundaries. Only external systems and databases are allowed to be mocked. Other than that, the SUT and all of its dependencies are real objects. The advantage of this technique is that they are more flexible in refactoring and better at verifying the end-to-end flow's behavior. They are also called behavioral tests. On the downside, they tend to be larger, and when they break, we can't be sure where the bug is located. A SUT can break because the output of one of its collaborators is erroneous. Therefore, it takes more time to investigate and debug the system until we can correct the defect. As a rule of thumb, mocks = white-box unit testing, no-mocks = black-box unit testing.

2. *Integration Tests or Integrated Tests.* In integration testing, software modules are combined and tested as a group. It can be a single module or an end-to-end flow. It's important to note that any external system, including a local database, is mocked in those tests. Those tests cannot run on the JVM; they require an actual emulator and are aware that they run on an Android or iOS platform. Therefore, they are not very easy to write and fast to run. We need to take care of the initial state of our emulators before we run them. Otherwise, we may not get the expected result. As external systems are mocked, when the tests fail, we know that the defect resides within the boundaries of our app. However, it usually requires investigation to locate it.

3. *End-to-End Tests (E2E).* They simulate a real user and test an application's workflow from beginning to end. Nothing is allowed to be mocked; we are talking to the actual backend system and a local DB. They verify that everything, end-to-end, behaves as a real user would expect. They obviously run on emulators and are affected by the backend behavior and response times. Consequently, they are very slow to run and sometimes flaky. Finally, when they fail, we can't instantly determine which system is defective.

The AAA pattern

The Arrange-Act-Assert (AAA) testing pattern has become a standard across the industry. It suggests that you should divide your test functions into three sections:

i. *Arrange.* We perform all the necessary object instantiations during arrange, whether we use real objects or mocks. Here, we also verify that our objects have the intended initial state.
ii. *Act* covers the execution of the function(s) we intend to test.
iii. *Assert* should verify that the actual outcome is equal to the intended outcome. It ultimately determines if the test passed or failed.

We should strive to pertain each A to a one-line implementation. When we require the instantiation of several objects, we can extract a function to take care of them. For act, we should aim to test a single function call in each test. And for assert, we should give each test one reason to fail, aka one assertion. It's not always easy to include each A in a one-liner, but getting as close as possible ensures that the tests are fast, focused, and easy to read.

The Testing Pyramid

The testing pyramid is a concept that Mike Cohn initially coined in his book *Succeeding with Agile*[3]. Later, it became viral with a Googler's blog post[4] authored by Mike Wacker.

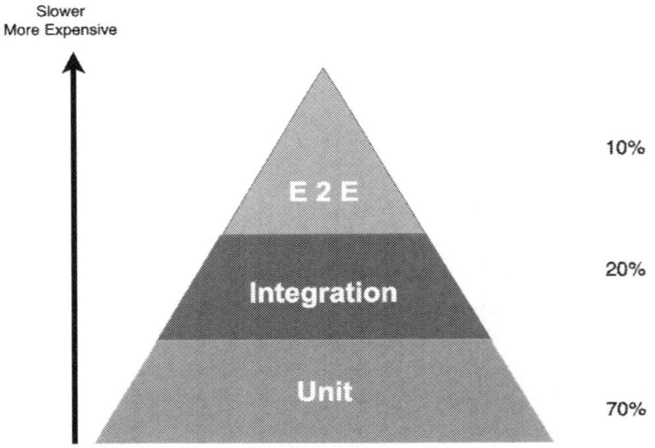

The Testing Pyramid.

The testing pyramid indicates that our testing strategy should include roughly 70% unit tests, 20% Integration tests, and 10% End-to-end tests. Mike Wacker advocates in favor of this strategy with the following argument: "While End-to-end and Integration tests are good at catching bugs, they are not good at indicating where the bugs are. A failing test is not beneficial for the user; the users only benefit from fixing the bug."

While each project's context and details are different, when it comes to establishing your own test suite, your best bet is to:

- Write tests with different granularity.
- The more high-level you get, the fewer tests you should have.

Testing strategies for Mobile apps

I generally recommend two testing strategies, particularly fitting to mobile applications.

1. For enterprise, complex applications, I suggest following the Testing Pyramid above, where the unit tests belong to the white-box category (including mocks). We put in place a massive testing suite apart from targeted unit tests that enable us to locate the defects fast and with high precision. We also benefit from the regression safety net that the Integration and E2E tests provide.

While this strategy is the safest, it also requires the most considerable effort to put in place and maintain. Non-flaky, E2E tests are pretty hard to write and slow to run. Sometimes they are flaky due to the backend response times or because the platform is lagging in displaying the screen elements. There are ways to deal with the flakiness, but it's by no means a trivial task.

Additionally, while great at indicating the defect's location, white-box unit tests require a lot of effort to maintain in the long run. As they need us to mock the public interface of the collaborators, we also have to refactor them when this changes. Some practices include generics and common interfaces that can reduce this side-effect. We should have the muscle power to deal with the effort when talking about a large enterprise app. The focus should be on fast-tracking defects in the massive codebase. This testing strategy is best at achieving this.

We can downscale this strategy a bit by omitting the Integration tests. The unit tests alongside the E2E can cover most of the cases.

2. A more pragmatic approach is to omit both the E2E and Integration tests that are hard to write. We also replace the white-box unit tests with black-box unit tests. Those will test the app's behavior from the View Model up to our service layer. The external systems and database

will be mocked. This more lightweight testing strategy offers the flexibility that larger refactorings require.

Of course, on the downside, this strategy is less safe. It's easier to allow bugs to slip into production as we don't test the UI in an automated way. Our app may also break for reasons outside our control, like a defect residing in the backend system. A unit test cannot possibly catch this. Remember, they cannot run on real devices or emulators. Finally, sometimes it may require additional debugging effort to track down the exact source of the errors.

You will find practical examples of the above strategies in Part III. Both for iOS and Android.

Many developers don't buy into writing tests. This mostly comes from the fact that we test our apps manually during development; why spend the time writing a unit test afterward? This is true; sometimes it feels like a complete waste of time. We would rather implement the next feature that will add value to our users.

There are two answers to that. First, it's context-dependent. Again don't think of every project only in regards to your personal efficiency but as a whole. The absence of a testing suite will slow down significantly another developer who will join later and have to deal with legacy code. Defects will slip into production unnoticed when adding new behavior. The same thing will happen to you in the next codebase that you'll move on.

The other answer is in the section below; write the tests before implementing the feature...

Test-Driven Development

Test-Driven Development (TDD) is a software development methodology in which tests *drive* the development of the application. The magic word here is *drive*. It requires automated tests to be written before the code they are supposed to validate. It was inspired by Kent Beck in the late 1990s as part of Extreme Programming.

* * *

TDD relies on the repetition of a concise development cycle:

i. Write a failing test for the intended new functionality.
ii. Make the test pass by implementing the functionality.
iii. Refactor the code to increase its quality.

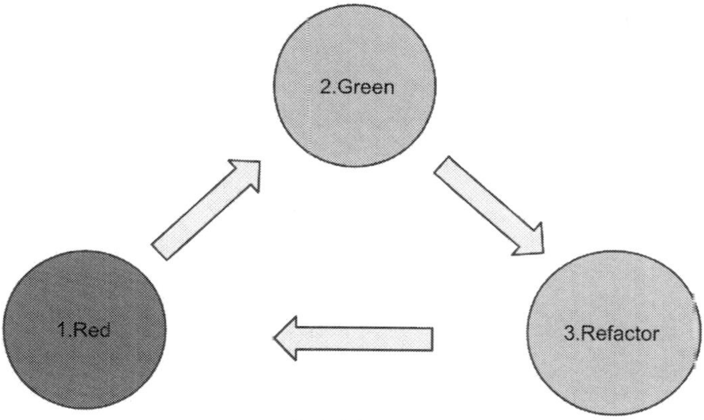

TDD lifecycle.

The initial test always fails as it is testing non-existent code. Imagine testing that a function returns one while the function doesn't even exist. Then, we write the minimum possible code to make the test pass. This is important. We should not go ahead and implement the full feature; we just make the first test pass. Finally, we refactor the code to improve the solution. Refactoring is an internal process that must not modify the observable behavior of the program, just enhance its quality.

We then proceed to repeat this cycle for all the parts of functionality our feature requires. When all the units of behavior are tested, implemented, and refactored, we are *done*.

> TDD encourages simple designs and inspires confidence. — Kent Beck

Types of TDD

There are mainly two different types of TDD. Possibly the hardest thing to grasp is the number of names that each type includes.

1. Classicist - Chicago School - Detroit School - State based testing - Inside out - Black box - Behavioral TDD. Yes, they all refer to the same TDD strategy. The main elements of this type include:

- We don't make use of mocks. Except for the system's boundaries, all objects are real. Hence the terms black-box and behavioral.
- We use the TDD cycle depicted above.
- The architectural design is supposed to emerge from practicing this cycle.
- Popular advocates of this technique include Kent Beck, Uncle Bob, and Ron Jeffries.

The advantages of this technique are pretty much the advantages of black-box unit tests vs. white-box. It's better at testing the behavior and enables easy and safe refactoring. On the other hand, the tests are usually larger, more complex, and don't indicate with high precision where the defect is hidden. I also don't like the idea of emerging design. Simply by following this technique, your design won't blossom into an enviable work of technical art. To implement a good design, you have to learn about design.

2. Mockists - London School - Outside in - White Box. The main elements are:

- Vast use of mocks.
- Testing the interactions (implementation details).
- Upfront design.
- Popular advocates include Sandro Mancuso, Steve Freeman, and Sandi Metz.
- This strategy uses a slightly altered lifecycle:

* * *

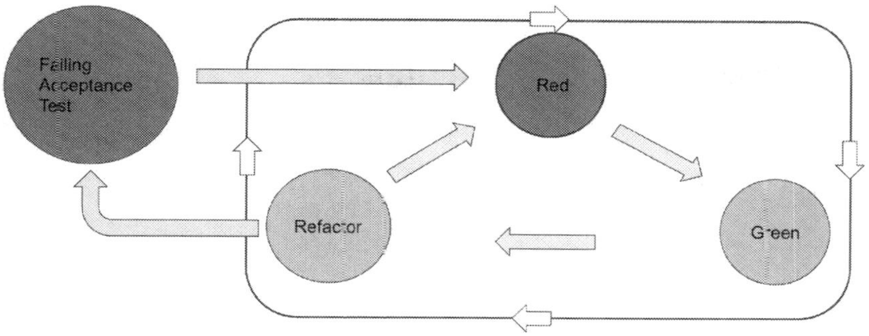

Outside-in TDD lifecycle.

Essentially, we have added one more step that comes at the very start, writing the Acceptance test. The Acceptance or E2E test is supposed to be a UI test that tests the feature as a whole. We proceed with the normal TDD cycle when we have this in place. In this TDD flavor, though, we implement white-box unit tests. Our job is done when the Acceptance test turns green after the repetition of one or more inner circles.

Again most of the pros and cons come from the pros and cons of white vs. black-box unit tests. We get simpler tests that predict the exact defect's location, but they are more rigid to refactoring. Another advantage is that it's easier to test error cases. We can easily mock error input in all of the components and see how they behave. I also prefer the fact that we have a dedicated time slot to think about the upfront architectural design. This comes right after we add the initial acceptance test.

* * *

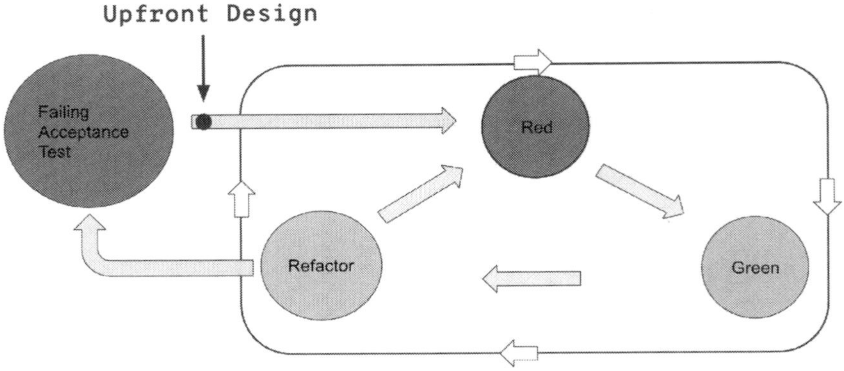

Upfront design in Outside-in TDD.

Why use TDD?

There are many advantages of using TDD; some come from the fact that we also inherit a testing suite alongside the feature implementation. All the benefits of a comprehensive testing suite, which we discussed at the beginning of that chapter, also apply here. But certain advantages apply *only* when following the TDD process and not when adding the tests after the feature implementation. Let's focus on them:

1. We get to think of error and edge cases. At the start of each cycle, we define the next part of the behavior that we need to test. We test error and edge cases when we are done with the happy path. This improves the system's effectiveness.
2. We save on annoying debugging effort. Writing tests after the implementation means that we have probably already spent considerable time working with the debugger and debug logs. TDD reduces and almost eliminates this effort.
3. Promotes a culture of technical quality. This is an important side-effect that is often ignored. Who wouldn't like to work in an organization where they can learn and practice top engineering practices?

Criticism

* * *

Regardless of how many pioneers advocate heavily in favor of it, TDD has yet to enjoy massive industry adoption. Evolutionary biology may be able to explain this.

I believe the number-one reason is that it's counterintuitive to human nature. There isn't a thing in the physical world that we can test before creating. We are wired to build something and then test if it works. Reversing this process causes us discomfort until we get used to it.

Furthermore, human behavior is described well by the Principle of Least Effort. The principle asserts that if there are several ways of solving a problem, people will eventually gravitate to the least demanding course of action. The effort stops as soon as minimally acceptable results are achieved. Also, this theory takes into account the person's previous problem-solving experience. The person will use the tools that they are most familiar with.

TDD is new and is also perceived to increase the overall effort to get something done. In reality, we have to figure out how to implement and test the feature in both styles. The issue with TDD is that it mandates us to maintain its lifecycle in our working memory consistently. This adds to the complexity we are already facing to implement the feature. It ends up feeling overwhelming, making us give up. It does get better in time, but it requires practice.

Many developers make the mistake of trying it out initially in a production project. I wouldn't recommend trying it in production if you have no prior experience. You will get overwhelmed by the app's complexity combined with the pressure of the deadlines and the TDD counter-intuitiveness. You will hate TDD without giving it a real chance.

First, I recommend mastering the testing tools of the platform you are using. Start with unit tests and become an expert in writing them. After you feel comfortable unit-testing anything, start practicing small TDD cycles in pet projects. Take all the time you need to apply it correctly. Then, you can begin to include Acceptance tests (which are hard to write on mobile platforms). Only after you master the above should you take on the challenge of using this process in your day-to-day professional work.

* * *

Of course, there are exceptions to the above. Certain companies have embraced this practice, and seniors there will help you immensely. But this is the exception rather than the rule.

Summary

Tests are a great tool to improve our effectiveness and the resilience of the app. When we feel like we are wasting our time writing them, we have to think about the bigger picture. The more complex the app is (including the size of the team), the more necessary they are.

We should avoid altering the production code for testing purposes. The codebase should be testable by design.

TDD is a development process that includes writing the automated test before the code they are supposed to test. It's counterintuitive and hard to get a good grasp of it, so avoid rejecting it prematurely. Start by mastering the testing mechanisms before you try it out. Pay the effort to master it, and it will pay you back with interest.

PART III

What - Clean Mobile Architecture

We have established the *why* we want to write high-quality software. We are also aware of *how* to write high-quality software. Let's now put everything together to build concrete mobile architectures that can set our mobile apps for success!

First, let's understand what software architecture is and what software architects do. We used to believe that being a software architect is the next career step for a developer. While it can be the case depending on how our organization is structured, nowadays, many advocate that those two responsibilities should belong to the same people. In other words, all engineers should design the system's architecture collectively. I am also supportive of the collective approach. However, it can prove beneficial to have a senior technical person who can make the tough calls when the team cannot conclude.

The critical part is that the software architect(s) do not cease to engage in developing tasks. They cannot do their jobs properly if they don't experience the problems they create for the rest of the team. The feedback loop has to close as fast as possible so the architectural issues get addressed quickly. Inspect and adapt.

The architecture of a system is the shape given to that system by those who build it. That shape comes from many conscious decisions that aim to facilitate the development of future requirements. Those decisions include:

i. The system's components & modules.
ii. The boundaries that separate them.
iii. How the above communicate.

> The architecture's purpose is to facilitate the development, deployment, operation, and maintenance of the software system contained within it. —Robert C. Martin

The Approach

The book's third and final part will define concrete ways to structure mobile apps. This will be driven by the objectives and principles that we learned in the previous parts. On a high level, we will follow the path described below:

1. We will start by comparing several battle-tested software

architectures.
2. Then, we will deep dive into Uncle Bob's Clean Architecture and see how it can help us structure our system.
3. Then, we will analyze several architectures that have become particularly popular in the mobile development industry—the MV family.
4. The main objective is to learn: how to make pragmatic and practical architectural decisions based on everything we learned in the context of a mobile app. We will explain the reasoning behind every critical decision. I have also prepared two repos that you can study.
    - The first contains a clean "textbook" approach. It's what I like to call *Mobile Microservices Architecture.* It's literally a microservices approach for mobile applications. It's helpful primarily for large-scale enterprise apps developed by several independent teams.
    - The other one is a more lightweight and pragmatic approach that can be used for most production applications. You may also decide to mix and match decisions from both approaches.
5. Finally, we will sum up the book with the Golden Circle of Software Development.

While writing this book, I doubted how to describe best the two mobile architectures that I am suggesting. Generally, when we learn new architectures, we face two significant challenges:
1. The first is when we blindly fork an architecture without spending the time and effort to understand it deeply. This, first of all, does not grow our engineering skills. Secondly, when we don't fully understand the reasoning behind the approach, we also can't recognize when we violate it. Soon our codebase will diverge from it, and we won't even notice. I have seen several "Clean Architecture" implementations that don't respect its basic principles. Furthermore, we may not be in a position to foresee any obstacles or deadends that the architecture has. Thus we only figure out much later that it is a bad fit for our needs. Then we often cut corners and apply workarounds to our issues.
2. The second point of failure is when we have spent the time

> and effort to understand an architectural pattern fully. But we don't have a practical example to guide us. The difference between theory and practice is called experience. Without experience, it may be tough to implement a correct solution based on the theory. Particularly when facing pressure to deliver results. Even though we understand that we are doing something wrong, we don't have the time and expertise to implement a clean approach. Having an example repo can help us quickly find a solution or simply validate that what we did, is indeed correct.

Therefore, in this book, I want to provide you with the theoretical background as well as practical implementations. I was skeptical on what's the most effective approach:

The first approach would be centered around the two specific architectures. I would devote a chapter to each architecture and explain the code and its reasoning. The second approach is centered around the challenges & solutions. We discuss the architectural challenges we face while architecting apps. Then, we lay down the possible solutions explaining their pros and cons. Finally, explaining the approach that I took in the two practical examples.

After careful consideration, I decided to follow the second approach for this book. The repos are public, and you are free to study them as much as you wish. An architect should be able to:

1. Think in an abstract way.
2. Acquire a deep understanding of the problems.
3. Be able to recognize them in different contexts.
4. Choose an adequate solution.

Therefore, I believe that it's more beneficial to focus on the challenges, the solutions, and their trade-offs rather than the specific implementations.

Again everything that we will discuss is platform-agnostic. They are applicable in Android, iOS, Flutter, and most of them even in web and backend apps. Thus, try not to pay too much attention to language details but rather understand the decisions and reasoning behind them. That's what this book is all about.

* * *

Enjoy the final part of it!

CHAPTER FOURTEEN

One Destination, Many Roads

This chapter will briefly discuss two software architectures that stand out. As you will notice, they are more similar than different. They aim to achieve the same fundamental objectives and comply with the principles described in the previous part. There is one last objective that most architectures try to gain. That is *framework independence*. As we will see, framework independence can increase the app's resilience and longevity.

Framework independence

* * *

One crucial objective that the software architectures are trying to achieve is to create systems independent of the framework used in building the app. The motivation behind this is the frameworks' instability. They often release major, backward-incompatible versions that break our apps.

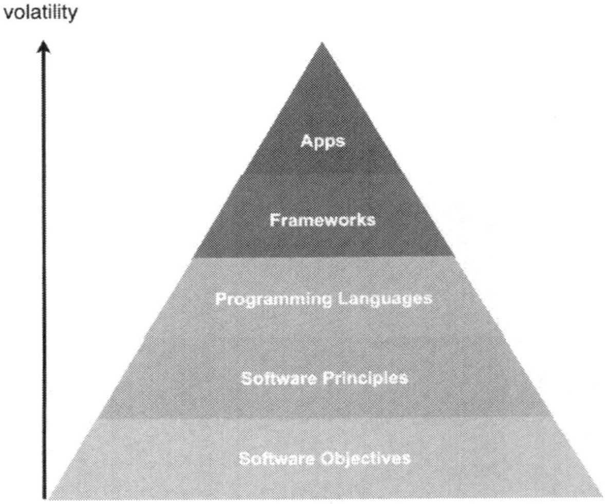

Software volatility.

This pyramid depicts software volatility. At the bottom, the most stable components are the Fundamental Software Objectives. We need the software to be readable, testable, extensible, maintainable, robust, and resilient, regardless of what kind of software it is. Those objectives are unlikely ever to change. We can also include the technical objectives such as separation of concerns, high cohesion, and low coupling in the same layer.

Above them, we have the Software Principles that help us hit those objectives. Those principles include Inversion of Control, Single Concern, and S.O.L.I.D. They are well established and not prone to change. It's a breakthrough when a brand new idea there gets widely accepted.

Just above sit the programming languages. New programming languages often come up, but those that stand out tend to stick for a long time. Take Java, for example; it came to the world in 1996[1], many "prophets" in the last 15 years have foretold that Java will die. As of today, it still is one of the most used languages. Most languages that managed to reach this magnitude have stuck around for a long. Still, languages do come and go over a decade.

Above that, we have the framework level—Android, iOS, Flutter, Spring boot, .NET, etc. Frameworks come and go often, and they also change dramatically every year. A popular framework typically includes several releases over a year, with one at least being major.

For us, who have been developing mobile since the early 2010s, we recall what the early Android and iOS platforms looked like. The initial development platforms were utterly different, immature, and far less efficient than now. The most volatile part of this layer includes the third-party libraries. We all use them to perform animations, networking, logging, etc. Things there are changing rapidly. And I don't even want to bring up the subject of JS frameworks (cough).

Finally, at the top, the most unstable layer includes our own applications. They are the least stable, as they are supposed to be. After all, we write software—soft products. They change in every release, which hopefully has a span equal to or shorter than two weeks. And they are supposed to change significantly to keep up with the evolving competition.

The point is that you want to base your app on stable ground. Objectives and Principles are pretty stable; they are not expected to change in the lifetime of your app. Programming languages do change; many of us faced the transitions from Objective-C to Swift and Java to Kotlin. But still, they are considered stable and interoperable with their successors. In any case, there isn't much you can do to achieve language independence.

Frameworks, on the other hand, are not that stable. The vast majority of our codebase should be framework-agnostic. A change in the iOS framework should not affect a big part of our codebase. When Apple, for example, decides to introduce new ways of performing navigation, like storyboards. It should not affect our business logic, presentation logic, or anything that has to do with the problem we are trying to solve. Equally, we must isolate third-party libraries. The majority of our app should be agnostic.

Framework-dependent code must be isolated from business logic and the rest of the app. Frameworks are also "soft" and cannot be used as a solid foundation.

There are several examples where third-party libraries caused severe harm to products. Like the Log4j library that was found to introduce critical security vulnerabilities to backend systems[2]. Another popular case[3] in the Javascript ecosystem was caused by Marak Squires, the engineer behind colors.js and faker.js. He intentionally sabotaged them, forcing them essentially to stop working. He was motivated by frustration over the level of support corporations provide to the open-source community. Whether you agree with him or not, if you used those libraries in your app, you would end up frustrated.

Uncle Bob calls this "asymmetric marriage." You must make a massive commitment to the framework, but the framework author does not commit to you. The author is free to change or even delete their framework altogether.

I am not advocating against using third-party libraries but try to isolate their usage in a particular layer. Don't let them tie up to a big part of your codebase. Contain cancer and be flexible to replace them at any point.

There is one more (potential) benefit that we can exploit when writing framework-independent software. The business code can potentially be ported to different frameworks. As we will see later, most of our application layers will be apart from pure Kotlin, Swift, or Dart code. Consequently, they can be ported to another system built on a different framework using the same programming language. This might not occur too often, but when it does, it works wonders.

It can take the form of code sharing between systems. For example, Kotlin data entities can be shared between the Android app and the backend system. Or it can take the form of transferring the same codebase to a different framework. For example, transporting java code from a deprecated EJB framework to a modern Spring boot application. That's something that we actually did in the Telecom company I worked for in the case study described in Part I.

We can take platform code-sharing to the next level by leveraging cross-platform frameworks like Kotlin Multiplatform (KMM)[27]. For this to function, though, most of the codebase has to be platform-agnostic. Any platform-specific parts will have to be duplicated.

Are frameworks that evil?

Are frameworks that dangerous for our system? As with everything, frameworks have a good side and a bad side. We, as engineers, should maximize the benefits that they have to offer while minimizing the negative consequences.

Frameworks and third-party libraries are remarkable for executing all the trivial, boilerplate tasks. Good examples of using frameworks:

- Performing HTTP requests.
- JSON serialization and deserialization.
- Drawing or animating UI elements on the screen.
- Handling security concerns, oAuth2, TSL, certificate pinning, etc.

Although trivial for the industry, those tasks are solved elsewhere; they are not trivial for anyone who hasn't encountered them before. Creating a custom solution takes time and effort, and there is no point in re-inventing the wheel. We should be using frameworks and third-party solutions here. Furthermore, all of those concerns do not sit at the center of our app. Our business logic has nothing to do with how JSON responses are deserialized. It's easy to move all those concerns to the sides of our architecture and make our business logic agnostic.

* * *

[27] Kotlin Multiplatform is a language feature that allows you to run Kotlin in iOS, Javascript, and native desktop applications, to name a few. And best of all, it's possible to share code between all these targets, reducing the time required for the development.

There are different types of frameworks, though; let's take Angular[28] [4] as an example. Those frameworks mandate that we develop our app using their architectural design. We call those opinionated frameworks. They don't just take care of boilerplate code but pretty much force us to build our app in a certain way. This has its pros and cons. Let's start with the pros:

i. It helps developers who don't have much experience architecting apps. An out-of-the-box architecture is probably better than an architecture conceived by an inexperienced developer.
ii. Gives a head start. You don't need to do too much architectural thinking; you can start writing code faster. This assumes that you have used the framework in the past.
iii. Consistency. The applications written with such frameworks will be similar. Therefore, it is easier to onboard new joiners.

On the other hand, there are cons to using architecture-opinionated frameworks too:

i. Lowers the bar. As the architecture is supposed to fit in any application, it is not taking into account our particular context and needs. An experienced engineer can consider the specific context and business requirements and develop an architecture tailored for the case. This architecture has a higher potential to enable the effective development of the app.
ii. Heavy maintenance cost in the long run. As we described earlier, frameworks are not stable pillars. In major releases, their APIs are often backward incompatible. Angular developers, for example, have felt the pain of migrating their apps to the latest Angular releases. This effort piles up over time.
iii. Vendor locking. If the framework code is spread all over our app, we are tightly coupled with it and cannot escape. Five years from now, we may want to migrate to a newer framework that offers some neat features. Or, in some cases,

[28] Angular is a TypeScript-based free and open-source web application framework led by the Angular Team at Google and by a community of individuals and corporations.
It is widely used to develop front-end applications.

the framework can prove to be inefficient or disastrous in our context, like the famous Twitter - Ruby on Rails case[295]. Generally, the more time we intend to keep our application alive, the more likely we will regret getting vendor-locked.

iv. Initial learning curve to learn the framework. Clean Architecture can be understood once and used everywhere. On the other hand, learning an opinionated framework is only helpful in the context of a particular platform.

So, to conclude:

I. We should use frameworks & third-party libraries to handle trivial tasks and reduce boilerplate code.

II. We can also use architecturally-opinionated frameworks to get a head start in developing simple applications. Particularly if we are not yet experienced in architecting systems.

III. I would avoid using opinionated frameworks in complex enterprise apps that are supposed to live long, healthy lives.

IV. We should isolate third-party libraries in our architecture's lowest/outermost layers. Contain cancer.

Let's now take a look at how popular architectures help us deal with those issues.

Hexagonal Architecture

* * *

[29] Twitter saw a rabid usage growth in 2008, which could not be supported by the Ruby-based app they had back then. This caused headaches to Twitter's engineering time as lagging and loading times increased dramatically.

From Spring 2007 to 2008, the messages were handled by a Ruby persistent queue server called Starling. Since 2009, implementation has been gradually replaced with software written in Scala. The switch from Ruby to Scala and the JVM has given Twitter a performance boost from 200–300 requests per second per host to around 10,000–20,000 requests per second per host.

As of April 6, 2011, Twitter engineers confirmed that they had switched away from their Ruby on Rails search stack to a Java server they call Blender.

Hexagonal Architecture was inspired by Dr. Alistair Cockburn[30]. It is also known as "Ports and Adapters Architecture." The intent, as he describes in his blog[6] is to "Allow an application to equally be driven by users, programs, automated test or batch scripts. And to be developed and tested in isolation from its eventual run-time devices and databases." The primary motivation is similar to the other architectures. It strives to separate business logic from UI and data concerns.

This architecture hasn't found much adoption in the mobile development industry; it's most popular in the backend ecosystem. But I still think it's worth studying it, as it will give us a 360 view of how great artisans approach the same puzzle. If you're looking to fast-track into the mobile stuff, feel free to jump to the next chapter.

The architecture refers to the business logic as the "inside" part of the app; the UI and data layers are the "outside" parts of the app. The rule to obey is that code pertaining to the ''inside'' part should not leak into the ''outside'' part. This is a concept that we will be seeing in the following architectures as well. They place the application business logic, the problem we solve, in the center. Everything else is a technicality.

The motivation behind "formalizing" this architecture was the need for a concrete, well-defined structure that would isolate the business logic from the rest of the system. As Alistair describes in his post, this is something that "almost" all architectures are trying to achieve. But what was lacking was a mechanism that could detect when we have violated this principle. Without such a mechanism, the systems will break this principle in time.

In fact, I have noticed that myself in several different companies and systems. As people come and go, it's not always clear what was the architect's initial intention for every module and layer. This can happen because the system was initially architected poorly. Or because

---

[30] Dr. Alistair Cockburn is an internationally known IT strategist, and project witchdoctor voted one of the "The All-Time Top 150 i-Technology Heroes." He is best known for agile methods and writing effective use cases; his latest work is the Heart of Agile.

the new team failed to understand it properly. Furthermore, new requirements may require significant system refactoring. The new team may fail to realize it. This can result in cluttering the existing layers with all kinds of concerns. Or newly introduced layers that fail to properly separate the concerns and adhere to the Single Concern Principle.

Furthermore, Alistair Cockburn realized that there wasn't much difference between how the UI and the database interact with an application. Essentially, they are both external actors. They are interchangeable with similar components that would, in equivalent ways, interact with the app. By seeing things this way, one could focus on keeping the application agnostic of these "external" actors. Essentially allowing them to interact via Ports and Adapters, thus avoiding entanglement and logic leakage between business logic and external components.

So pretty much the whole purpose of the architecture is to separate the business logic from the rest of the code. The main idea can be described by the diagram below:

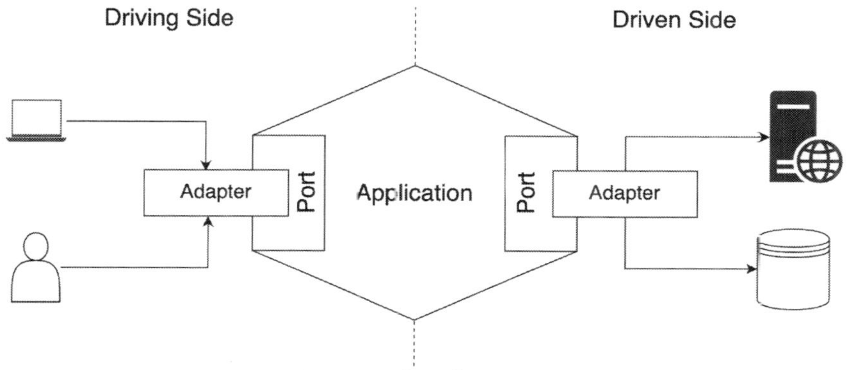

Hexagonal Architecture.

First of all, the diagram is split into two sides, the driving and the driven. The driving side is close to the actors who initiate the flow of control. For a mobile app, it's usually a user or another application calling ours. For a backend system, it can be a mobile, web, or another backend client. The driven side is the last one to receive the flow of control. As we saw previously, the data layer sits outside of our main application business logic, but the application depends on the data.

The *Application* represents the system's business logic. It contains the domain entities as well as the use cases. Please note that the whole application, meaning the one that we will upload to the App Store, contains all the Application, Ports, and Adapters components. The "Application" in the diagram refers to the "application layer."

The *Ports* are interfaces/protocols. Via them, we allow anything outside the Application to interact with it. To correlate with the previous Inversion of Control example, the ports here are the data source interfaces tailored to the use case needs. We are using Dependency Inversion in the Hexagonal Architecture as well. The open port on the driven side is an example of Dependency Inversion. It doesn't have any knowledge of who is going to implement it. Thus, the outer side depends on the inner.

Another thing to note is that there is no restriction on how many ports each side will contain. In the example above, we have one for the driving side and one for the driven. But we usually include several per side. The architecture itself does not provide any restrictions; the API can be segregated into one port per use case or one port per side. It's a design decision.

Hint: Use the Interface Segregation Principle wisely to define the number of ports.

Next to the ports, we have the *Adapters*. An adapter can "plug into" a port and initiate the interaction with the Application. Technically, this means that an adapter is implementing a specific port interface and consequently can interact with the Application by sending or receiving information. For a backend application, a driving adapter would typically be a Rest Controller that can "plug" into a Service via a specific interface. For a mobile application, the driving adapters bridge the UI with the Application. Usually, it would be a View Model or Presenter. Again, many adapters are allowed to plug into a single port. The system can select the appropriate adapter to handle the case at runtime. (Cough) Open-Closed Principle.

* * *

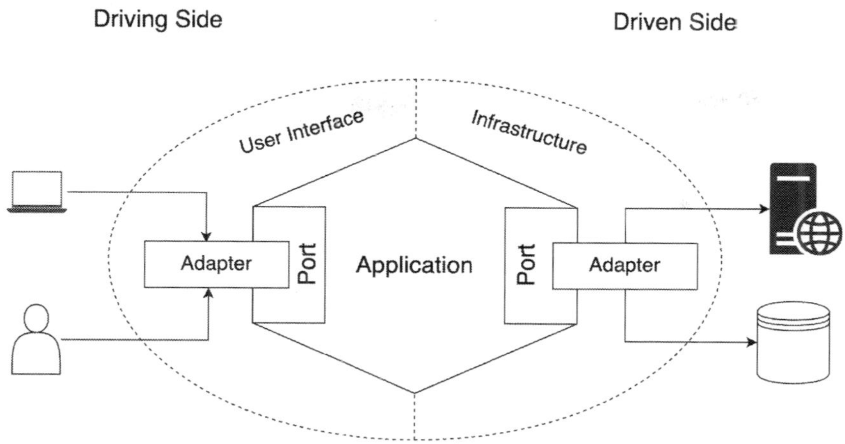

Hexagonal Architecture.

We can see that the UI is sitting on the driving side. On the driven side, we have the Infrastructure layer, which includes a database and our HTTP services. Understanding the flow of control vs. the "flow" of dependency is essential. And how we invert the dependencies on the driven side to protect our application layer.

The flow of control points inwards from the driving side, and so does the dependency flow. The UI uses an adapter; then, a use case implements the port. We don't have any objections to this as the port lives inside the Application and is an interface. So both layers depend on an interface, and the dependency arrows point inwards/upwards to the Application.

On the Driven side, though, we have the same problem we faced earlier. As the control flow points outwards towards the infrastructure, we need to invert the dependency. How do we do that? We force the adapter to implement the port and the use case to depend on the port. Precisely, as we demonstrated in the Dependency Inversion and Inversion of Control chapters.

* * *

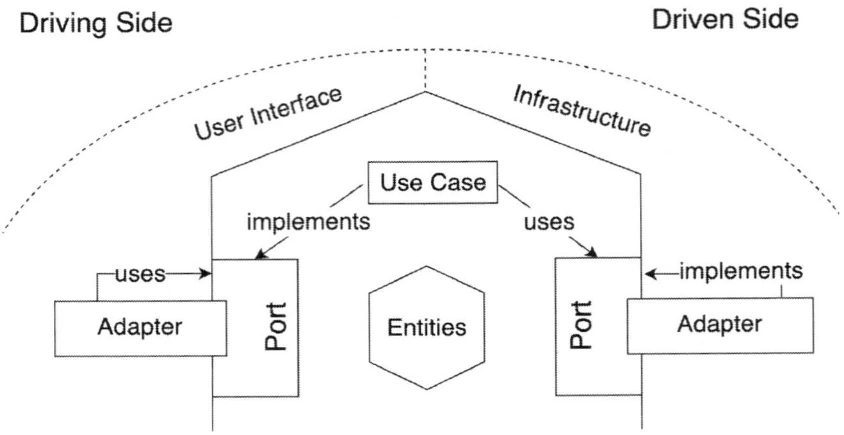

Dependency Inversion on Hexagonal Architecture.

Hexagonal Architecture Benefits

Using Hexagonal Architecture, we isolate business logic from the rest of the system. Therefore we fortify it from changes in the UI or the infrastructure layers. This also helps us design our interfaces by purpose rather than by technology. The third-party libraries and frameworks for the UI or database are irrelevant to the core logic. If the backend API changes or we decide to introduce a database, it will not affect our core app. Same if the UI designer chooses to recolor the UI.

By isolating the business logic, we also improve its testability. It allows us to mock all the external dependencies quickly. Thus, enabling us to test the business logic with unit tests instead of instrumentation tests.

You will notice that all the well-designed architectures provide the above advantages. So how does Hexagonal Architecture differs? The Hexagonal Architecture is focused solely on business logic. By defining the ports and adapters, we make it crystal clear when we break this separation of concerns. It is harder to violate than the other architectures and more apparent to identify the violations. This is a solid advantage when writing backend systems. The backend apps are almost exclusively focused on business logic.

* * *

On the other hand, a mobile application focuses more on UI/UX and state management. It includes more types of logic, like presentation logic. The Hexagonal Architecture is not particularly addressing those needs. Therefore, I believe it is better fitting for backend systems rather than mobile or front-end apps. Still, understanding its reasoning will help us understand Clean Architecture better and provide us with a 360 view of the topic.

The Onion Architecture

The Onion architecture was described by Jeffrey Palermo in 2008 in his blog post series[7]. By the time he wrote the blog post, it was not a new concept, but his motivation was to define it as a named architectural pattern. Patterns are helpful because they give software professionals a common vocabulary to communicate. As he suggests, this architecture is inappropriate for small "websites." It is suitable for long-lived corporate applications and applications with complex behavior. It emphasizes the use of interfaces for behavior contracts and forces the externalization of infrastructure.

He intended to break the traditional layering that he encountered in most systems:

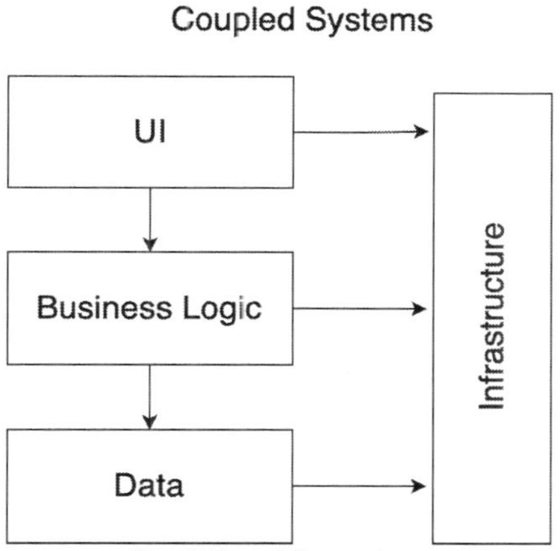

Traditional Layering.

This diagram represents the case that we saw earlier, where the flow of dependencies matches the flow of control. The UI is coupled to the business logic, the business logic to the data, and often all the layers also depend on shared infrastructure code.

This architecture creates unnecessary coupling. As you know by now, the worst kind of coupling has the business logic depending on the data and other framework code.

Onion architecture separates the code into several layers resembling onion scales.

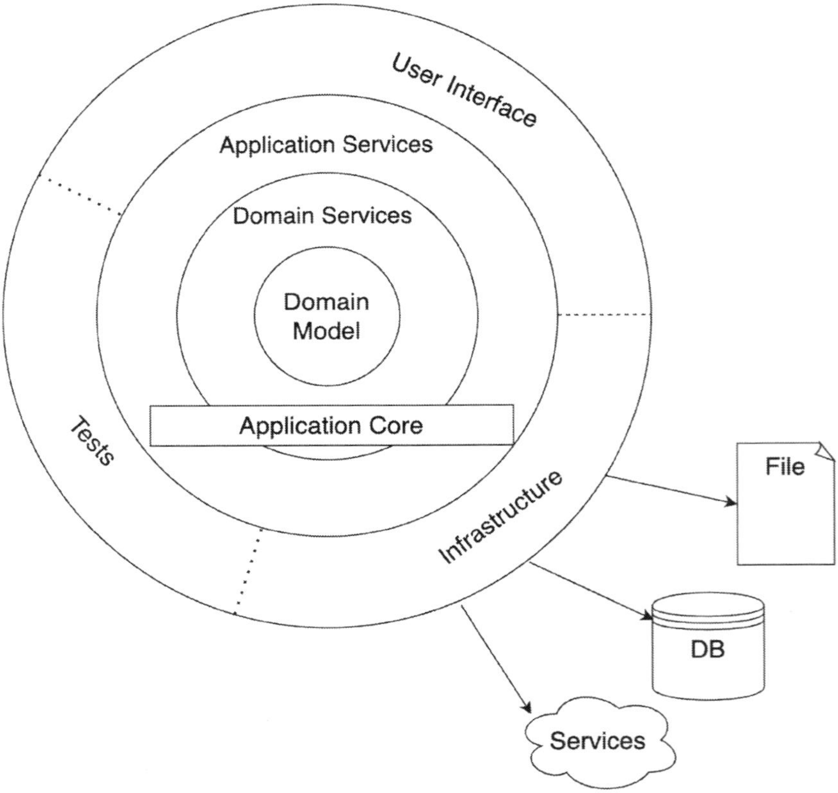

Onion Architecture.

In the diagram, we can see the Onion Architecture's layering. The number of layers inside the application core can vary depending on our specific needs. The central premise is that it controls coupling. The fundamental rule is that all code can depend on layers more central, but code cannot depend on layers further out from the core. Therefore the Onion Architecture relies heavily on the DIP. We revert the dependencies wherever the flow of control points from an inner layer to an outer layer.

I will not take deep dive into the Onion Architecture further. Honestly, it is identical to the Clean Architecture except for layer naming. I decided to include Onion Architecture in the book for historical reasons. Jeffrey Palermo came up with it in 2008 to name and define ideas that pre-existed, as he described. After Uncle Bob's Clean Architecture blog post in 2013, it seems like the Onion Architecture name got overridden entirely, even though the two sets of principles are almost identical. Therefore I believe mentioning Onion Architecture as a predecessor and giving it some credit is worth a few pages.

Summary

Diachronically, software architectures are trying to tackle the same issues. The most important ones are:

i. To separate the app's concerns and achieve high cohesion and low coupling.
ii. To build framework-independent systems.

Opinionated frameworks can boost productivity early on, particularly for simple apps. On the other hand, they couple themselves with the entire codebase, which can prove problematic in the long run. Particularly for complex, large-scale apps.

Hexagonal architecture isolates the business logic from the rest of the code. Its advantage over the others is that it's architecturally more robust. It helps us identify violations better than the others.

The Onion Architecture is identical to Clean Architecture.

CHAPTER FIFTEEN

Clean Architecture - The theory

This chapter will present the theory of Clean Architecture (CA), as formed by Robert C Martin. It was initially introduced in 2012 in his blog post[1] and later in his book - *Clean Architecture.* I will also provide criticism and feedback obtained by applying it to production projects of varying complexity. By the end of this chapter, you will clearly understand how CA can help us in mobile development.

The Clean Architecture

The intent behind CA is to protect high-level business code from low-level implementation details.

Below is the world-famous diagram that you have probably come across in several blog posts on the web.

* * *

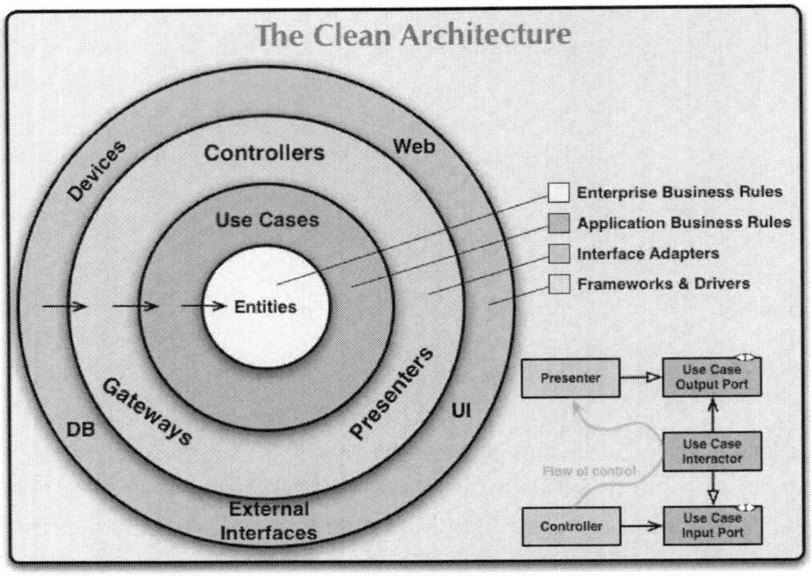

There are three main concepts to understand. You are ready to structure your app by CA if you get those right:

1. Code separation in layers of different levels.
2. The Dependency Rule.
3. Dependency Inversion.

Let's break them down…

Separation in Layers

We can see in the diagram that the original version of the CA contains four distinct layers. Let's go ahead and study them one by one.

In the center, we have the *Entities* layer. The entities encapsulate the enterprise-wide business rules. They usually are classes that contain data—variables and values and the core business functions. They encapsulate the most general and high-level rules. They are supposed to be reusable throughout different applications of the same organization. For example, both the Android app and backend system should be able to share the following entity:

* * *

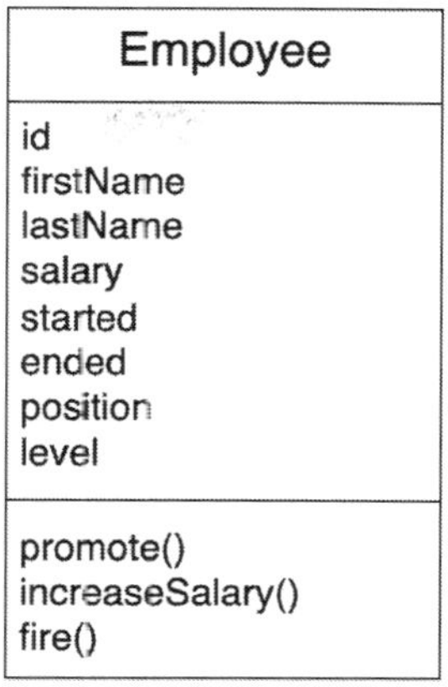

The entities are the most valuable and well-protected classes. We don't expect them to be affected by changes in the UI, database, or other layers. They change only when the business changes.

The second layer from the center contains the *Use Cases*. The software in this layer includes the application-specific logic and rules. The use cases orchestrate the flow of data to and from the entities. It directs them to use their enterprise-wide business rules to achieve the goals of the use case. For example, we could be developing a screen with a button that is firing an entire team. Cough, ok, let's change this to a button that increases the salary of the whole team!

The flow of control will start from the UI, where the director will push the button to approve the raise and go up to our IncreaseTeamSalary Use Case. Then the Use Case will call the *increaseSalary* function for each Employee entity of this particular team. Once all the operations are carried out, the Use Case will instruct the data layer to save the data, of course, using Dependency Inversion.

* * *

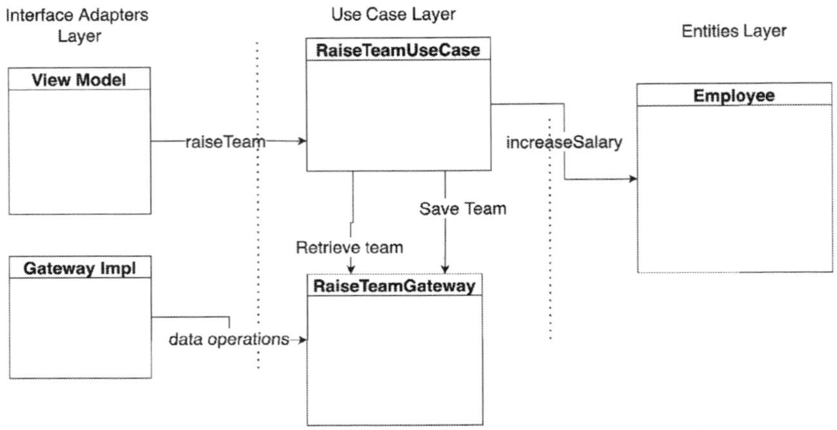

The flow of control between Interface Adapters, Use Cases, and Entities.

As you can see, the View Model and the implementation of our data source, whether it's an HTTP service or a DB-access object, both belong to the interface adapters layer. Via Dependency Inversion, the Data Gateway depends on the use case layer to which it provides data access. And the use case layer orchestrates the application logic. It depends on the entities and uses them for business-related operations.

Jumping to the *Interface Adapters* layer, it contains all the code that glues the UI, DB, and backend with our Use Cases. The "gateways" seen on the diagram refer to the actual implementations of the data source interfaces. They are classes that orchestrate the communication with our backend server. They can also be the data-access objects that direct the operations to our local database. This layer also contains the "driving adapters," aka the View Models and Presenters. Those facilitate the communication between the UI and the Use Cases.

It's a glue layer, and it's essential to be platform-agnostic. The classes in this layer aren't aware of whether they belong to a mobile, web, or backend application. They are not Activities, Fragments, Android background services, View Controllers, etc. They can be tested with unit tests. This is important as unit tests are easier to write and faster to run.

This layer is also responsible for transforming the data from the outer layers to a convenient format for the inner layers. For example, we may receive a lot of unnecessary fields in a backend response. This layer will map the response object to an object that is convenient to the Use Case. The same applies to a local database query that returns unused info.

Finally, the outermost layer is the *Frameworks & Drivers*. This contains all the mobile framework code. The Android or iOS-specific classes like Activities, Fragments, View Controllers, or Flutter's Widgets. This code is tightly coupled with the platform that is running our application. It usually includes the UI, the actual database, code responsible for low-level communication with external devices, access to the file system, etc. Third-party libraries are also isolated here.

This layer is hard to test. It requires an emulator for a mobile app or a server instance for a backend system. Those tests are harder to write; there are a lot of factors that must be taken into account. Like:

i. The device details: hardware, OS version, screen size, etc.
ii. Asynchronous tasks and concurrency. We have to pause the assertions until an HTTP request or a DB query completes.
iii. Current state of the database. Our assertions may fail when the initial DB state is different from what we assume.
iv. The external systems must be up and running.

They are also slower to run since instantiating an emulator and bringing it to the required state takes time. Therefore, the Frameworks & Drivers layer code must be dumb, meaning it must not contain any logic at all. Any conditionals that make decisions based on the data are forbidden in this layer. For example:

```
if (employee.annualSalary > 100.000)
  text.color = Colors.Green
```

This is forbidden inside an Activity, Fragment, View Controller, or Widget. A screen must only know how to draw the ready-to-consume information that it receives.

When I explain Clean Architecture, a question that often comes up is: "Are we allowed only to have four layers?". The answer is no. You are allowed to include as many layers as you need. But you must:

1. Navigate from more generic and business-related code to more

concrete and framework-specific code.

2. Respect the Dependency Rule.

The Dependency Rule

The Dependency Rule suggests that source code dependencies can only point inwards. Inner circles must not be aware of the existence of outer layers. In other words, an inner layer class should not reference any class that lives in an outer layer. It must also not call static functions or use static variables that belong in an outer layer. Inner circles must be completely agnostic of who is using them. This enables us to either modify or completely replace the outer rings easily. We can, for example, migrate to another database or redesign the UI without affecting the core app.

There are two popular ways to interpret the Clean Architecture diagram; as a sphere (the one we saw earlier), or a pyramid:

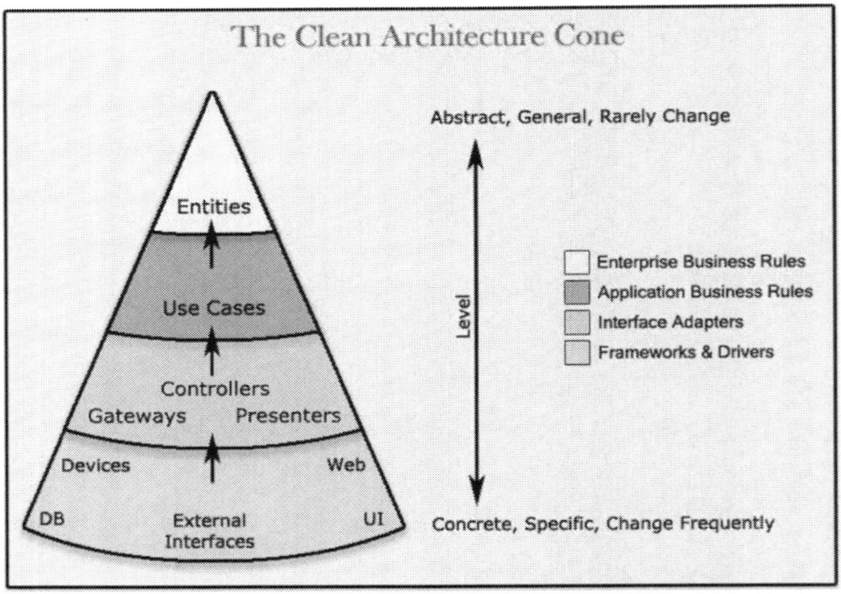

Turning the diagram by 90 degrees, we can identify the level of each layer. The main takeaway from this diagram is that CA allows lower layers to depend on higher layers but not the other way around. Furthermore, the top layers are more abstract and focused on the business. At the same time, the bottom layers are more concrete and will reference particular tools, third-party libraries, framework APIs, and implementation details. At the top of our castle, we place the code that we want to fortify from invasions of Product Owners, designers, and third-party vendors!

It's not that the entities don't ever change. The thing is that they change less often and for more important reasons. They change when the business changes. The UI is very volatile and changes for less critical reasons. We all have been asked mid-sprint to modify the size of a UI element "because it takes no time." We don't want those low-importance changes to affect more critical parts of our business and cause a high-priority bug in the next release.

Finally, the third ingredient and enabler of Clean Architecture is Dependency Inversion. Without DI, we wouldn't practically be able to apply the Dependency Rule as the use cases would depend on the interface adapters.

What data crosses the boundaries?

We explained the Dependency Rule, but we haven't explained what actual data can pass through our layer's walls. Typically the data that crosses the boundaries are simple data structures, preferably immutable. It can be Kotlin data classes or Swift structs. The important thing is that isolated, simple data structures are passed across the boundaries.

Specific frameworks, third-party libraries, and databases use their own data structures that extend from a superclass. For example, Room is using the @Entity annotation. We don't want to propagate this class all the way up to our use case layer. If we do, we make our application logic aware of such external dependencies, reducing our ability to replace them in the future.

Generally, the interface adapters layer is responsible for transforming/

mapping third-party data structures to pure data structures used by our application and business logic. It acts as a firewall to block the frameworks' intruders from reaching our headquarters.

As a rule of thumb, when we pass data across a boundary, it is always in the form most convenient to the inner circle.

Benefits

Separation of Concerns. We isolate the business logic and practically every high-level concern using a layered approach. Each concern pertains to its own cohesive layer.

Testable application. By isolating the framework code to the outer-most layer, we make the rest of the application easy to test. As we described earlier, pure Kotlin/Swift classes can be tested by unit tests.

Robust application. With the layered approach, we protect the inner layers from changes in the outer layers. Outer layers are more volatile and change for less critical reasons. Thus we implement a more robust core application that is harder to break in each release.

Readable application. By separating the code into well-defined layers, we make our application easy to read. New joiners will have certain expectations of a Use Case class; they will more or less know what they will find inside. Note that there is a catch here. First of all, the newcomers must be familiar with Clean Architecture. Secondly, the implementation must be "Clean." I often find poor implementations of CA that violate its principles. This actively hurts the app's readability as the expectations are not met.

Open for extension, closed for modification. The OCP applies not only for classes but for whole layers as well. Using Dependency Inversion between the layers, we have them both depending on abstractions rather than concretions. This enables us to swap the concrete implementations without affecting the rest of the layers. Most importantly, we can easily swap framework-dependent code like databases or third-party libraries.

* * *

Criticism

Okay, we praised CA a lot but are there any downsides? Or maybe occasions where we should avoid using it?

I personally don't believe in silver bullets. Some solutions solve specific problems while introducing problems that didn't exist before. There isn't a single architecture, methodology, framework, or library that doesn't introduce its unique downsides to the equation. It falls on us to identify whether, in our context, it solves more problems than it creates. Let's examine Clean Architecture's downsides:

Learning Curve

There is a steep learning curve to deeply understand CA and its ingredients: separation of concerns, dependency rule, code layering, and dependency inversion. Junior devs with no prior exposure may struggle to get onboarded.

Complexity & Verbosity

CA can unnecessarily increase our projects' complexity, verbosity, and file count. Drawing boundaries and inverting dependencies carry an overhead. This overhead is well-worth in complex projects but sometimes unnecessary for simpler ones.

Additionally, specific layers can end up carrying zero responsibilities. For example, certain features may not require any application logic at all, but to be consistent with Clean Architecture, we implement a Use Case class. This Use Case will simply act as a middle-man between a View Model and a data service without really carrying out any concern. Let's take a look at an example:

```
class GetArticles(private val articlesGateway: ArticlesGateway) {

    fun getArticles(): List<Article> = articlesGateway.getArticles()
}
```

The Use Case above does not carry out any concern. It simply wires up a single

View Model to a single Gateway.

```
class GetArticles(private val articlesGateway: ArticlesGateway) {

    fun getArticles(authorId: String): List<Article> =
        articlesGateway.getArticles().map { article ->
            article.copy(
                editable = article.authorId == authorId
            )
    }
}
```

This Use Case applies application logic. Thus, it's useful.

```
class GetArticles(
    private val articlesGateway: ArticlesGateway,
    private val authorsGateway: AuthorsGateway
) {

    fun getArticlesAuthors(): List<ArticleAuthor> {
        val articles = articlesGateway.getArticles()
        val authors = authorsGateway.getAuthors()

        return articles.map { article ->
            val author = authors.find { it: Author
                article.authorId == it.id
            }

            ArticleAuthor(
                articleId = article.id,
                articleTitle = article.title,
                articleDesc = article.desc,
                authorName = author?.name
            ) ^map
        }
    }
}
```

This Use Case aggregates information from two gateways and combines them into a single model. It also carries out a concern.

Keep in mind that if a Use Case both applies application logic and aggregates information, it violates the Single Concern Principle. We probably need to break down the layers even further.

In any case, the point of the example is to clarify that if we find ourselves implementing many Use Cases like the first one, we probably should avoid Clean Architecture in this app. It just unnecessarily increases its complexity. The same applies to the rest of the layers; simple apps generally don't benefit much from Clean.

> Don't use a cannon to kill a mosquito. —Confucius

Paying up-front, Over-Engineering

This point is similar to the one above but from another angle. A key advantage of CA is the replaceability of the outer circles, particularly the framework's layer but not exclusively. However, don't think that this comes for free. It increases the complexity and file count as we have to draw interfaces and apply data transformations to cross the boundaries.

Someone here can argue that this is some sort of over-engineering, speculations about the future. We pay the price now to swap outer layers in the future easily. But we may never need to change our database, for example. This point is valid, but there are two things to consider:

First, particularly for the isolation of the framework layer, we do enjoy the benefit of enabling unit tests for the majority of our codebase immediately.

Second, if we don't draw boundaries from the start, we risk having the cancer spread. In this case, we need to make sure that we use practices to contain cancer and leave the doors open for upscaling our architecture to Clean later. Such practices include the Repository pattern, the Facade pattern, and generally implementing a single point that abstracts the exterior details from the core logic.

Generally, in *complex* applications, more often than not, a full or partial application of CA is beneficial. In simple apps, we just need to contain cancer with soft boundaries, so we reserve the option to toughen them when we identify the need to do so. Think in terms of MVA.

Misunderstandings

One of the main benefits of assembling standard practices and patterns under a named principle or architecture is that it serves as a shared vocabulary for engineers. This vocabulary can significantly increase the efficiency of our communication. It also makes us sound weird to non-engineers, but well… It's much easier to explain that our app is built by Clean Architecture rather than list all the patterns included one by one.

What happens, though, when people have misinterpreted CA? And I see this happening a lot in the industry, which is one of my main motivations for writing this book. What happens is.. misunderstanding. People use the same words to describe different things. Devs jump into projects having expectations of classes named Use Cases and Interactors, only to get frustrated when they figure out that they have been used for a different purpose here. Sometimes without even following the Dependency Rule.

Honestly, this is not an issue of CA specifically but rather an issue of all named architectures and principles. I am mentioning it here as I have noticed it happening very often with Clean Architecture in particular.

Mitigating the cons

The next thing that comes to one's mind is how to mitigate the cons. Regarding the learning curve and misunderstandings, we can only improve our technical onboarding. And make sure that the newcomers and we understand CA correctly. I hope that this book can also facilitate this process effectively.

Regarding complexity, verbosity, and paying upfront, they all are very context-specific. A good system analysis will show whether applying Clean Architecture in your context will solve more problems than it will create.

* * *

I will try to help you as much as possible in the following chapters, where we will see all the above in code.

Summary

To sum up, Clean Architecture is the manifestation of three practices:

1. Separate the code into cohesive layers belonging to different levels. Put at the top (center) code that is more abstract and business-specific and at the bottom (out) code that is more concrete and platform-specific.
2. The Dependency Rule. Outer layers are only allowed to depend on/know about the inner layers. An inner layer must be utterly agnostic of the outer layers.
3. Apply Dependency Inversion wherever the flow of control goes against the Dependency Rule.

CA is a great tool and should be in the toolset of every engineer. Whether to apply it and to what degree is context-specific. Generally, the more complex the app is, the more it can benefit.

CHAPTER SIXTEEN

MV(C,P,VM,I)

Introduction

In the short lifespan of the Mobile development industry, we have observed specific architectures prevailing over the years. It all started with "Let's throw all the code in the Activities/View Controllers buckets." Soon, as the apps' complexity increased, this proved unviable.

The first revolution came alongside the adoption of the Model View Controller (MVC) pattern. Or at least an interpretation of it. Model View Presenter (MVP) came shortly after and dominated for a while until more modern reactive patterns like MVVM and MVI took the lead.

We call those the MV architecture family or simply MVs. We use the word architecture, same as Clean Architecture and Hexagonal Architecture. Does this mean that they all belong to the same level and solve the same problems? Are they mutually exclusive, or can we use them in combination?

Those are questions that often stay with us until we reach a certain level of seniority and, to be honest, never get fully answered. By the end of this chapter, you will better understand the MVs. What problems they solve, and how they relate to the previously described architectures.

* * *

MVs Vs. Clean Architecture

First, I would like to compare the MVs with Clean, Onion & Hexagonal Architectures. Clean Architecture and its siblings are higher-level architectures. Their primary purpose is to define high-level rules that guide us in implementing well-structured systems.

Clean Architecture is generic and system agnostic. It is intended to be used in any system, whether a front-end, mobile or backend application. It's flexible as we can define our own layers as long as the basic principles are followed. Therefore, the final software products based on CA will vary greatly. And this assumes that they have been implemented correctly, following the rules properly.

The MVs, on the other hand, are lower-level architectural patterns. They are more pragmatic and hands-on. They are also centered around the separation of concerns but aim to provide more specific ways to structure code.

The key point is that the MVs and CA are not mutually exclusive. We can, for example, apply MVVM combined with CA. I like to consider the MVs as kickstarter for MVAs.. no MV pun intended. Then, when complexity grows, I gradually upscale to a more layered Clean implementation.

The MVs are generally a good and pragmatic starting point.

MVC - The original

Model View Controller (MVC) is one of the most quoted (and most misquoted) patterns around. —Martin Fowler[1]

Before we discuss how MVC got interpreted in the mobile industry, I want to describe the initial intent of Trygve Reenskaug[31]. He coined MVC in the late 1970s. It's important to keep in mind that software engineering back then was not as advanced as it is today. The essential purpose of MVC, as he describes[2] is to bridge the gap between the human user's mental model and the digital model that exists in the computer. He depicts this with the following diagram.

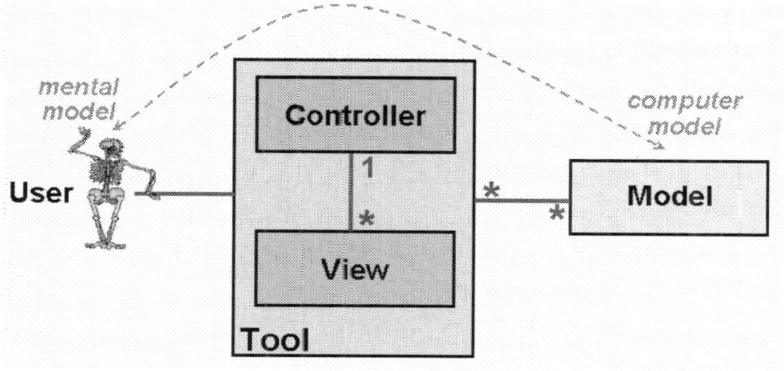

We identify three elements in MVC. I will briefly describe them here; if you wish to deep dive into them, feel free to study the original paper[3].

Models represent knowledge. A model could be a single object, or it could be some structure of objects. The proposed implementation supports knowledge represented in something resembling semantic nets.

Views. A view is a (visual) representation of its model. It would ordinarily highlight certain attributes of the model and suppress others. It is thus acting as a presentation filter.

Controllers. A controller is the link between a user and the system. It provides the user with input by arranging relevant views to present themselves in appropriate places on the screen. The Controller also receives user output, translates it into the right messages, and passes

---

[31] Trygve Mikkjel Heyerdahl Reenskaug (born 21 June 1930) is a Norwegian computer scientist and professor emeritus of the University of Oslo. He formulated the model–view–controller (MVC) pattern for graphical user interface (GUI) software design in 1979 while visiting the Xerox Palo Alto Research Center (PARC).

them on to one or more views.

For the sake of space, I intentionally omitted a lot of details included in the original paper. If we put all the pieces together, the original MVC pattern looks like this:

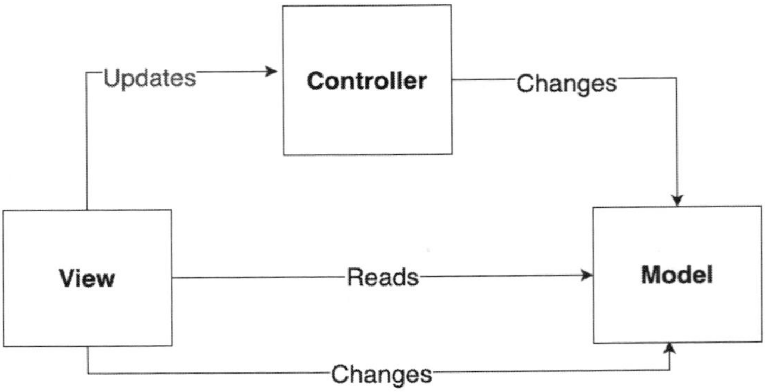

The original MVC.

Does it look clean? Well, not in particular. It violates two fundamental principles:

1. It breaks the Single Concern Principle since both the Controller and the View are responsible for updating the Model.
2. The components are tightly coupled. The Controller depends on both the View and the Model. The View depends on the Model as well.

To mitigate the disadvantages above, it evolved over the years to the diagram below:

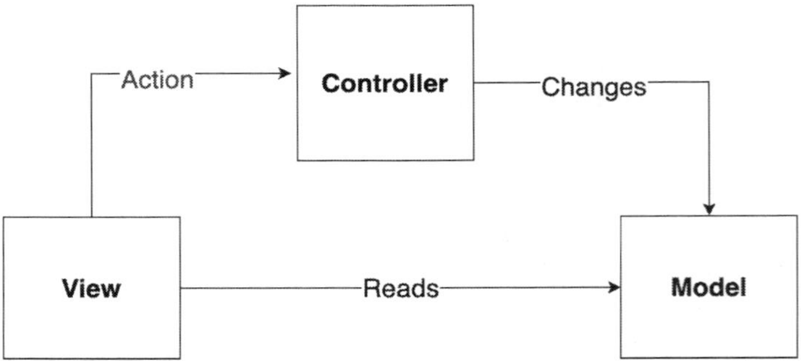

MVC, one of its variations.

It was primarily used as a low-level design pattern rather than a full-blown architecture. The Model was a single class responsible for the data of a specific screen element. Several MVC circuits composed the whole screen. More recently, it moved again from a micro to a macro solution and is used as a full-blown architecture.

MVC eventually became a buzzword, meaning well-designed software that separates the concerns. Since its initial conception, the same abbreviation has been used to describe irrelevant architectures and patterns. "If it's MVC, then it must be something good." The buzzword was used to market solutions and frameworks, like Spring MVC and ASP.NET MVC. Clean Architecture now enjoys a similar status in the mobile industry and microservices in the backend ecosystem.

In any case, enough with the history lessons. Let's see how MVC got interpreted in the mobile apps.

MVC - The Mobile Version

Getting back to the mobile world, MVC, well, one of its variations, was the first attempt to structure the newly born mobile applications properly. The diagram below describes the main idea:

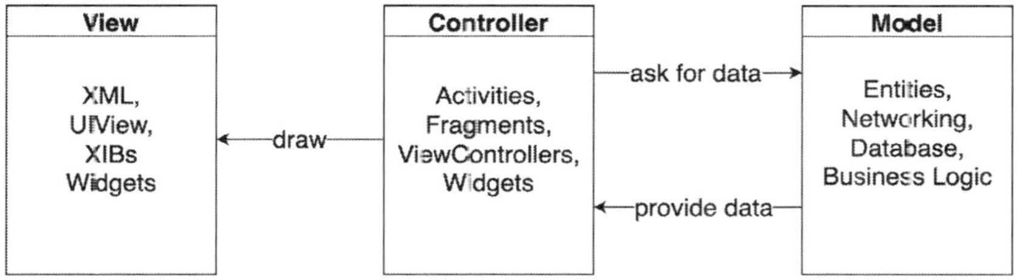

MVC, the Mobile variation.

The code is split into three layers; first, we have the view layer. This layer is supposed to be "dumb," meaning it must not contain logic. It simply knows how to display UI elements within a specific framework. For Android, this layer typically contains XML files and classes that extend from the View class. For iOS, this layer has anything that extends from UIView and Xibs. For Flutter, just Widgets. It is not supposed to contain any logic; it typically is very thin.

The second layer contains the Controllers. For Android, those are the Activities and Fragments. For iOS, well, the name gives it, the View Controllers. And for Flutter, it's again Widgets. The code here is responsible for controlling the View based on:

- The user interactions.
- The data received from the Model.

It orchestrates user interactions via click listeners and requests for the data from the model layer. As we can see, it is tightly coupled to the Model, and both are aware of each other. This can be improved with Dependency Inversion. The MVs and CA are not mutually exclusive. We can apply MVC and use practices like layering and the Dependency Rule to enhance our system further.

Finally, we have the Model, which contains, well, the rest of the application. Most importantly, it contains the entities and the business logic of our app. It also includes the data layer. It basically receives requests from the Controller, locates the data, applies the logic, and returns it back. It may or may not be agnostic of the Controllers depending on whether we have inverted the dependencies.

MVC Concerns

Uneven layer distribution. In an enterprise MVC-based application, the Model contains most of the code. The Model does everything as we keep the View dumb and the Controller thin. It lacks a boundary between the business logic and the data persistence concern. They are both included in the Model.

The biggest drawback is that the Controller is tightly coupled to the views and, therefore, hard to test. Fragments and View Controllers are not unit-testable; they require an emulator.

Finally, the presentation logic is not distinguished from business logic. Presentation logic like:

* * *

```
if (owedAmount > 100)
    textColor = red
```

Is mixed with business logic like:

```
if (owedAmount > 100)
    canTakeLoan = false
```

The architecture does not make this distinction by design. This often leads to:

i. Adding the presentation logic inside the Controller. This reduces the logic's testability as the Controllers require instrumentation tests.
ii. Mixing both types of logic inside the Model, reducing its readability.

MVC Conclusion

MVC can be a good fit for low-complexity applications like CRUD apps. We should avoid MVC when we need to include large chunks of presentation & business logic. Even though for simple apps, there is nothing wrong with using MVC, I wouldn't ever opt-in because:

a. There are better options.
b. It is considered outdated. Sometimes it's essential to keep up with the industry hype. Not solely for technical reasons but for people's motives as well. It may be hard to attract developers willing to work on an MVC application, which is crucial for the product's success. Most of us prefer working on codebases where:
    - We learn from.
    - They boost our future employability.

When the industry collectively feels that something is outdated, regardless of whether it truly is obsolete or not, it becomes.

Model View Presenter (MVP)

Looking at the MVP diagram, it appears similar to MVC. However, there are some key differences that we will discuss.

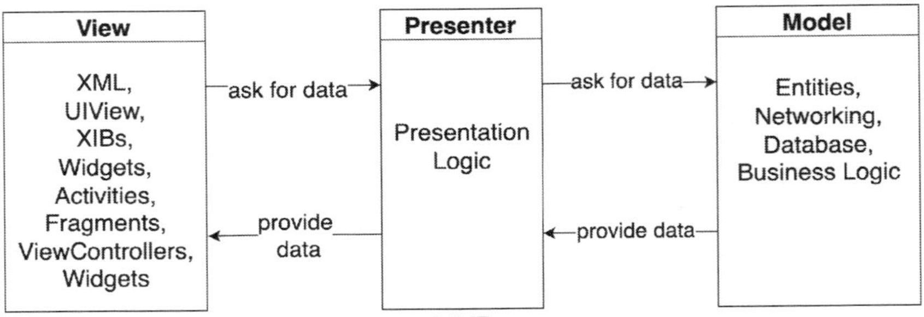

MVP.

The elements that used to belong in the controller layer, like the Fragments and View Controllers, have now been moved to the view layer. The concern of those classes is essentially to interact with the View; it made sense to move them over along to the view layer.

We have added a new layer called the Presenter. The Presenter now owns the responsibility to apply the presentation logic. We now can adequately separate the presentation from the business logic.

The Model remains as it was, with the difference that it no longer contains any presentation logic.

MVP Concerns

The MVP pattern has mainly two downsides. First of all, the Presenter is coupled to the View. This makes our Presenter hard to test as we cannot mock Fragments and View Controllers. This can be resolved, and in many MVP implementations, has been resolved with Dependency Inversion. By making the Presenter depend on a view interface rather than a concrete class, we somehow decouple the two layers. This looks like this:

* * *

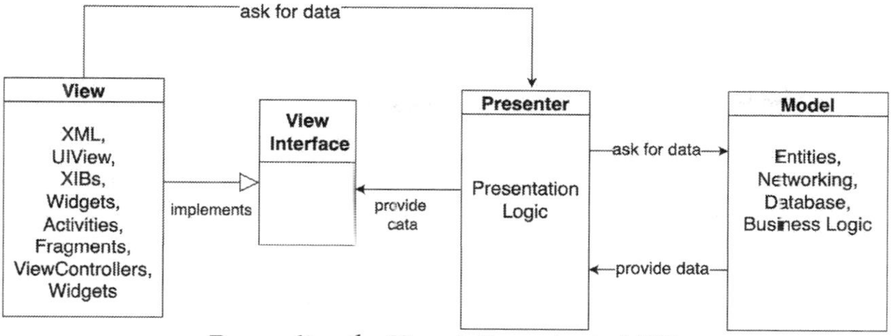

Decoupling the View & Presenter in MVP.

With this solution, we have kind of decoupled the Presenter from the View. I am saying kind of because the View still depends on a concrete Presenter implementation. And the Presenter is still holding on to an interface reference of the View.

The second MVP downside is implementing either over-complicated or duplicated Presenters. When multiple screens require information about the same entity, it makes sense to have them all implement the same view interface and depend on a shared Presenter. This is a case of accidental duplication. Eventually, the screens will require the data in different formats; thus, we will have to create several interfaces. One per screen. This is forcing the shared Presenters to hold onto multiple view interfaces, which leads to overly-complex and thick Presenters:

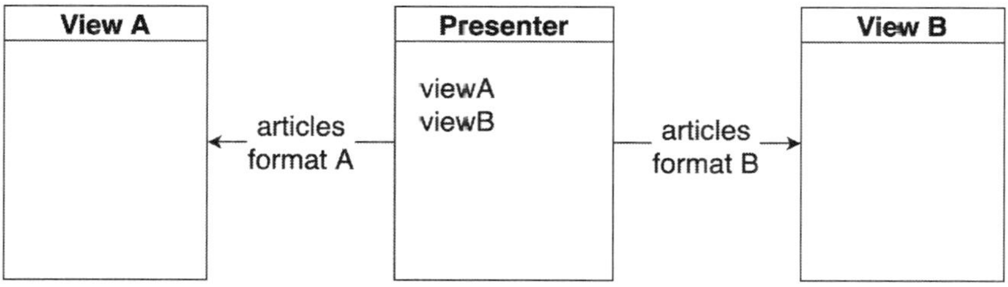

When to use MVP

MVP is an enhancement of MVC and has pretty much rendered MVC deprecated in mobile development. Every application "worth mentioning" will eventually require some sort of presentation logic, and having a dedicated layer for it helps.

* * *

Again though, MVP is considered outdated compared to later architectures such as MVVM and MVI. I would suggest using MVP only when the team does not have any prior experience or the will to learn Reactive Programming (see next section).

Model View View-Model (MVVM)

MVVM is essentially MVP, with a renamed Presenter to View Model and the addition of Reactive Programming. Now it is arguable whether another name was required to describe this. Essentially, nothing prevents the introduction of RP in MVC, MVP, or any other architecture. In any case, this naming has been adopted, so we will stick to it to avoid further confusion.

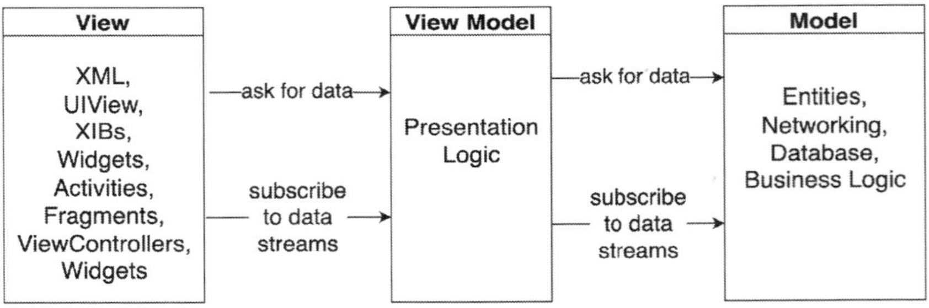

MVVM.

The first thing to notice is that the Presenter is now called View Model. There is nothing more to that; it still owns the same responsibility—to apply the presentation login.

The important thing is the introduction of Reactive Programming. As you can see, now all the arrows point from left to right. There is no View reference inside the View Model whatsoever, nor a concrete implementation or interface. This is achieved by leveraging data streams. Streams are also used to facilitate the communication between the Model and the View Model.

Note that this is not 100% Dependency Inversion. The driving layers depend on concrete implementations rather than abstractions. We can draw proper boundaries and apply DI with the introduction of interfaces. As we discussed earlier, MVs and CA are not mutually exclusive but complement each other.

Again the views are supposed to be "dumb" and must not contain any logic like:

```
if (amount == 0)
  textView.hide()
```

The View is supposed to receive a ready-to-consume model containing the boolean field *textViewVisibility*.

MVVM Concerns

The biggest downside of MVVM is that the final state of the View is a composition of multiple stream inputs.

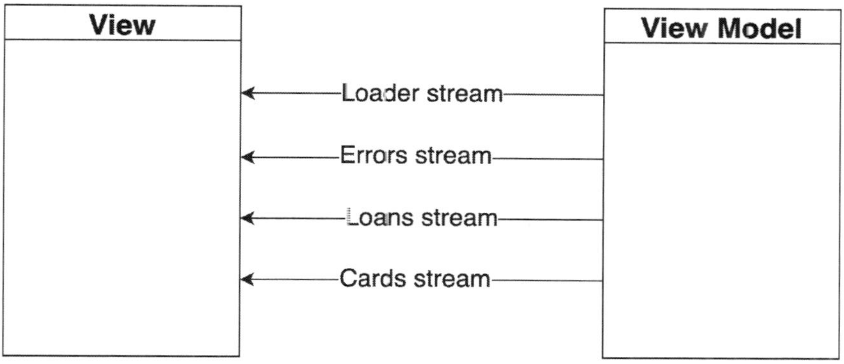

Multiple streams in MVVM.

Usually, views end up subscribing to a stream that controls a loader, another stream to receive errors, and another to obtain the actual data. If a screen displays unrelated data, like Loans and Cards, it ends up subscribing to a dedicated stream for each entity. The view layer must cater to all the possible combinations of stream emissions. This complexifies it, effectively reducing the testability of our app. We have to run instrumentation tests to check that the final result, under several combinations, matches the expected result. Simply testing that every stream in isolation behaves correctly is not sufficient.

Another concern is that Reactive Programming has a steep learning curve. It will take a while for developers who haven't come across RP in the past until they can fully understand it and feel comfortable using it broadly. On the other hand, it's a powerful tool that comes in handy in many situations.

As with all the MVs, I will add that the model layer is too thick, and we need to break it down into thinner layers. At least to separate the data operations from the business and domain logic.

When to use MVVM

MVVM is currently the industry's go-to. It is widely adopted, and sooner or later, every mobile engineer will have to get familiar with Reactive Programming. It usually is a good candidate for the initial MVA. Avoid it in the scenario that your team members are unwilling to explore RP. In this case, you can downscale to MVP. More importantly, in complex applications with *many* data streams per screen, I would opt-in for MVI.

Model View Intent (MVI)

MVI is a unidirectional, cyclical, and Reactive architectural pattern inspired by front end Redux[32] and Cycle.js[4]. In regards to the Android platform, it was introduced by Hannes Dorfman in his blog post series[5]. This MV differentiates most from the others and, in my opinion, is the best one. It comes with several key differences. Most importantly, it addresses the multiple-stream issue in MVVM. Let's

---

[32] Redux is an open-source JavaScript library for managing and centralizing the application state. It is most commonly used with React or Angular libraries to build user interfaces. Similar to (and inspired by) Facebook's Flux architecture, it was created by Dan Abramov and Andrew Clark. For additional informations visit: https://en.wikipedia.org/wiki/Redux_(JavaScript_library)

take a look:

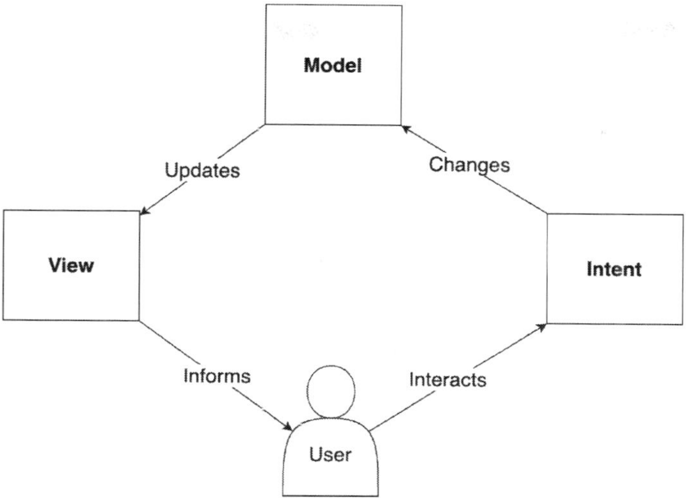

MVI.

As you probably noticed, this diagram doesn't look much like the previous MVs. That's because MVI uses the same terminology to describe different concepts. This has caused a lot of confusion in the industry. To be honest, MVI is making more proper use of the term "Model" but not following the same conventions as the other MVs is confusing.

Everything starts with the user who interacts with our app. In our example, let's assume that a user has two ways of interacting with the screen. First, they can view all the articles, and second by tapping on an article, they can "like" it. In MVI, those two intents are described in a single Intent-model. For iOS, we usually make use of enums:

```
enum HomeIntent : ViewIntent {
    case viewAllArticles
    case likeArticle(id : String)
}
```

For Android, we usually use Kotlin's sealed classes.

* * *

```
sealed class HomeIntent : ViewIntent {
    object ViewAllArticles : HomeIntent()
    data class LikeArticle(val id: String) : HomeIntent()
}
```

Let's compare the advantages of this vs. the traditional approach. Normally, we would implement two separate functions:

i. `viewAllArticles()`
ii. `likeArticle(id: String)`

First of all, by having a single class that describes all the supported intents, we help the code-reader understand the options included on the screen.

Secondly, MVI uses unidirectional data flows, which means using streams both ways. The View Model's public API does not include any functions; it exposes a single public stream accepting intents from the views. After the Intents are received, they are privately handled inside the View Model.

```
private func handleIntent(intent: HomeIntent) {
    switch intent {
    case .viewAllArticles:
        getAllArticles()
    case .likeArticle(let id):
        likeArticle(id: id)
    }
}
```

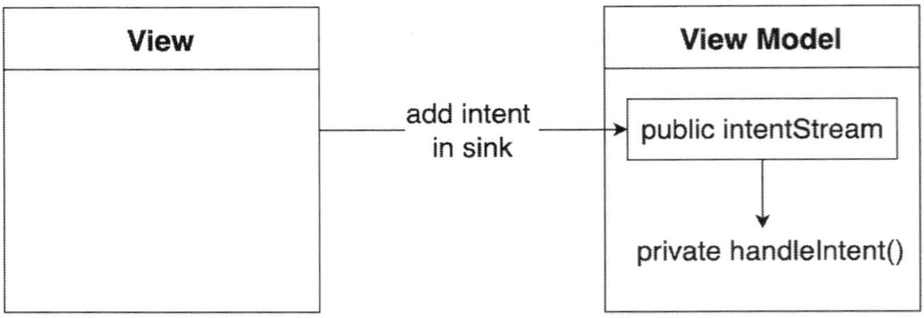

In MVI, layers communicate via public streams. They add requests in the stream's sink.

* * *

The Model in MVI is not a layer responsible for applying the business logic. It is a class that represents the application state. While this is confusing, considering that the rest of the MVs use the same term to describe a different thing, Hannes Dorfman chose to do this on purpose. He is right; the other MVs should not use the term "Model" to describe a whole layer, including the data & business logic. However, in order to avoid confusion, we will refer to it as the State-model. Let's see what the State-model is in MVI.

For iOS, the State-model is represented again by an enum, and for Android, we leverage Kotlin's sealed classes:

```
enum HomeState  {
    case loading
    case allArticles(articles: [Article])
    case empty
    case failed(Error)
}
```

```
sealed class HomeState {
    object Loading : HomeState()
    data class AllArticles(val data: List<Article>) : HomeState()
    object Empty : HomeState()
    data class Failed(val exception: Exception) : HomeState()
}
```

As you can see, the State-model describes all the possible situations that the screen can be in:

Possible screen states.

This is the most important element of MVI. The View is supposed to receive all the information it requires in a *single* object. A single stream emits this object which simplifies our View a lot. Particularly for the cases where we need to consider the previous state to calculate the new state. For example, we may want to display an animation only if the View transitions from the loading state to the data state. Previously this state-logic would live inside our views.

Here I want to mention that there are generally two approaches regarding the state. It can describe the state of a screen or the state of the whole app. Both are viable, though I find that a model describing the state of the entire app eventually becomes overly complex. Therefore, I usually go with the approach of one State-model per screen.

If the business requirements require an offline mode, you can persistently store a conglomeration object. This object can hold a reference to a State-model per screen as well as which was the last visited screen. This way, users can instantly resume from where they exited the mobile app.

Finally, we need a reducer or a reduce-like function to assemble the ready-to-consume State-model:

```
private func reduce(
    previousState: HomeState?, articlesResult: [Article]?
) -> HomeState {

    guard previousState != nil else {
        return HomeState.loading
    }
    guard let articles = articlesResult else {
        return HomeState.failed(NSError())
    }
    if(articles.isEmpty) {
        return HomeState.empty
    }
    return HomeState.allArticles(articles: articles)
}
```

* * *

This function can consider several factors like the previous state of our screen or the user's last intent. No matter what needs to be considered, all the logic that calculates the new State-model must be pertained here, in a single function. This function is pure Swift/Kotlin code; thus, it's easy to test and maintain.

MVI works well with declarative UI builders like Jetpack Compose, SwiftUI, or Flutter. As a matter of fact, Flutter's BLoC architectural pattern is identical to MVI.

To sum it up, MVI is the manifestation of three main concepts:

1. A single State-model that contains *all* the information the View requires to display the UI.
2. A single Intent-model (per screen) that contains all the supported user actions & information.
3. Unidirectional reactive flow. The State-model, as well as the Intent-model, are communicated via single reactive streams:
    - The Intent stream: View -> ViewModel.
    - The State stream: View Model -> View.

Keep in mind that both streams are declared inside the View Model. The View Model is not allowed to depend on the View while the View references the View Model. Therefore, both streams are declared in the VM, but they differ on who observes them.

MVI Concerns

Steep learning curve. MVI is more complex than the rest of the MVs. It contains the complexity of unidirectional streams and reduces the information into single streams. Newcomers who haven't any prior experience may need longer until they get fully onboarded.

Does not define layering. Model and Intent are not layers; they are rather "models" or data classes representing the transmitted information. MVI does not introduce any layering or separation of concerns. This is not necessarily a bad thing as we can combine it with MVA & Clean Architecture to define proper layering for our applications.

The unidirectional flow of streams can unnecessarily increase the complexity of the app. This issue, due to the previous point, is not immediately visible. Applying unidirectional data streams between only two layers, the View and the VM, is fairly simple. Multiple layers participate in a more complex app like View, View Model, Use Case, Repository, Service, etc. Each layer has to expose two streams, one to receive and another to pass data. This increases the boilerplate code without providing a clear benefit. The streams flowing from the view to the data layer are particularly unnecessary. It's perfectly fine if they are simple function calls. Let's compare the two approaches:

Example A, function calls that return streams:

```
class GetArticles constructor(
    private val source: GetArticlesSource,
) {

    suspend fun getArticles(): Flow<List<Article>> = source.articles()
}
```

Our Use Case has a simple suspend function that can be called from within any coroutine like this:

```
getArticlesUseCase.getArticles()
```

Example B, unidirectional data streams. Both for input and output:

* * *

```
class GetArticles(
    private val source: GetArticlesSource,
    private val scope: CoroutineScope
) {
    val action: MutableSharedFlow<HomeAction>
        = MutableSharedFlow()

    private val _state: MutableStateFlow<List<Article>>
        = MutableStateFlow(listOf())

    val state = _state.asStateFlow()


    init {
        scope.launch {  this: CoroutineScope
            action.collect { action ->
                when (action) {
                    HomeAction.ViewAllArticles -> {
                        source.articles().collect { articles ->
                                _state.value = articles
                        }
                    }
                }
            }
        }
    }
}
```

Now the Use Case has the action stream to receive input and the state stream to expose output.

In order to call our Use Case now, we need to use the sink of the action stream:

```
getArticlesUseCase.action.emit(HomeAction.ViewAllArticles)
```

The second implementation contains large amounts of boilerplate code. And similar boilerplate code has to be introduced in every layer. Even though the boilerplate code can be reduced with Generics,

Inheritance, and the Template Method design pattern[33], it's probably still not worth it. We don't receive significant benefits by exposing streams instead of functions that flow from the driving side to the driven.

On the other hand, the streams flowing from the DB to the views provide the advantages such as:

i. Safe concurrency.
ii. Having a single source of truth that updates all the views simultaneously.

The streams that flow from the driving towards the driven side can be replaced by:

i. Simple function calls.
ii. Coroutines.
iii. Async/await.

When to use MVI

MVI - like - systems are my way to go for complex applications. They provide several advantages, but I mostly like the fact that single State-models, delivered by single streams, describe the complete state of a screen. I personally often choose not to adopt the unidirectional data stream approach. I only use streams to facilitate the communication from the driven side (data) back to the driving (UI).

I would only advise avoiding MVI in low-complexity apps that do not need to combine several data streams. Additionally, you may want to avoid it when the team cannot or does not want to go through the initial learning curve. In those cases, it's OK if you downscale to an MVVM-based architecture. Other than that, MVI works well with complex mobile apps.

---

[33] The Template Method is a behavioral design pattern identified by Gamma et al. in the book *Design Patterns*.
The template method is a method in a superclass, usually an abstract superclass, that defines the skeleton of an operation in terms of high-level steps.
A subclass must override this method and add the intended behavior.

* * *

Summary

Since the early years of mobile development, it became evident that architecting mobile apps properly is crucial to their success.

MVC - even though viable for minor apps, has become obsolete.
MVP - is still considered decent, though over-shined by MVVM.
MVVM - use it in small to medium complexity applications.
MVI - use it in complex applications. You can choose to go MVI - like rather than pure MVI to mitigate its cons: boilerplate code and complexity.

CHAPTER SEVENTEEN

Mobile Clean Architecture

The Approach

Now let's try to transform everything we learned into actionable items that will drive the development of our next production application. That's what the following chapters are all about.

As I explained in the introduction of Part III, our focus is centered around the decisions that constitute an architecture rather than discussing specific architectures. A particular architecture is a conglomeration of multiple design decisions. We need to learn how to identify the issues and choose solutions rather than blindly following what we see on the internet.

Nevertheless, I have also prepared two repos suited for different scenarios. Practical code examples can give you a head-start and clear up theoretical ambiguities. Theory-only does not provide the complete picture either.

Before we get to the examples, let's first discuss the business requirements of the mobile app that we will build together.

The Minimum Viable Product

So, we are a lead mobile engineer hired to build a green-field app.

After analysis and exhaustive conversations with the team, our Product Owner has defined the Minimum Viable Product. It includes three user stories:

i. As a User, I want to see all the relevant articles so that I can stay up to date with my interests.
ii. As a User, I want to see the number of likes each article has, so I can identify which ones are popular.
iii. As a User, I want to like an article so that my feed gets more relevant to my preferences.

The UI designer has just finished with the wireframes; the screen looks like this:

It's a list of items that include the:

i. Article title.
ii. Article description.
iii. Author.
iv. Article image.
v. Likes/stars count. Clicking this element adds our like to the article.

* * *

We have everything we need to start working on the architectural design of our app. Or maybe not? Here the story splits into two parallel universes.

In-universe A, we are working for the largest news agency in the world. It's the international colossus "World News." It operates worldwide and employs tens of thousands of employees on every continent. Its value streams as of today are the TV news, the website, and a print newspaper that is distributed globally. Given the recent rise of mobile devices, they decided to build a native mobile app.

Initially, we are only interested in the MVP described above, but the organization already has enormous plans for the mobile app. Given its large customer base, it is guaranteed to have a large volume of users. The stakeholders already have plans to stream their TV programs, add live chat, games, etc. You get the idea. Additionally, many of our customers often travel. Therefore, the application should work offline while in airplane mode.

World News has already hired five mobile-dedicated development teams. By the end of the year, they plan to double the size of the mobile development department. Technically, the focus now is to lay the foundation of a large-scale, enterprise mobile application that will thrive through the following decades. We have the firepower, and it is only expected to double up. We need to lay down a solid structured foundation that will enable the teams to work effectively & efficiently.

— — —

In-universe B, we work for a newly-founded startup called "Disruptive News." It aims to revolutionize the way people consume the news. We are currently one of the two native mobile developers. If everything goes well, the plan is to hire two more devs per platform, iOS, and Android, by the end of the year.

We have secured seed funding until the end of the year. However, To achieve a successful series A we need to deliver results soon. The investors demand to see a working product. Technically, the focus is split between immediate results and slowly laying down the foundation of a future large-scale production app. We won't run solo for long, but we also have to get the ship going.

Do the two cases above require the same architecture? Not! Even though the initial MVP scope is identical, the situations above are fundamentally different from an architectural perspective. The initial MVA for universe A should:

i. Enable multiple development teams to work independently and in parallel. We should enable them to:
    - Make their own choices in third-party libraries without affecting the other teams.
    - Minimize cross-team merge conflicts. Each team's boundaries of control should be clear.
ii. Make as much of the codebase as possible, framework independent. The Android/iOS platforms and their APIs are expected to change dramatically in the years to come. The same applies to third-party libraries. Those changes should not affect a large chunk of our codebase. Updating to AndroidX, for example, should be easy and risk-free.
iii. The velocity should be steady and maintained in time. Our huge corporation does not depend on meeting tight deadlines to secure funding. Therefore, we should avoid piling up technical debt as well. We mainly care about maintaining a steady velocity, regardless of the team's composition, new hires, and leaves.
iv. The contribution guidelines should be strict and precise. We must discourage on-the-fly improvisations, as this can get out of hand with the number of developers who will be contributing.
v. Add offline support.

On the other hand, in the startup's universe, the objectives are quite different:

i. Architectural flexibility is key. We should be flexible to make big decisions on the fly. In a startup, variables like the number of developers, requirements, product pivots, etc.. change rapidly. Therefore, we should be flexible to make significant decisions about the design alongside them.
ii. We should put proper boundaries in place, but the boundaries should not be rigid. Hard boundaries also increase the number of classes and code lines, while they are not as valuable for a

small team of a few developers. Here, it's arguably easier to solve a merge conflict with a person sitting next to us rather than drawing rigid boundaries between us. On the other hand, *soft* boundaries should be in place to contain cancer and reserve the option to upscale later should the need arise.

iii. We are okay with taking a few loans early on, technical loans as well. Every startup runs on a cash runway countdown[34]. There is a burning need to catch set milestones to secure funding. Cancer has to be contained, though. We should not let those loans cripple the future of our product. The architecture must be based on solid ground, enabling later refactoring to a cleaner approach.

I have prepared two repos, each targeting one of the cases above. For the World News agency, the *Mobile Microservices Architecture*. It's inspired by the respective backend microservices approach. The code is split into multiple modules that can be developed and deployed independently.
Android: https://github.com/petros-efthymiou/Mobile-Android-Microservices-Architecture
iOS: https://github.com/petros-efthymiou/Mobile-iOS-Microservices-Architecture

For the disruptive startup, the *Pragmatic Clean Architecture*. A more lightweight approach with flexible boundaries that are open to becoming rigid later on.
Android: https://github.com/petros-efthymiou/Android-Pragmatic-Clean-Architecture
iOS: https://github.com/petros-efthymiou/iOS-Pragmatic-Clean-Architecture

The purpose of those repos is educational; we will use them as examples to discuss the architectural concerns and solutions. You are free to fork them and do whatever you please with them. As long as you understand their reasoning. And that they are just one conglomeration of educated choices rather than a global truth.

* * *

[34] The amount of time before the company runs out of money.

Before you move to your laptop to check the repos, let's make sure you understand the reasoning behind them. Let's kick off the discussion...

Easy Decisions

I want to start with the - easy to make - architectural decisions to get them out of our way and focus on the ones that require some thinking.

MVWhat?

We will follow an MVI-like architecture combined with Clean Architecture on a high level. We will take some aspects from MVI, like:

- Reactive Programming. The previous chapters explain that it helps us deal with two of the most critical issues we face in mobile development. Concurrency and coupling.
- A State-model that contains all the information required to draw the screen. It simplifies our view layer, making the whole application easier to develop and test.
- An Intent-model contains all the available screen interactions. It helps with readability & maintainability.

We will skip the unidirectional reactive streams, as they unnecessarily complexify the codebase. Of course, we will also combine it with Clean Architecture. Specifically, we will:

- Separate the code into layers. Each layer will belong to a different level.
- Follow the Dependency Rule. Inner/high-level layers are not supposed to know anything about lower-level layers.
- We will apply Dependency Inversion wherever the flow of control goes against the Dependency Rule.

We will discuss the exact layers and boundaries in the following chapters. Those decisions require a lot of thinking, and we need to consider the context and details of each scenario. The two scenarios require different layers and boundaries, but the general rules apply to both.

* * *

Dependency Injection

Not much to argue about here; we will properly inject all the dependencies using third-party libraries in both apps. We enjoy benefits like testability and separation of concerns, almost for free.

Technicalities

We eventually also have to decide on low-level decisions, like selecting a reactive framework, networking library, database (scenario A), etc. Those are technicalities. When designing the system's architecture, we should leave those decisions last. They are platform and details specific. Here, for the purposes of this book, I will present them now to get done with the details so that we can focus on the critical matters.

- Dependency Injection.
  - Android: I would normally opt-in for Hilt, which is super easy to use. However, it comes with limitations when segregating the codebase into independent modules. Thus, I picked Koin, which is also easy to use and doesn't have such constraints. Dagger2 is complicated and hard to use. Hilt is an option for the startup scenario where we avoid rigid boundaries, but we will face issues if we decide to draw strict boundaries later.
  - iOS: I went with Resolver. It is simple, fast, and straightforward to use.
- Database. We only need to support offline mode in scenario A. In B, we don't have such a requirement. If we identify the need to improve the performance later, we can achieve it simply with HTTP caching. Therefore, I have only included databases for scenario A. The choices here are pretty obvious:
  - Android: Room. Dramatically reduces the boilerplate code.
  - iOS: Core data. Fast, reliable, and battle-tested.
- Reactive frameworks. The choice here lies between the native solutions and the Rx family. Both options are equally viable, in my opinion. The native solutions are better performant and

save us from adding third-party dependencies. On the other hand, the Rx API is more powerful and almost identical in all programming languages. You learn it once, and you can use it everywhere.

  - Android: Kotlin Flow & State Flow combined with Kotlin Coroutines. Flow is easy to adopt, plus it benefits from the coroutine's Structured Concurrency[35] [1].
  - iOS: RxSwift. I choose RxSwift instead of Combine because I am more familiar with Rx, and Combine is still immature. Feel free to opt-in to Combine if you want to hit better performance.

- Networking. Again, the choices here are pretty obvious. We just need a library that is reliable and minimizes the boilerplate code. The community points at:
  - Android: Retrofit.
  - iOS: Alamofire.
- UI. The community is moving fast toward Declarative Programming. It is easier to read and maintain, plus it works well with Reactive Programming. Our only option here is to adopt the native solutions:
  - Android: Jetpack Compose
  - iOS: SwiftUI

It's not that those decisions are of low importance. Specific libraries and frameworks offer advantages over others. We should investigate before making up our minds. Usually, the most important criteria for selecting a library are:

- Ease of use. How convenient their public API is.
- Performance.
- Power. How many options the library is offering, and how many problems it solves.
- Stability. We don't want to base production apps on libraries that are still in alpha or beta.

---

[35] "Structured concurrency" refers to a way to structure async/concurrent computations so that child operations are guaranteed to complete before their parents, i.e., no child operation is executed outside the scope of a parent operation.
This helps avoid memory and work leaks.

- Industry adoption. The community's adoption of a library is always important. It's easier to find and onboard engineers familiar with Retrofit, for example, than a library used by a small part of the community. Furthermore, popular libraries are less likely to get discontinued.

Those decisions should come last in a typical scenario and not in a book. We first draw the high-level picture and then the technicalities. We leave the external libraries' decisions for the last responsible moment[36] when we have as much information as possible about what exactly we are going to build.

Finally, as we discussed, our architecture should banish third-party libraries at the edge of the design. Effectively protecting the rest of the codebase from their volatility.

> Delay design decisions until it's necessary. Architecture is an art, not a science. Don't architect for things you don't know. Your design decisions should always be built on facts, not guesses. —Pierre Pureur

Summary

The architectural design is context-dependent. We should take into account factors like:

- Complexity.
- App size.
- Team size.
- Company budget.
- Company plans.

..and decide how elaborate our initial MVA should be.

Facts, not speculations, should drive the decisions.

---

[36] LRM - A strategy of not making a premature decision but instead delaying commitment and keeping important and irreversible decisions open until the cost of not making a decision becomes greater than the cost of making a decision.

When we don't have enough facts, we should wait until the last responsible moment to make the call.
The decisions should change when the facts change.
A good architecture allows us to delay and even change decisions quickly.

CHAPTER EIGHTEEN

Logic & Validations

Types of Logic

If I asked you to explain, "On a high level, what software programs do?" what would be your answer?

They are systems that manifest four main concepts:

i. Input: They receive data from other systems.
ii. Validations & error handling: They validate that the data meets certain conditions. When it doesn't, they handle the errors.
iii. Logic: They apply logic by transforming the data.
iv. Storage: They potentially store data.

The logic & validations of the data are the driving factors that shape our architecture. As Uncle Bob states, "The database is a detail." "The web is a detail, a delivery mechanism."

What matters is the application logic. Deeply understanding the types of logic and validations is critical in making educated architectural decisions. The following diagram sums up all the types of tasks that an application *may* need to execute:

* * *

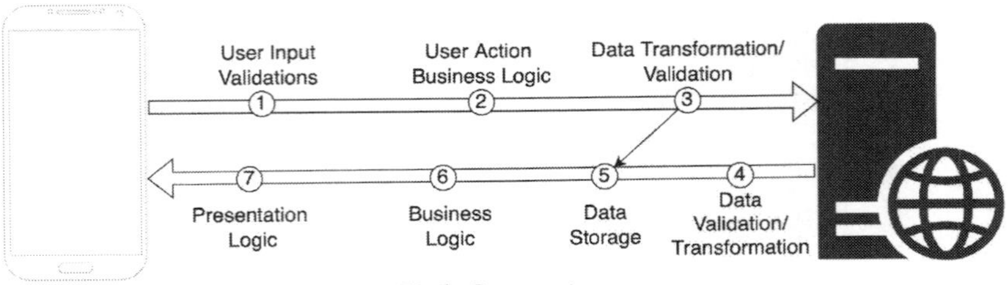

Task Categories.

Do all applications require all of them? Nope, some of them can be omitted in certain apps. Let's examine them one by one.

1. *User input validations*. We normally validate that the user input meets certain preconditions. If it doesn't, we provide instant feedback to the user. It's not a must to have those validations in the client, as the backend must reject forbidden actions. But having them in the client improves the UX and relieves our system from unnecessary traffic.

2. *User action business logic*. This is the logic applied after a user action. For example, when a user clicks to like an article. It includes increasing the article's like-count by one. Do we need to have this logic in a mobile app? Well, it depends. Usually, the backend should perform such operations. The mobile app, instead of calculating the like-count, should rather just call an endpoint "/like-article/{id}." In this endpoint, the backend will query the article in the DB, increase the like-count and return the updated article. It's preferable this way because:

   i. We avoid duplicating or triplicating the business logic into multiple clients (Android, iOS, Web). All those apps would have to include the same code in three different programming languages. We are effectively multiplying the effort & risk. It's better to rely on the backend as a single source of truth.
   ii. For security purposes. Clients generally cannot be trusted. Hackers can perform malicious HTTP requests that increase the like-count by, say, x1000. This must be validated and rejected by the backend code. As the backend will query for the article anyway to prevent malicious data input, why not include the logic altogether?

In specific situations, though, when we depend on pure RESTful APIs, solutions like Firebase, or we manipulate our local database, this kind of logic has to be added to the client. Let's understand the difference between having the backend apply this logic vs. including it in the client.

In the two snippets below, we have included the business logic in the mobile client.

```
class LikeArticle(
    private val source: LikeArticleSource,
    private val mapper: ArticlesMapper
) {

    suspend operator fun invoke(id: String) {
        val articlesAuthorsLikes = source.findArticle(id)
        val articlePlain = articlesAuthorsLikes.articlesPlain[0]
        val article = mapper.mapArticle(
            articlePlain,
            articlesAuthorsLikes.authorsPlain,
            articlesAuthorsLikes.likedArticlesIds
        )
        val updatedArticle = article.likeArticle()
        if (updatedArticle != null)
            source.updateArticle(
                mapper(
                    updatedArticle,
                    articlePlain.authorId,
                    articlePlain.words
                )
            )
    }
}
```

```
fun likeArticle(): Article? {
    return if (canLike)
        Article(
            this.id,
            this.title,
            this.desc,
            this.date,
            this.readTime,
            this.category,
            this.imageUrl,
            likes: this.likes + 1,
            this.authorName,
            canLike: false
        )
    else
        null
}
```

In this example, we are working with a RESTful CRUD backend like Firestore. We also manipulate a local DB to instantly make the new information available to the user. We initially retrieve the article from the DB and map it to a convenient format. Then, we apply the business logic by calling the *article.likeArticle* function (second code snippet). Finally, we update the Article to both the server and our DB.

When we are working with a backend that includes all the business logic, the previous Use Case looks like this:

```
suspend fun likeArticle(id: String) =
    source.likeArticle(id)
```

The clients don't have to do anything. They just call an endpoint and let the backend retrieve the article, increase the like-count and update the result. It also comes with enhanced security for free!

3-4. *Data transformation & validation*. Steps 3 & 4 are similar; in no 3, we ensure that the data about to be sent is in a format that the server can consume. In no 4, we validate that the data that we received from the backend is valid and transform it into a convenient form for our application. Let's assume that we receive from our backend the following data regarding the articles:

```
data class ArticleRaw(
    val id: String,
    val title: String,
    val desc: String,
    val date: String,
    val words: Int,
    val category: String,
    val imageUrl: String,
    val stars: Int,
    val authorId: String,
    val otherJunkTheBackendIsSending: List<Any>?
)
```

Our mobile application is not interested in the field *otherJunkTheBackendIsSending*. So we transform the raw data into a plain model that does not contain it:

```
data class ArticlePlain(
    val id: String,
    val title: String,
    val desc: String,
    val date: String,
    val words: Int,
    val category: String,
    val imageUrl: String,
    val likes: Int,
    val authorId: String
)
```

Regarding error handling, if a required field is missing or comes in an unexpected format, we must return an error object or throw an Exception. Usually, I prefer having wrappers around errors, like Kotlin Result, for example. Throwing exceptions may lead to undesired crashes.

5. *Data storage*. This step includes transforming the data to a convenient format for our database and the actual data storing (ORM). This can

range from saving user configurations in local files or having a complete relational database. Again not all applications require persistent storage. We receive everything, including user configs, from the backend in some cases. Other apps require offline support and a complete relational database. For an Android app, the ORM layer with Room looks like this:

```
@Entity(tableName = "article")
data class ArticleDb(
    @PrimaryKey
    val id: String,
    val title: String,
    val desc: String,
    val date: String,
    val words: Int,
    val category: String,
    val imageUrl: String,
    val likes: Int,
    val authorId: String
)
```

6. *Business Logic*. We can also call this application logic as parts of the logic may only be relevant to our app. This includes processing and transforming the data in a meaningful, for the user, shape. We often need to both aggregate data and apply calculations to produce those models. For example, in the article models above, the *authorId* field does not hold any significance for our users. The users are interested in the name of the author. Additionally, the domain model includes calculated fields, like whether the current user can like an article or how much time it takes to read it. The full article model looks like this:

* * *

```
data class Article(
    val id: String,
    val title: String,
    val desc: String,
    val date: String,
    val readTime: Int,
    val category: ArticleCategory,
    val imageUrl: String,
    val likes: Int,
    val authorName: String,
    val canLike: Boolean
)
```

Is it necessary to have business logic in our apps? Again, not in every situation. Not in the case where the backend aggregates and processes the info appropriately.

7. *Presentation logic.* Besides the data transformations with business significance, we also have UI-related transformations like decisions related to a text field's size, color, or opacity. All this information should be calculated before the model reaches the UI. The UI must be dumb. The final model that is ready to consume:

```
data class ArticlePresentation(
    val id: String,
    val title: String,
    val desc: String,
    val date: String,
    val readTime: Int,
    val category: String,
    val imageUrl: String,
    val likes: Int,
    val authorName: String,
    val canLike: Boolean,
    val likeActionAlpha: Float
)
```

It contains one additional field, the *likeActionAlpha*. This represents the opacity of the like-button based on whether the current user can like the article or not. Additionally, even though not visible here, the date has been formatted to match the user's locale. Presentation logic is not supposed to live in a backend system. Again, for simple applications, we may not need it, though. We don't have presentation logic when the data does not affect UI decisions. E.g., all texts have a predefined, static size, color, and attributes.

Finally, here we have to decide on the presentation of the errors or exceptions. Do we want to display a popup informing the user that something went wrong? In modern apps, I often notice that they avoid popups. Sometimes they avoid displaying anything at all. We have to map the error in an object that the View knows how to display. Or omit the error altogether. In any case, this decision has to be taken together with the product designer.

So based on the above:

- We (may) have data transformations on the driving side - user actions.
- We (most likely) have data transformations on the driven side. The data must be processed to get to a meaningful for the user form.

We have also agreed to use Reactive / Functional Programming; thus, all those models will be immutable. Consequently, applying any kind of logic or error handling involves mapping from one model to another that includes the calculated values.

As we explained, an app may require a subset of the task categories described above. Identifying the exact subset and how thick each set is, is key in defining our architecture. It's a big part of the technical context—the technical complexity of our app.

According to the Single Concern Principle, our components are either:

- Executors.
- Orchestrators.
- Data holders.
- Data holders+executors.

Here, we are only discussing the executors. Those are the ones that apply logic. The orchestrators serve as glue to enable the cohesive executors to worry only about a single concern.

It's not absolutely necessary for all executors to pertain to a single concern; we can implement a transformation mapper that applies both the presentation and business logic. Especially when the app is simple, and the logic is small. However, it has to be an educated decision and consciously take this loan. We may have to break it down later into two executors.

Getting back to our story, for scenario A - World news, I am suggesting the following data transformations:

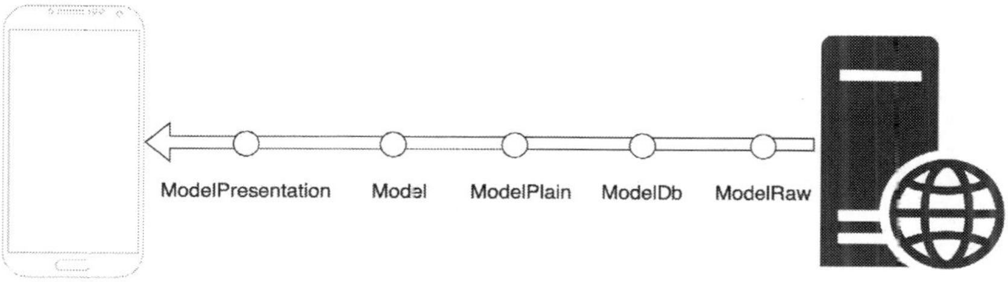

Model types, Enterprise.

Let's discuss the purpose of each transformation:

- JSON -> ModelRaw: we validate that we have all the information we need, and it is in the expected format. We can also rename fields.
- ModelRaw -> ModelDB: we remove unnecessary fields.
- ModelDB -> ModelPlain: we don't include any logic; it's a plain data class. We use it to invert the dependency of the Model to the ModelDB. Remember our domain must not depend on ORM/third-party models. Our business logic must be framework-agnostic.
- ModelPlain -> Model: The Model refers to the domain model. We add all the domain/application logic.
- Model -> ModelPresentation: we apply the presentation logic.

For scenario B - Disruptive News, I have selected the following mappings:

* * *

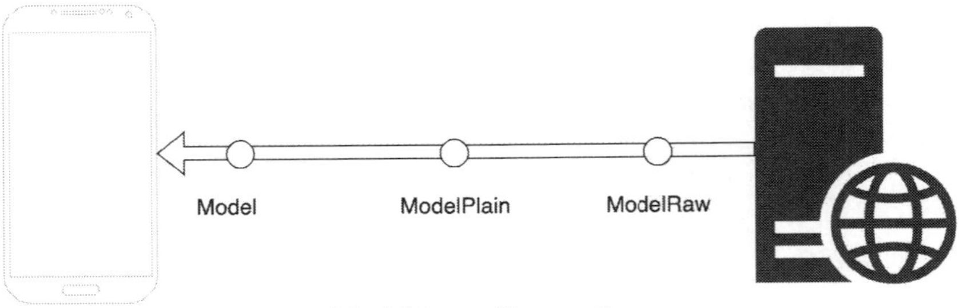

Model types, Pragmatic.

A simpler approach. We don't need the ModelDB (ORM) as we don't include a relational DB. We have also merged the business and presentation logic inside the Model. It's okay for small and flexible applications. Finally, we have kept the ModelPlain to decouple the Model from ModelRaw and invert the dependencies. We want to be able to scale this architecture; later on, this inversion will help us. Our Model should be agnostic of the databases, external APIs, and anything like that. Imagine that we may be basing our MVP on a Firebase backend, while later, we'll want to scale it up to a fully-fledged backend system. This layer has to be isolated to enable us to switch quickly.

Okay, so we discussed how to choose the number of transformations in an application. We now need to discuss how those transformations will be applied. In dedicated mapper classes or inside the models themselves? We briefly touched on this dilemma a few times earlier in the book. I promised you that we would discuss what it means to mix OO and Functional Programming and how we don't fully respect Data Encapsulation. It's time to fulfill my promise and discuss this topic in detail.

Rich vs. Poor models

We have mentioned earlier in the book that we should avoid having data/POJO classes representing the business entities in a pure OO design. One of the core OO concepts is Data Encapsulation, which states that data and operations should sit together, not in separate classes. To explain this with an example:

* * *

```
data class Article(
    val id: String,
    val title: String,
    val desc: String,
    val date: String,
    val readTime: Int,
    val category: ArticleCategory,
    val imageUrl: String,
    val likes: Int,
    val authorName: String,
    val canLike: Boolean
) {
    fun likeArticle(): Article? {
        return if (canLike)
            this.copy(
                likes = this.likes + 1,
                canLike = false
            )
        else
            null
    }
}
```

The *likeArticle* function lives inside the Article domain model. The logic is together with the data. Encapsulation is respected. Below we move the *likeArticle* function to a Use Case:

* * *

```
class LikeArticle(private val source: LikeArticleSource) {

    suspend operator fun invoke(id: String): Article? {
        val article: Article = source.getArticle(id)
        return likeArticle(article)
    }

    private fun likeArticle(article: Article): Article? {
        return if (article.canLike)
            article.copy(
                likes = article.likes + 1,
                canLike = false
            )
        else
            null
    }
}
```

The like-article business logic lives inside a Use Case and outside the Article model. The Article model only contains data, while the operations on the data reside elsewhere. This is not respecting the Data Encapsulation OO principle.

Should we care? Well, yes and no…

> The fundamental horror of this anti-pattern is that it's so contrary to the basic idea of object-oriented design; which is to combine data and process together. —Martin Fowler [1]

Many people, including Martin Fowler, consider data domain models an anti-pattern and call them "anemic" models. Mainly because we spend the effort to map the data model into a domain model without getting the benefits of a domain model. Let's compare the arguments and counterarguments on having a rich domain model while focusing on the mobile development perspective.

We spend the effort mapping the data model to a domain model without yielding any of the benefits. The benefit is having a centralized source of truth, which enforces all the rules and validations on the business entity. Since everything is encapsulated in a single class, no one can bypass the rules even if they want to. Furthermore, it helps us find the business rules. We know that any logic related to the Article model will reside inside the Article entity.

Countering the above, since we use Reactive Programming in mobile development, and for a good reason, we are going to spend the effort mapping between two models regardless of whether we use an " anemic" or rich model. Remember everything in RP is immutable; thus, the domain model cannot have a mutable state. Whether we opt-in for rich or poor models, we have to implement a mapping function. It will either live in a mapper or in the model itself. This pretty much cancels most pure OO motives, as we mix OO and Functional Programming by definition.

Regarding the other point, which is the single source of business rules enforcement, this is semi-true for our case. An external mapper can also be a single source of truth that we can instantly locate. If we design the app like this, we will know that any business logic related to the Article model will live inside the ArticleMapper. However, we can't enforce those rules on a developer unaware that they have to use the mapper. As the Article constructor is public, anyone can create an instance without respecting the rules defined inside the mapper. Well, this is something that I can live with. If the team is not aligned on how we have architected the app, such violations will happen all over the codebase anyhow. I am not saying we should not be architecting to maximize robustness; I prefer the pure OO way here. OO scores a point.. or half a point.

Another counter-OO argument is that a domain model holding all the logic, both the driving and the driven, will become overly complex in a complex application. There are ways to break it down into collaborators & design patterns like the Facade[37]. This does not come for free, though. It increases the number of classes and overall complexity.

On another note, sometimes, we don't need to add any domain logic in

[37] The facade pattern hides the system's complexities and provides an interface for the client to access the system. This design pattern comes under structural patterns as it adds an interface to existing systems to hide its complexities.

our app as the backend handles most of it. Therefore, we end up with "anemic" models by definition.

For the case of mobile development, I will call this a draw. A poor or rich model is a situational decision based on the specific context of our app. Practical guidelines that you can follow:

- Add the *driving logic*[38] inside the models. There should be hardly any driving business logic in the mobile client with a decent back-end API. We don't need to introduce extra mappers for that.
- For the *driven logic*[39]:
    i. For a medium to high complexity application, add it inside dedicated mappers. You will eventually need to include large chunks of it, and it helps to have them in dedicated classes.
    ii. For simple apps, you can add the *driven logic* in the model. This will reduce the number of classes as you won't have to implement and inject mapper classes.

Remember that we still need the Use Cases regardless of rich or poor models. We still need to communicate the changes to other layers even if the transformation logic is added inside our rich models. Like save the data to a database or send it to a backend system. All this orchestration must happen in the Use Case and never inside the Model. The models must not have any external dependencies at all. This would be a severe violation of the Single Concern Principle. With rich models, we can only omit to implement logic mappers; we can't omit Use Cases.

Summary

We can identify seven distinct types of logic that a mobile app *may* need to include. We may need to apply all categories or a subset of them in our application.

---

[38] Driving logic flows from the user to the backend system.
[39] Driven logic flows from the backend to the user.

* * *

Besides the different types, it's essential to weigh the complexity of our app to understand how much of each logic is necessary.

The above factors are key in deciding our architectural design.

The design changes when the above change.

CHAPTER NINETEEN

Boundaries & Layers

Boundaries & Packages

Let's now discuss how to draw proper boundaries in our application. "Proper," as always, is context-dependent.

The system's boundaries are essential. Besides their direct effect on cohesion & coupling, they form the facade of our architecture. What is the first thing they see when a newcomer joins the team? It's the modules and packages that our application contains. Can you recall your excitement when you enter a new team and open up the project for the first time? We are all eager to assess the codebase that we will spend the following months or years. Will it be love at first sight or regret joining the team?

The facade of our architecture: the modules, submodules, and packages is crucial. There are two questions to answer:

a. Where do we draw the boundaries?
b. How rigid are those boundaries?

First, let's assume that all the boundaries are hard, and we only need to answer where to draw them. The meaningful, strict boundary strategies are the following:

* * *

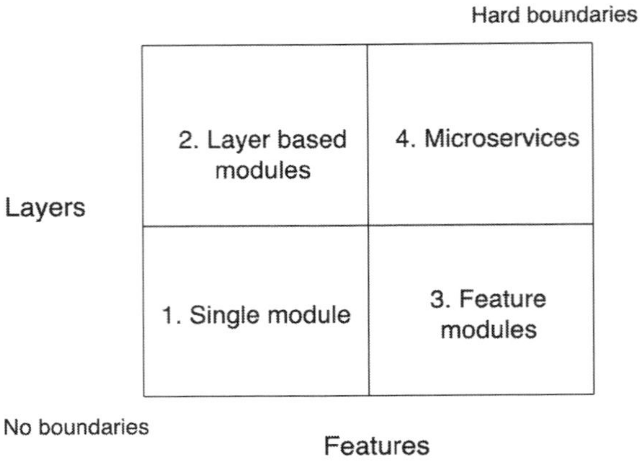

Architecture categorization based on hard boundaries.

1. *Single Module.* This is the simplest case; we don't have any boundaries. All the code is placed under a single module.

2. *Layer-Based Modules.* When the segregation factor is the layering, we implement layer-based modules, e.g., PresentationModule, DataModule, etc.

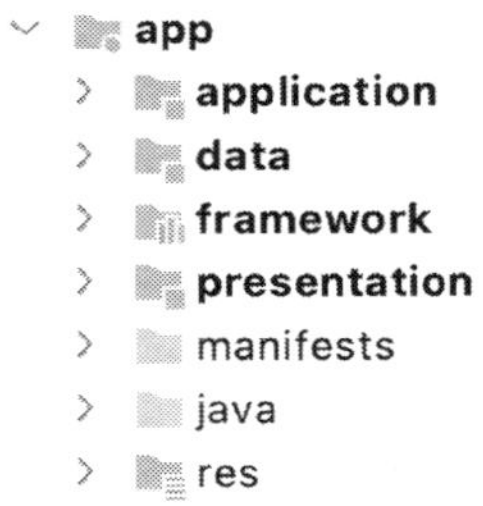

Layer Modules. Notice how only the Framework layer is an Android module. The rest are pure Kotlin modules - Android agnostic.

By drawing hard boundaries between the layers, we effectively prevent architectural violations. An inner layer is blocked from importing dependencies from an outer later. Cross-module imports must be explicitly defined in the build.gradle or Architecture.xcodeproj files. This way, a junior dev cannot accidentally import a class belonging to the framework module in the domain module:

* * *

```
implementation project(path: 'application')
```

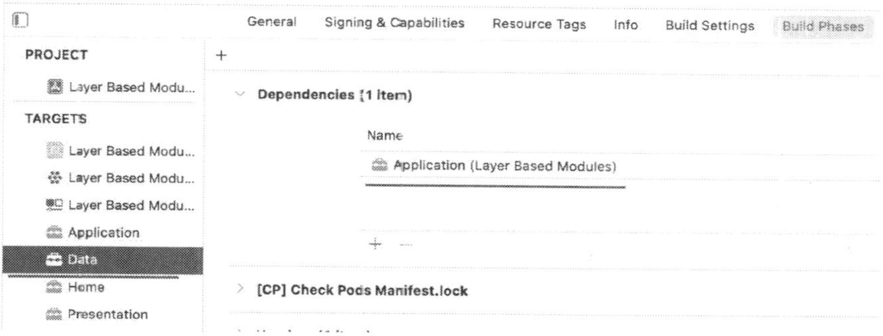

Furthermore, this approach also communicates well that we have adopted Clean Architecture and the specific layering that we have chosen.

On the downside, it doesn't scale well. In a large app, those modules will eventually turn into code buckets. As the number of features increases, we will have to add too many classes in each layer. Another disadvantage is that this project's facade says nothing about the system's intention. It does not express whether it belongs to a banking or healthcare app. It's the opposite of what Uncle Bob refers to as Screaming Architecture[1]. Overall I don't recommend this approach.

> Your architecture should tell readers about the system, not about the frameworks you used in your system. —Robert C Martin

3. *Feature Modules*. The other separation axis is per feature: e.g., home, chat, settings, etc. Then we produce feature modules.

* * *

Feature modules.

There aren't any strict guidelines on what constitutes a "feature." Like designing back-end services, we have to make educated decisions on where to draw the boundaries. The most rigid option is to opt-in for one feature module per screen. However, it's more advisable to group several related screens into a cohesive module. A feature module can include a whole user journey. Or screens that are somehow logically related.

With this approach, our app scales much better. As the number of features increases, so do the boundaries and modules. Therefore, we can maintain low coupling. Each module can be completely independent and agnostic of all others. The app/main module depends on all of them and orchestrates the navigation between them. This way, we can enable independent teams to work in parallel; each team can own specific module(s). Consequently, each team can also decide on third-party libraries and coding styles.

If that's something that we don't want, we can also introduce a shared module that every other will import. The shared module can contain parent classes, Generics, shared UI elements, colors, etc. It's a tradeoff between the teams' independence (minimizing merge conflicts, etc.) vs. the app's consistency and development speed.

On the downsides of the Feature module approach, we lack rigid boundaries between the layers. For example, Fragments and Use Cases live under the same module. Thus, they can both import and use each other directly. This is something that we can address with proper onboarding and code reviews. Overall, this approach fits well with most *complex* applications. On simple apps, we don't really need hard boundaries at all.

4. *Microservices*. Finally, when we draw hard boundaries on both axes, we opt-in for the *Mobile Microservices Architecture*.

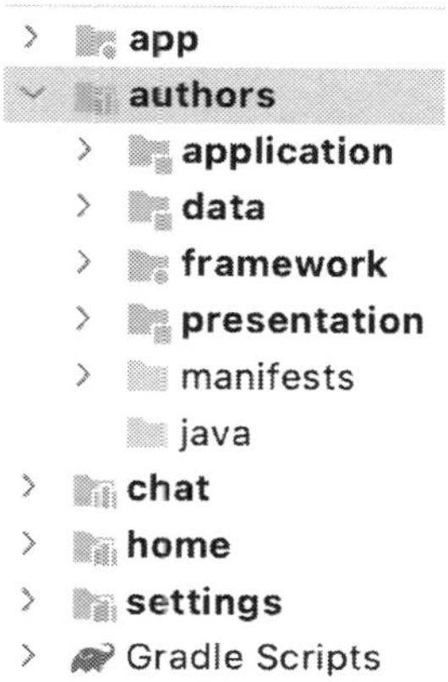

Microservices Architecture.

This approach draws rigid boundaries both on features and on layers axis. We get the benefits of both, and we produce the minimum possible coupling. On the other hand, it increases the app's complexity and reduces its flexibility. Everything is isolated. Honestly, I would not choose to go down this road unless we talk about a project with ~50+ engineers on each mobile codebase and more than one team per feature.

The examples described above include only hard boundaries. Hard boundaries mean that the code is segregated into independent modules. We can also use soft boundaries, which translates to separation into packages. All the possible combinations can be described in the matrix below:

* * *

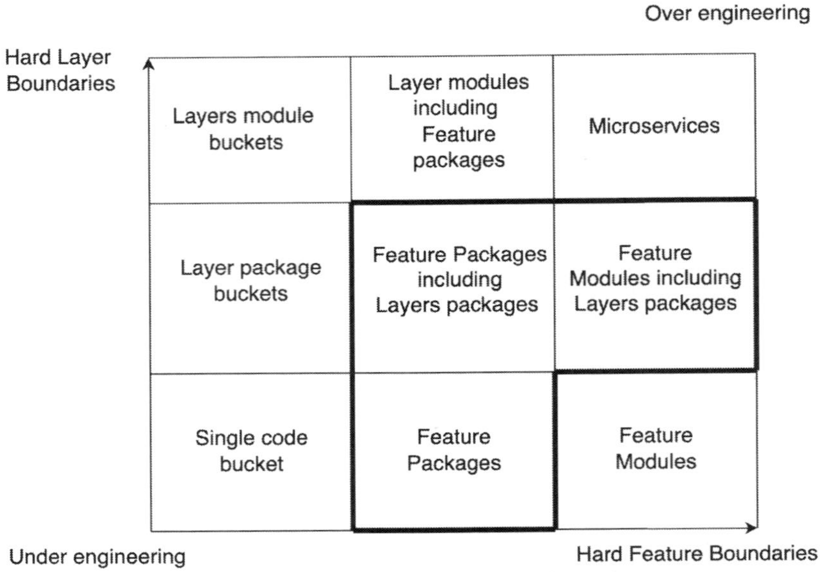

Architecture categorization based on boundaries.

The highlighted area contains the options that I recommend. Package means soft boundary while module means hard boundary. More specifically, for:

- Medium complexity apps: Feature packages, including layer packages. The end result is a single, flexible module without hard boundaries:

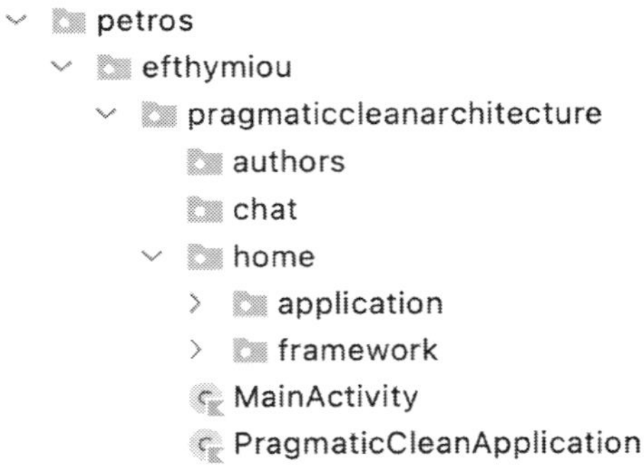

- High complexity apps: Feature modules including layer packages. The same as above with the difference that we draw hard boundaries between the features. Each team can be responsible for a group of features and remain autonomous.

* * *

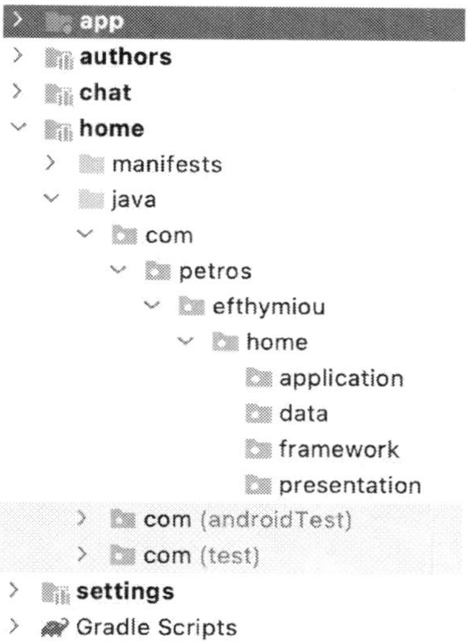

Note that the combinations presented in the diagram are the combinations that make some sense. I often see in production applications meaningless boundaries that don't serve any purpose. Those fall under the category of low cohesion and low coupling described in Part II.

Getting back to our story, for the promising startup, Disruptive News, I chose: Feature Packages, including layer packages. It's an overall flexible pick that reserves the ability to scale up later on.

In the parallel universe, for World News, I chose Microservices. Honestly, for most enterprise apps, I would opt-in for Feature modules, including layer packages. I did choose Microservices, though, for demonstration purposes. To demonstrate how to achieve the extreme scenario. You can easily fork it and downscale it if you want.

Layers & Levels

Let's now discuss the layers and levels we should include in our architectural design. Like everything, it's situational. For World News,

I have selected the following layers:

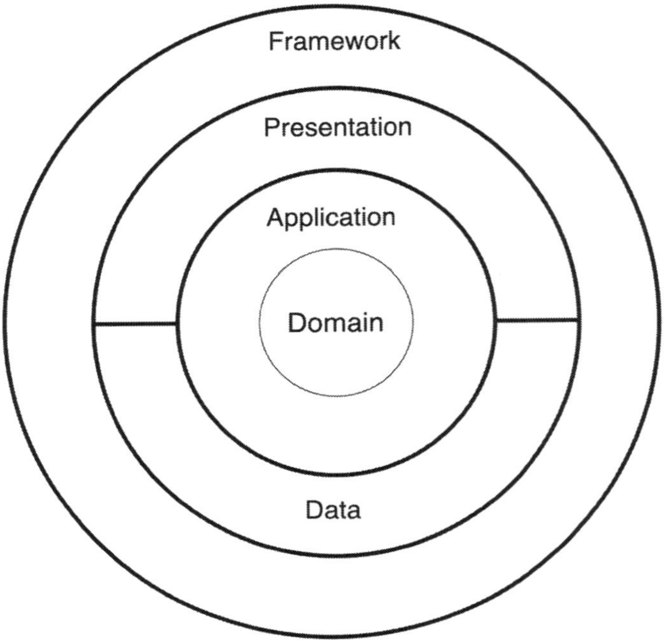

Enterprise Mobile Layering.

First of all, notice that the diagram has thick and thin walls. The thick walls represent hard boundaries while the thin walls soft boundaries. Let's break it down:

1. *Domain* Model & Logic. This includes the domain models (Article) and the domain logic mappers (ArticleMapper). Those two represent the business and must not have any external dependencies.

2. *Application* layer. It includes all the application Use Cases, ViewArticles and LikeArticle. The boundary with the domain layer is thin. The domain classes, by definition, do not have any dependencies. Therefore, I tend to add those two layers under the same module to avoid over-engineering. Additionally, most Use Cases describe business actions. Thus the two layers are logically connected.

3. *Presentation* & *Data* layers. The next circle includes both the

presentation and data layers. Does this mean that those two are allowed to depend on each other? Not! There is a hard wall that separates them. They both are only allowed to depend on the application layer. Therefore, it would be inaccurate to place one outer to the other. That would signify that the outer is allowed to depend on the inner. In our design, those two layers must be utterly agnostic of each other. No direct communication is allowed at all.

- The data layer includes data aggregation and manipulation. It provides access to local DB and/or remote servers. It is also responsible for aggregating and transforming the data in a format most convenient for the application layer. It does *not* include the actual database or the HTTP client. Those are framework specific.
- The presentation layer includes data transformations to deliver the optimal UI/UX. It's also responsible for assembling the State-model and Intent-model. Its logic is based on the way we want to present the data.

4. *Framework* layer. This is the only layer aware that it belongs to a mobile codebase. It's the only layer with Android or iOS dependencies. As you can see at the repos, the rest of the layers are pure Kotlin modules/Swift targets. They can be included - as is - in any kind of system that supports those programming languages. The framework layer is not supposed to contain any type of logic. It includes details like:

- The actual database.
- Our third-party networking library (Retrofit & Alamofire) and HTTP client.
- File-access code.
- UI.
- View Model. This is a questionable decision. For iOS, the View Model belongs to the presentation later. For Android, if we extend it from the Android View Model, then we have to add it inside the framework layer. If not, it's best to add it to the presentation layer.

Now, let's switch universes and discuss the layer cake we baked for our disruptive startup.

* * *

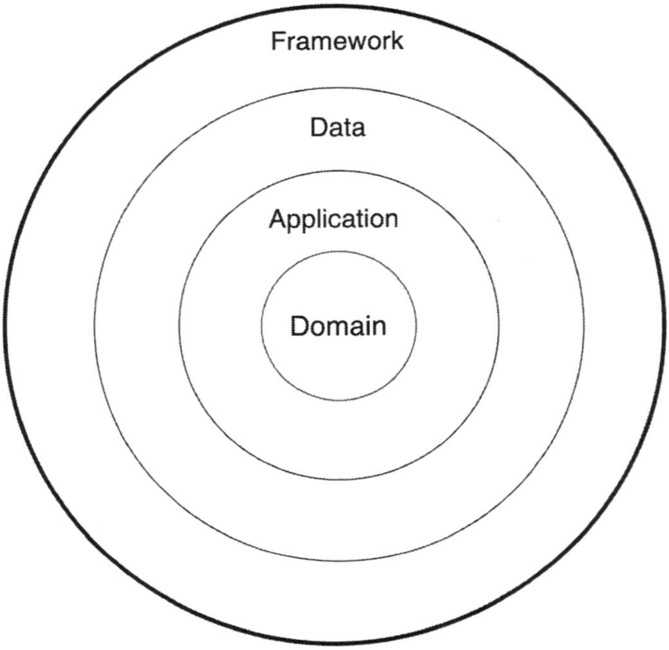

Clean Pragmatic Mobile Layering.

It's similar to the previous one, with two key differences. First of all, we have merged the application and presentation layers. We no longer separate the business from the presentation logic; we apply it all together for a single entity. This can simplify our application and reduce the number of classes. For flexible and straightforward apps, this is ok.

Secondly, we have turned all the boundaries soft. The layers are not segregated in different independent modules but rather in packages. An app developed by a couple of engineers does not benefit from borders. It's easier to solve a merge conflict with a person sitting next to you rather than draw rigid ownership boundaries.

Testing strategy

The testing strategies are also vital for the product's long-term success.

For World News, I have opted-in for white-box unit tests for all the framework-independent layers. And UI end-to-end tests that verify that the whole system behaves as expected. As we explained before, this strategy enables us to trace defects fast and effectively. We are testing each layer in isolation while its neighbors are mocked. It requires a lot of mocking effort, but we have the muscle power to deal with this.

As we want every microservice to be independent, the tests reside within each module. This way, each team is enabled, if they want to, to use a different testing strategy for the modules they own.

For Disruptive News, I used black-box unit tests that test all the layers except for the framework layer. Black-box unit tests provide the flexibility we need to refactor our system. We avoid the overhead of having to refactor the mocking code. And refactoring our architecture is something that we are expected to be doing a lot in the following years. Furthermore, since they test the behavior, they serve as an excellent regression test-suite in every release. They verify that the latest release is not breaking past behavior. Adding instrumentation-UI tests here is optional; they are hard to write, and the UI is expected to be very volatile.

Workflow

You may be wondering why I have diverged from the norm of this book, which is to navigate from the more abstract to the more concrete. Initially, we made some easy decisions and selected the external libraries. The previous chapter discussed the types of logic that our application needs to apply and defined the specific transformations and data models. Finally, in this chapter, we closed by drawing the boundaries, layers, and testing strategies. The layers are a more abstract concept than the boundaries or the types of logic.

Except for selecting the third-party libraries, which we always do last, this is the workflow that I use in my day-to-day work. As we discussed earlier, the purpose of exemplary architecture is to leave decisions open for as long as possible, ideally, until the last responsible moment.

* * *

How we can conclude the layers and their boundaries if we don't first take a look at the specifics our system needs to achieve. Whether it requires a database or not. What kind of backend API do we depend on, and what types of logic are left to be taken care of in our app. Do we need to perform data aggregation, or will our fellow back-end developers? Do we need to include domain logic, or will it reside inside the backend system? All those small details combined draw the bigger picture and enable us to make educated decisions on high-level designs.

In the past, "high-level" "master" architects started the project by drawing countless UML diagrams. Those depicted how our system needs to be structured. They based those decisions on theory, imagination, and speculations about the future. I say no more. To draw the bigger picture, we need to consider the small details. The more details, the better understanding we have. The better understanding we have, the better fitting high-level architecture we design. And this is a continuous thing. We keep *inspecting* what goes well and wrong and keep *adapting* our MVA.

After making those educated, high-level decisions on our architecture, we document them in order to quickly onboard new devs. We don't need to spend the time documenting everything, just the essential diagrams. And most importantly, we keep them updated when we make high-level changes.

Connecting the dots

We have already made up our minds on all the crucial decisions. We need to break our design down into concrete classes and interfaces. Usually, I don't spend much time doing this in UML; I either sit together with my team on a whiteboard or simply start coding and refactoring.

The high-level decisions, the Single Concern Principle alongside S.O.L.I.D, and all the best practices that we learned in this book will eventually show us the way. For the context of this book, I decided to draw some diagrams to help you go through the repos. They don't contain all the classes and mappers for practical reasons, but they should give you the main idea.

For World News:

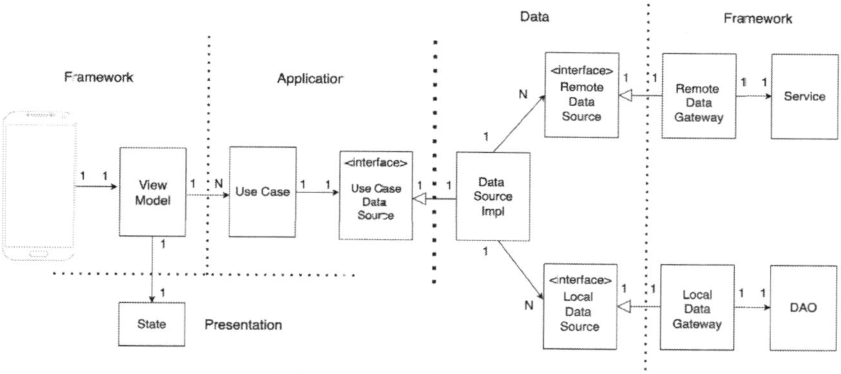

Microservices Architecture.

Notice the Dependency Inversion between the data and the application layers, as well as between the framework and the data layers. All the arrows are pointing inwards to the Use Case. Or upwards if you prefer. Another thing to notice is the strong cut line in the middle. Everything to its left is all about the user and UX; to its right, it's all about the data and its topology. *All* the boundaries are rigid here; I just wanted to make this distinction clearer.

For Disruptive News, we downscale it to:

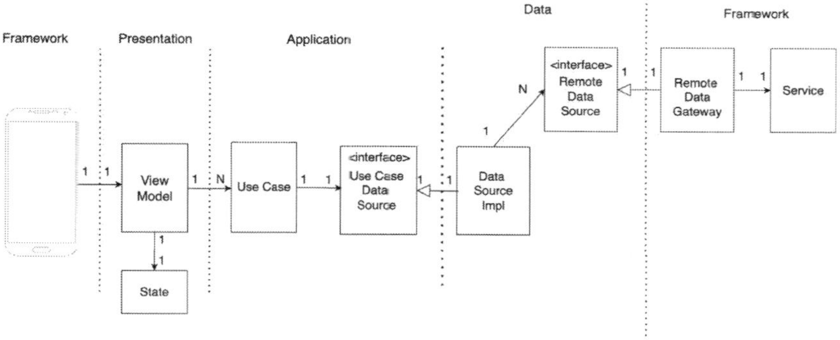

Pragmatic Clean Architecture.

* * *

We don't need a database. Therefore, all the local data sources have been removed. Additionally, the boundaries are not rigid, which allows us to add the View Model under the presentation layer. Even for the case that we extend from the Android View Model.

I also want to clarify that our design for Disruptive News is not the simplest possible MVA. You can choose a more simple architectural design for a startup and be successful. However, this design enables our startup to scale quickly and scale well. We take the minimum possible loans. It's Pragmatic yet Clean.

Can you develop a successful application without Clean? Of course, there are hundreds of examples out there. Will it be able to maintain its velocity and robustness in the years? Not as well.

You can now visit the repos and study the code. You know the reasoning behind all the critical decisions. Enjoy playing with the code!

Summary

The boundaries that we choose to draw in our app are among the most important architectural decisions. This includes where we draw them as well as how rigid they are.

There are mainly two axes that we can draw boundaries. Layers and Features. We can combine those axes with boundaries of different toughness to achieve the *desired* decoupling.

The testing strategy is mainly a decision between black-box and white-box tests. Whether we want to include mocks or not. Including mocks provides effectiveness in tracking down the specific location of the defects. On the other hand, they make refactoring more rigid.

Finally, we can conclude our layers & levels diagram and proceed to the implementation.

Keep inspecting and adapting.

CHAPTER TWENTY

The Golden Circle of Software development

Condensing everything we learned in a single diagram, we get the Golden Circle of Software Development!

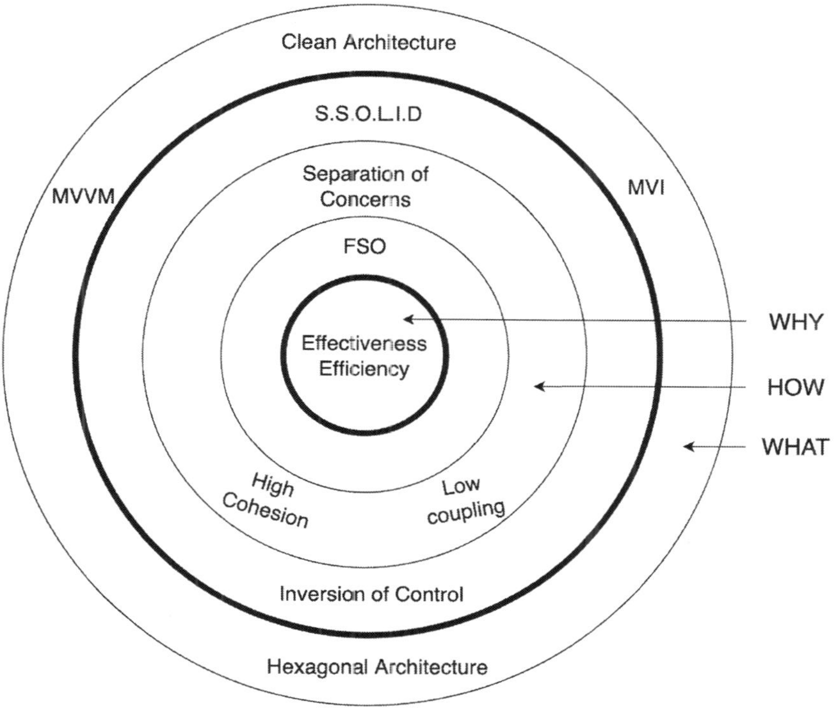

The Golden Circle Of Software Development.

FSO stands for Fundamental Software Objectives: Readability, Testability, Robustness, Extensibility, Maintainability, Resilience. In S.S.O.L.I.D, the first S stands for Single Concern Principle.

In accordance with the DRY principle, I won't repeat everything here. It's essential, though, to keep the above diagram clear in your memory. It sums up most of what we learned in this book. You can jump to the respective chapter whenever you need to refresh the details.

By Combining:

- The Golden Circle Of Software Development.
- Our experience.
- The specific context and details, like requirements, team size, and the systems we depend on.
- Continuous inspection and adaptation.

..we produce a successful product not only in the short term but also in the long run.

The formula is simple:

Golden Circle Of Software Development + experience + context + inspect & adapt = Successful product!

Don't forget that successful products require both technical skills and communications skills. We should adjust our communication patterns depending on who we are talking to. When talking to business people, remember to correlate any technical point with its *why*. Technical people may also require different depths of explanations based on their experience. A junior person won't easily comprehend the importance of cohesion, coupling, S.O.L.I.D, etc. A connection with the FSO will help them get aligned.

We understood *why* writing quality software matters. Then, we learned *how* to write quality software. Finally, we saw *what* quality mobile software is.

Now go out there and change the world with your software!

PART IV

References And Related Reading

Chapter One - Loans are generally a bad idea

1 Definition of what is a project from the PMI org: https://www.pmi.org/about/learn-about-pmi/what-is-project-management

2 Definition of what is a software product: https://en.wikipedia.org/wiki/Product_(business)

Chapter Two - Expensive code is also expensive

1 Understanding Software book by Max Kanat-Alexander: https://www.amazon.com/Understanding-Software-Kanat-Alexander-simplicity-programmer/dp/1788628810

2 KISS software principle: https://en.wikipedia.org/wiki/KISS_principle

3 The Dunning-Kruger effect: https://en.wikipedia.org/wiki/Dunning%E2%80%93Kruger_effect

4 The Strategy Design Pattern: https://en.wikipedia.org/wiki/Strategy_pattern.The

5 Preparatory refactoring: https://martinfowler.com/articles/preparatory-refactoring-example.html

Chapter Three - Minimum Viable Architecture

1 Lean startup, minimum viable product: http://www.startuplessonslearned.com/2009/08/minimum-viable-product-guide.html

* * *

Chapter Four - So, Why?

1 Science and engineering definitions: https://blog.eie.org/4-simple-ways-to-explain-the-difference-between-science-and-engineering
2 How to estimate velocity: https://www.lucidchart.com/blog/how-to-estimate-sprint-velocity
3 The most expensive software bugs in history: https://u-tor.com/topic/the-most-expensive-software-bugs-in-history
4 History's most costly bugs: https://www.ibeta.com/historys-most-expensive-software-bugs/

Part ii - How - S.S.O.L.I.D Principles

1 Design Principles and Design Patterns written by Robert C Martin: https://docs.google.com/file/d/0BxR1naE0JfyzV2JVbkYwRE5odGM/edit?resourcekey=0-bu4KRwWrpeIPAMrNL1812g

Chapter Five - Fundamental Software Objectives

1 Clean Code by Robert C Martin: https://www.goodreads.com/book/show/3735293-clean-code
2 The Law of Demeter: https://en.wikipedia.org/wiki/Law_of_Demeter
3 Information hiding principle: https://en.wikipedia.org/wiki/Information_hiding
4 Principle of the least privilege: https://en.wikipedia.org/wiki/Principle_of_least_privilege

Chapter Six - Single Responsibility

1 The Single Responsibility Principle: https://en.wikipedia.org/wiki/Single-responsibility_principle
2 Martin, Robert C. (2003). Agile Software Development, Principles, Patterns, and Practices
3 Clean Architecture in clean coders blog: https://blog.cleancoder.com/uncle-bob/2014/05/08/SingleReponsibilityPrinciple.html
4 Uncle Bob on Single Responsibility Principle: https://blog.cleancoder.com/uncle-bob/2014/05/08/SingleReponsibilityPrinciple.html

Chapter Seven - Open Closed

1 Bertand Meyer's book, "Object-oriented Software Construction," published in 1988: https://en.wikipedia.org/wiki/Object-Oriented_Software_Construction
2 Software design patterns: https://en.wikipedia.org/wiki/Software_design_pattern
3 Refactoring to Patterns by Joshua Kerievsky: https://www.goodreads.com/en/book/show/85041.Refactoring_to_Patterns

4 The Strategy design pattern - Problem, Solution, and Applicability". w3sDesign.com. Retrieved 2017-08-12.

Chapter Eight - Liskov Substitution

1 The Liskov Substitution principle: https://en.wikipedia.org/wiki/Liskov_substitution_principle
2 The LSP similarity with design by contract by Thorben Janssen: https://stackify.com/solid-design-liskov-substitution-principle/
3 Jamles Gosling, the founder and lead designer being Java: https://en.wikipedia.org/wiki/James_Gosling
4 James Gosling interview: https://www.artima.com/articles/james-gosling-on-java-may-2001

Chapter Ten - Dependency Inversion

1 Clean Architecture by Robert C. Martin: https://www.goodreads.com/book/show/18043011-clean-architecture

Chapter Eleven - Reactive Programming

1 Reactive programming: https://en.wikipedia.org/wiki/Reactive_programming
2 The observer design pattern: https://en.wikipedia.org/wiki/Observer_pattern
3 Reactive X: https://reactivex.io/intro.html
4 Event-driven programming: https://en.wikipedia.org/wiki/Event-driven_programming
5 RxSwift: https://github.com/ReactiveX/RxSwift

Chapter Thirteen - Testing & TDD

1 Michael Feathers book, Working Effectively With Legacy Code: https://www.goodreads.com/book/show/44919.Working_Effectively_with_Legacy_Code
2 Principle of Least Effort: https://en.wikipedia.org/wiki/Principle_of_least_effort
3 Mike Cohn's succeeding with Agile: https://www.goodreads.com/book/show/6707987-succeeding-with-agile
4 Testing pyramid by Mike Wacker: https://testing.googleblog.com/2015/04/just-say-no-to-more-end-to-end-tests.html

Chapter Fourteen - One Destination, Many Roads

1 The Java programming language: https://en.wikipedia.org/wiki/Java_(programming_language)
2 Log4J Security Issues: https://cyberint.com/blog/research/log4j-incident-

update/
3 Colors.js & Faker.js incident: https://mariosfakiolas.com/blog/open-source-chaos/
4 Angular official website https://angular.io/
5 Twitter to move away from Ruby: https://techcrunch.com/2008/05/01/twitter-said-to-be-abandoning-ruby-on-rails/
6 Hexagonal Architecture by Alistair Cockburn: https://alistair.cockburn.us/hexagonal-architecture
7 Jeffrey Palermo on Onion Architecture: https://jeffreypalermo.com/2008/07/the-onion-architecture-part-1/

Chapter Fifteen - Clean Architecture - The theory

1 Clean Architecture original blog post: http://blog.cleancoder.com/uncle-bob/2012/08/13/the-clean-architecture.html

Chapter Sixteen - MV(C,P,VM,I)

1 Martin Fowler on MVC: https://martinfowler.com/eaaDev/uiArchs.html#ModelViewController
2 Trygve Reenskaug on MVC: https://folk.universitetetioslo.no/trygver/themes/mvc/mvc-index.html
3 Original MVC paper: https://folk.universitetetioslo.no/trygver/1979/mvc-2/1979-12-MVC.pdf
4 Cycle.js: tps://cycle.js.org/
5 Hannes Dorfman on MVI: http://hannesdorfmann.com/android/mosby3-mvi-1/

Chapter Seventeen - Mobile Clean Architecture

1 Structured Concurrency: https://proandroiddev.com/structured-concurrency-in-action-97c749a8f755

Chapter Eighteen - Logic & Validations

1 Martin Fowler on anemic models: https://martinfowler.com/bliki/AnemicDomainModel.html

Chapter Nineteen - Boundaries & Layers

1 Uncle Bob, Screaming Architecture: https://blog.cleancoder.com/uncle-bob/2011/09/30/Screaming-Architecture.html